W9-DJA-134

PARENT EDUCATION
Toward Parental Competence

EVELYN PICKARTS
Los Angeles City Schools

JEAN FARGO
University of Hawaii

New York

APPLETON-CENTURY-CROFTS
Educational Division
MEREDITH CORPORATION

CARL A. RUDISILL LIBRARY
LENOIR RHYNE COLLEGE

649.107
P58P
76857
Dec. 1971

Copyright © 1971 by
MEREDITH CORPORATION

All rights reserved

711-1

This book, or parts thereof, must not be used or
reproduced in any manner without written per-
mission. For information address the publisher,
Appleton-Century-Crofts, Educational Division,
Meredith Corporation, 440 Park Avenue South,
New York, N. Y. 10016.

Library of Congress Card Number: 72-136490

PRINTED IN THE UNITED STATES OF AMERICA

390-70755-4

ACKNOWLEDGMENTS

To Elizabeth B. McCandless, my friend and colleague, who
gave freely of her knowledge, understanding, and time to repeatedly
read the developing manuscript and to make valuable critical anal-
yses, helping suggestions and contributions from her own understanding of the field; to the teachers of Parent Education of the
Adult Education Division of the Los Angeles City Schools for their
many contributions of ideas deriving from their own practice and
their commitment to the field of parent education; to my son for
his encouragement and assistance.

E.P.

To my husband, whose constant support and insightful evaluation were essential to any closure of this effort; to my children
whose tolerance maintained an unflagging and resolutely high level;
to the entire staff of the Department of Family Life, Seattle Community College, for the tremendous stimulus that generated from
staff interaction; and to Dr. William Sherman, who enabled me to
define "toward" with such nurturing clarity.

J.F.

Contents

Preface

The purpose of this book is to propose a framework and methodology for meeting the crucial need for broadly available parent education programs. Before we reach the point of program recommendations, a sequence of concerns will be explored. This sequence moves through five main steps: (1) the impact of great social change on the role of parents today, (2) the increased significance of the parent as the prime teacher of his child, (3) the effect of parent-child interaction on learning a way of viewing the socialization process, (4) the question of "what is teachable" to parents in the mass of information dealing with the nature of parent-child interaction, and (5) the melding of that "teachable" content with an educative process based on sound principles of adult learning.

The book is addressed to the people in the educational and mental health fields who deal in some way with the confusion parents feel about child-rearing, and who see the preventive task that confronts them. We have attempted to come to grips with the difficult problems facing those professions and agencies as they search for effective approaches.

Brim, in his book, *Education for Child Rearing* (New York: The Free Press, 1965), provides an incisive analysis of the conflicts in purpose and procedure that beset the field of parent education. Brim's work provides the underlying structure of the book. We will not attempt to comprehensively summarize his observations, rather, our effort has been to accept the challenges he so explicitly poses and to move toward a possible solution.

We assume that the reader has a working knowledge of the

basic principles of child growth and development, family interaction, and the helping process. We attempt to reassess these principles in the light of new information. We try to weave these findings into a content clearly relevant to parents' concerns and toward
the goal of increasing parental competence.

We strongly emphasize that throughout the book, the term
"parent" refers to both mother and father. Most parent education
efforts, for all their earnest endeavor, have not succeeded in speaking
to fathers, nor has the general modus operandi effected the involvement of fathers. We firmly stress that our concern not be seen as
solely mother-oriented.

The title of the book has special conceptual significance. The
phrase "toward parental competence" was chosen explicitly to indicate our concern that the reader conceive of the educative process
described here within the context of *becoming*. There are no
rigidly specified terminal behaviors for which we are educating;
there is no proscribed maze that, once maneuvered, earns one the
badge of "good parent." Child-rearing is seen as an ever-evolving
dimension of the adult growth process that should deepen in meaning and effectiveness throughout one's lifetime. We are concerned
here with competence in the *becoming* process, and with the parent's capacity to nurture the competent *becoming* of his child.

In order to develop our primary premises, we necessarily
consider the dynamics of the learning process in the early years, and
the application of these understandings to working with parents of
young children. We also apply the proposed framework and methodology to a wide range of settings in which parents are exploring
their role, examining their confusion, and searching for meaningful
answers.

E.P.

J.F.

Introduction

The family's main task has always been the socialization of its children. But the requisite skills for this task have radically changed over the centuries, and changed at an accelerating rate. It is no longer possible for parents to concern themselves simply with their child's nutrition and general health, see to it that he plays well with his peers, and trust he will follow in his parents' footsteps. The socialization process is far more complex today than ever before.

In the society in which our children are growing up the common base of knowledge has expanded with great rapidity, and the expansion is still accelerating. This explosion of knowledge deeply affects today's children; they are bombarded with such a welter of vivid and varied experiences that they cannot, without their parents' help, understand what their experiences mean or how they are to adjust to it.

This complexity has invaded the ethical sphere as well. Values have become so diffuse and conflicting that parents must define a clear, personal ethic to guide the child's own growing search.

From the beginning of life, what children learn is grounded in what parents teach. Parents must recognize and accept this teaching role. They must want to develop skill in using the substance of daily life to enhance the child's capacity to deal with his world and find meaning in it. These are the skills that determine parental competence today.

These are new requirements, new skills, that parents must

master if the next generation is to cope with our highly advanced, constantly changing, problem-ridden society. In most vocations, when old methods become obsolete, training programs in new methods quickly appear. New knowledge is analyzed for essential concepts and sound teaching methods are sought. Educators are trained to meet the unique learning problems.

The parent's vocation is perhaps the most important in society. If his skills have proved ineffectual, where are the vocational retraining programs? Where are the essential concepts, the sound teaching methods? Where are the structures wherein parents can come to terms with the problems they face and gain new perceptions of the changing demands of their job? Where are the educators capable of guiding the kind of person-oriented, clarifying, decision-making process that would generate a higher level of parental effectiveness?

Parent educators have worked long and hard to deal with the overwhelming confusion most parents feel as they try to prepare their children for a world they themselves have never known. We have engaged in long and vigorous debate over the most basic questions: What should we educate for? What is the good parent? And if we know the answers, how do we go about training parents from a multitude of backgrounds, to be more like the ideal we have settled upon? In our view, the first question is the only one that will lead us to a sound philosophical base, a teachable content, and a workable methodology. The other two questions have led us into disparity and despair.

The premise of this book is threefold: First, we would educate for autonomy as the foundation for parental competence. This concept provides a philosophical base for meaningful educational effort. Second, there recently has been a recognition both of the pervasive role of learning in the child's capacity to deal with life effectively and of the significant role of the parent in enabling that learning. We understand enough about the dynamics of this process to make it visible to parents. There is also a new recognition of the urgent need for parents to be aware of their own values, so that their daily judgments be consistent with the growth goals they really care about for their children. We understand enough about the valuing process and about the current value paradoxes to make this visible to parents. This is teachable content.

Third, parents' decisions define family style and the dimensions of children's growth. These decisions cannot come from books, from back-fence conversation, from experts. They are sound to the degree that they are arrived at thoughtfully, personally. They must evolve from the parent's clear understanding of his own convictions. The capacity for self-direction increases with each conscious consideration of alternatives and consequences—each choice. Thus, the goal of education aimed at improving the quality of family life is to encourage individual decision-making. By making the existing data available and guiding the problem-solving process, we can provide a structure which will stimulate personal choice. This is workable methodology.

This, briefly, is the substance of our contention: an effective approach to programming for the education of parents will involve a focus on the processes of learning and valuing within a structure based on individual choice. Such an approach, rather than relying on expertise, will have as its object the provision of direction and skills for parents whereby they will be enabled to define what they want the child to learn from his experience and relate this to the way in which children do learn.

This book attempts to justify these contentions and work out a plan of action. The task demands both an extensive validation of premises in the findings of current research and a description of practical applications in the findings of experience. The authors approach it with zest but also with humility, presenting the results as only a beginning.

Chapter 1 explores the impact of social and technological change on the family. These changes necessitate a redefinition of the teaching role parents play in guiding how their children learn to learn from their experience and to derive their value systems. Criteria for education programs are based on the competencies our society demands of its individual members. Criteria are also based on the recognition that the fostering of these competencies demands concepts and skills parents have had little opportunity to learn.

Chapter 2 relates these assumptions to current research in preschool learning and in the meaning of readiness for formal learning; and to parents' mediating role in their children's learning process. The role of values in parental decision-making—the valuing process as a dimension of parental competence—is explored. These two themes are combined in a "learning-valuing focus" for parent education programs based on a structure that educates for individual choice.

Chapter 3 considers the goals, content, and methods in current parent education programs, and their effectiveness. Differences in the way parent educators perceive their role are assessed in the attempt to arrive at a clarified description of their task. The group discussion method is explored in the search for a structure that will provide maximum potential for guided consideration of information, alternatives, and individual decision-making.

Chapter 4 presents an application of the learning-valuing focus to the problems of selection, training, and supervision of personnel needed to staff effective parent education programs.

Chapter 5 relates the authors' experience in a public-school-based adult education program for parents and preschool children in the Los Angeles area, with a primary emphasis on working with parents in advantaged communities.

Chapter 6 explores some dimensions of programming to meet the needs of parents in low income areas and presents the authors' experience in designing programs, primarily in Head Start and with parents of preschool children.

Chapter 7 demonstrates ways in which a learning-valuing focus can be utilized in programs reaching the parents of infants, programs in other preschool settings, programs dealing with the concerns of parents of older children, and programs preparing young people for parenthood.

Chapter 8 considers innovations in programming, problems in program development, and recommendations for future growth.

1

The Need for Parent Education

There are many factors, in what the child brings to the world and in the nature of that world, that affect how the young child grows. One factor upon whose basic importance most authorities agree is parents. Whether we study physical growth, personality patterns, social behavior, or value systems; whether we are concerned with the impact of poverty or the effects of affluence; we see human ability as a social product that gets its start, for better or worse, in the environment parents provide.

The key role of the family in the physical, emotional, and social well-being of the young child has long been recognized. Parents are the prime factor in enabling healthy growth of their children's bodies. Parents build the groundwork for a child's positive feelings about himself. Parents set the stage for developing a child's capacities for effective interaction with the world of people and things.

PARENTS ARE THE PRIME TEACHERS OF THEIR CHILDREN

To these understandings we now add a new and twofold dimension. From the wealth of recent research into the nature of the learning process has evolved a far sharper awareness of the influence of learning on behavior we once thought "just came naturally." Indeed, the way in which we learn may well be the basis for integrating all our behavior and experience, whatever its emotional,

motivational, or intellectual emphasis at the moment. At the same
time, new knowledge has placed marked emphasis on the environmental determinants of that learning as they are reflected in the
parents' style of interaction with the child. There is new comprehension of the pervasive effect of this interaction style on how the
young child learns to learn, as a key to understanding the whole
developmental process.

While our primary focus on parental influence has, until
recently, been on emotional factors and their impact on the child,
we now see parents as the teachers of their children in much the
same capacity as school teachers. A comparison is made between
the strategies, methods, and materials—as well as the content—usually associated with the role of the school teacher and those used
by the mother in her daily interaction with the child.[1]

The work of Hess and Shipman, Bernstein, Deutsch, and
others has shown that the way in which the parent communicates
with the child—the choice of words; the ideas; the underlying feelings and values in the communication; the degree to which the
parent leads the child to experience and gives meaning to that
experience; the control techniques that define the child's place in
the world—all have primary importance in the child's developing
capacity for growth.

That the parent teaches the child, often without being aware
of it, is not a new idea. This has always been seen as the automatic
function of an adult in a stable society. The parent is the trans-
mitter of the culture. He is the instructor and model for a vast range
of attitudes, behaviors, values, and ideas that reflect both the cultural norms and his own unique response to his experience. What
is new is our understanding that the *way* in which he teaches has
a pervasive effect not just on *what* children learn, but on *how* they
learn to view their experience and to use it. From the beginning of
his life the child is continually organizing all the information he
receives, both from his own inner responses and from his environment. Later experience has a decided modifying effect (a variety
of factors impinge on people's lives), but the way in which parents
perceive the world, interpret it to the child, and define the dimensions of their lives and their parental role is of paramount importance. The extent to which the parent provides, or fails to
provide, meaningful experiences for the young child and—more

crucially—helps him to discover the meaning and interrelatedness of his own experiences has far-reaching implications for how well that child is prepared to use his unique potential. In other words, how the young child learns to think, use language, feel about himself and others, view the world and his place in it, and unpack the meaning of his experience is significantly affected by the way in which the parent interacts with him. These learnings are not the result of didactic teaching but are implicit in the content of daily interaction between parent and child.

We will explore some dimensions of this interaction process in Chapter 2. At this point, we wish to stress the fact that whether or not the parent is aware of this process, by the simple act of becoming a parent he suddenly takes on a totally new function—the task of teaching. This task begins at the child's beginning. Children learn from everything the parent is and does, from every nuance of the parent's response to his experience and his sociocultural milieu. The parent teaches, perhaps more significantly than those formally trained to "teach." Skillful teachers perceive the potentials for learning and are aware of what is known about how children learn. They find providing a stimulating environment and guiding the natural zest of children a rewarding challenge. They feel competent and effective as enabling people in the lives of children. Parents need this same kind of awareness, the same kinds of enabling skills, so that they can feel the same kind of competence in guiding the fullest growth of their children.

However the quality of teacher-training programs may vary, they do exist within the structure of education. But parents, despite the vigorous efforts of educational and mental health agencies and even the thrust of the antipoverty program, are to a large extent thrown on their own resources. They do the best they can—teach what they know and translate to their children what their lives have taught them about the way things are.

SOCIETY AND ITS IMPACT ON PARENTAL TEACHING

Taking a brief look at "how things are" may sharpen our awareness that the world in which today's American parent functions refuses to stand still long enough for one to get one's bearings. This fact alone makes being a parent a very difficult task.

THE WORLD WE LIVE IN

In the course of one generation—or at the most, two—there have been such radical structural changes in American society that we can no longer rely on tradition to guide behavior. While urbanization has raised living standards, it has also served to concentrate poverty. Technology and the great explosion of knowledge have increased our ability to control the environment, but to channel this knowledge and make it work for people, far more complex organizational forms are required. The higher levels of industrial organization that have produced a great abundance of material goods and the mass media through which this prosperity is reflected combine to render more acute the sense of alienation and loss of identity experienced by those large numbers of people for whom this much advertised promise is never realized. The tremendous growth of science, even while it expands our vision of what is possible, reverses the rightful order of our feelings: it turns us toward loving things and using people.[2] The rapid growth of instant worldwide communication systems is bringing the complex problems of many different peoples, with their varying solutions, immediately to bear on our daily thought, with effects that are edifying yet highly disturbing. The growth of nuclear power holds the key to the future, and at the same time it poses a threat to the world's survival and undermines our former reliance on nationalism. The worldwide revolution in human rights is forcing a positive move toward the rethinking of social attitudes and behavior, but it is engendering the violent resistance that accompanies most change.

A developing force that has had a resounding impact on families is the solidifying of a critical style among the youth. As the first generation to consider and attempt to assimilate the constant outpouring of the mass media into their evolving perception of the world, they have a far greater grasp of the vast common base of knowledge than their parents have. They look more squarely at the profound issues of war, discrimination, and poverty and seek new solutions. Old answers are no longer acceptable, and our youth are employing tradition-shaking methods to inform the adult world that it must reconceptualize what it means to be civilized. Their rejection of the validity of established authority is gradually forcing those of us who are over thirty to perceive the obvious shift in value systems that happened from one generation to the next.

Parents are asking themselves the painful yet exciting question, "In the face of all this change, what do I have to teach that is meaningful to my child?" The question is painful because at first glance the answer is "I no longer know." It is exciting because, at second appraisal, the answer can be "I don't fully know, but I will struggle for some answers and grow in the process."

What did parents teach in the days when cultural change was slow, and the roles of men and women were more clearly defined? In the "good old days," the role of the family was defined by tradition, a tradition that provided specific norms, shared and supported by a stable community in a world that remained relatively unchanging from one generation to another. A man's identity was simply handed to him as a concrete symbol of his family's history to carry steadily and according to a predetermined pattern throughout his cycle of life. Parents taught their children that the role of the man was to provide and the task of the woman was to nurture. Poverty was the result of the individual's own deficiencies, and the way to success was through thrift, hard work, honesty, and rugged individualism. Sex was sternly confined to the seclusion of the marriage bed. Learning was valued when it contributed to personal achievement.

What the parent had learned from his own experience provided him with adequate tools for enabling his child to take a meaningful place in the world. He had skills that were visible to the child, both in terms of teachability and their relevance to daily life. Parents generally felt they knew what lay ahead, what children were like—what kind of adults they wanted them to become and what they wanted them to believe in.

Social changes of mammoth proportions, occurring with ever-increasing speed, have disrupted both the structure and the function of traditional family life, and the parent often finds himself functioning in a world he does not know. All the basic relationships he used to depend on are in the turmoil of change: that of man and woman, husband and wife, parent and child, man and fellowman. Social and geographic mobility has detached the family from its traditional supports, forcing it to work out its own guidelines. Many families are trapped in a self-perpetuating poverty cycle that isolates them from the major currents of social life. Many health, education, and welfare functions that were historically the province of the family have been yielded to the community. Old values from which one did not depart now exist side-by-side with their opposites in daily life. National crises threaten the validity of old ways of handling the problems of the poor, the culturally different, the nonconforming. Thus, what was reality for the parent, what worked for him, does not always make sense to his child.

The movement of women toward increased autonomy both within and outside the home, and the impact of poverty on parents' freedom to assume traditional family roles have blurred the previously clear distinction between the roles of men and women. Movement away from the earlier pattern of the extended family has focused the role of child-rearing on two people, or single parents, who are often unsure of their task. It is hard to stress the value of thrift when one is laboring under the yoke of installment payments, or when there is nothing to save. It is hard to work unceasingly to provide material comforts for one's family when children do not appreciate those comforts because too many human values have been sacrificed in the struggle to obtain them. It is improbable that parents demonstrate the efficacy of hard work when its only gain is marginal physical survival. It is difficult to provide meaningful work experience for children amid the welter of labor-saving devices, or to present the models of the good provider when employment is not available. It is bewildering to talk of individual worth when personality and social contacts seem to be more relevant to success, or when discrimination and joblessness deny the value of integrity.

The traditional approach to sexuality is being battered by the titillations of the mass media, by new concepts of freedom and responsibility; it is collapsing under the weight of the solutions to which the poor are driven when they find middle-class mores meaningless in conditions that preclude normal family life. We are often overwhelmed by the immense growth of technology. Suspicious of those who attempt to master it, we deny the urgency of that mastery by limiting the quality and availability of good education.

THE CHANGING ROLE OF THE FAMILY

Thus we see that in the face of tremendous change, the role of parents including their teaching task joins the increasing number of traditional patterns that are up for reassessment. All this movement, combined with the growth of a large, complex, and often conflicting body of knowledge about human development, has meant that the parent is no longer certain about what children are like, what lies ahead for them to become, or what he thinks they should believe in. When we look at the family in terms of its earlier functions and relationships, it seems relatively without function, characterized by few roles and core relationships and with few norms on the basis of which its members can interact.[3] At first glance there are few stable values, attitudes, behaviors, skills, or concepts about which parents feel deeply secure.

Whether it is within the capacity of today's family to respond to this confusion with clarity has been roundly debated for some time. Is its loss of function sufficient to indicate that the family is on its way out? Is it outdated, or does it remain essential to the survival of society? Generally, theorists differ about the meaning of the losses in function suffered by the family unit as a result of social change, but there is a broad area of agreement among those who find heartening evidence of the family's capacity to adapt externally to societal demands and internally to the needs of its own members,[4] provided it has sufficient access to the products of that society to make commitment possible.

Many theorists feel strongly that the losses in function that the family has undergone, and the breakdown in tradition roles can be seen as gains. For those families not incapacitated by poverty are freed from health, welfare, education, and daily maintenance functions that once absorbed their energies; they can concentrate in a more conscious way on their humanizing, socializing function. Social change has created a whole new set of needs that perhaps only the family can meet. The family can lay the groundwork of attitudes, values, and skills that the child will need to take his place in a highly complex society. It can protect, nurture, and heal, provide ever-renewing energy for commitment to more clearly delineated societal values.[5] It becomes a unit that mediates between its members and the welter of community services and demands,[6] and provides a pattern for the larger social framework of meaningful, involving relationships.[7]

Criteria for effective family functioning, however, are hard to come by in our pluralistic society. There is a bewildering array of findings from studies of the impact of particular family structures and behaviors on personality development. In the last analysis, the best indicator of a family's success as a socialization agent may be the child's eventual competence as an adult in society.[8-7]

It is the extensive quantity and quality of the skills needed to function in contemporary society that must be recognized before the complexity of parents' socialization task can be fully appreciated.

Effective participation in a modern industrial and urban society requires certain levels of skill in the manipulation of language and other symbol systems, such as arithmetic and time; the ability to comprehend and complete forms; information as to when and where to go for what; skills in interpersonal relations which permit negotiation, insure protection of one's interests, and provide maintenance of stable and satisfying relations with intimates, peers and authorities; motives to achieve, to master, to persevere; defenses to control and channel acceptably the impulses to aggression, to sexual expression, to extreme dependency; a cognitive style which permits thinking in concrete terms while still permitting reasonable handling of abstractions and general concepts; a mind which does not insist on excessively premature closure, is tolerant of diversity, and has some components of flexibility; a conative style which facilitates reasonably regular steady and persistent effort, relieved by rest and relaxation but not requiring long periods of total withdrawal or depressive psychic slumps; and a style of expressing affect which encourages stable and enduring relationships without excessive narcissistic dependence or explosive aggression in the face of petty frustration.[9]

Inkeles [10] presents us with an exhaustive list of the attitudes, values, behaviors, and skills a child will need in order to find life meaningful in present-day society. How does a family go about this hydra-headed process? Perhaps it would be worthwhile to assess the recent resounding social changes in terms of their specific meaning for the parental teaching task.

A NEW LOOK AT THE IMPORTANCE
OF LEARNING

The common body of knowledge and concepts about the world that must be mastered before any specific skills can be acquired has grown a hundredfold in this century. Knowledge has been amassed so fast that the meaning of "readiness for learning" must be reassessed in terms of this concept's meaning for parents and their socialization task in the child's early years.

THE URGENCY OF MASTERY

It is generally agreed that the kind of human being needed to function in the world of today and tomorrow is an autonomous individual, concerned for others, who can adapt to change and who is able to see and consciously choose from the broad range of alternatives present in his reality, exercising a great sense of freedom and responsibility in the process.[11]

There is a new reality that must be added to this concept of the person who must cope with today's troubled and swiftly moving world: the long apprenticeship required to master the skills essential to the qualities of autonomy, commitment, adaptability, and choice. Now we come to one of the least recognized truths of our time: the more highly skilled and specialized the jobs which Americans perform, including homemaking and the rearing of children, the more dependent are all these pursuits upon the mastery of a broad, shared, common base of knowledge.[12]

The sheer increasing complexity of our society is such that for each succeeding generation there is an ever-increasing heritage of knowledge basic to a wide variety of occupations which must be passed on. Only after this basic heritage has been learned can the special skills of specialized occupations be taught. Many of the so-called unskilled occupations of our society which take so little time for an American to learn, actually take so little time because of the basic heritage that has already been imparted. For example, the woman who sells tickets in a bus station can be taught that occupation in a short time only because she has already learned to read, write and figure, has a basic knowledge of the transportation system of our society and of geography, and because she knows something about people and how to handle them.[13]

We are beginning to recognize the implications of the ever-increasing complexity of the task of passing on the "broad, shared, common base of knowledge" to each succeeding generation. Bruner [14] points out that there are obvious specifications that can be stated about how a society must proceed in order to equip its young:

It [society] must convert what is to be known—whether a skill or a belief system or a connected body of knowledge—into a form capable of being mastered by a beginner. The more we know of the process of growth, the better we shall be at such conversion. . . . All societies must maintain interest among the young in the learning process, a minor problem when learning is in the context of life and action, but harder when it becomes more abstracted. And finally, and perhaps most obviously, a society must insure that its necessary skills and procedures remain intact from one generation to another.[15]

EMPHASIS ON THE PARENTAL TEACHING ROLE

The development of the kind of adult who can function effectively in our increasingly complex society, who can master knowledge and learn from his experience, has been seen too exclusively as the province of the school. The massive growth of knowledge demands that parents take a new look at the preschool years and the foundations for learning that begin there.

Today's child at birth does not differ greatly from his ancestors of the late Stone Age. His brain is neither larger nor more complex. His senses are no more acute. He inherits nothing more in the way of moral propensity or social awareness. Yet we expect him, within a few short years, to behave as a civilized adult in a complex society. If he is to do so, his learning cannot be left to chance. . . . Every child who is to live in a civilized society must learn some of the things that adults have to teach him. That is why we have homes; that is why we have schools. If both reject their responsibility, the results can be disastrous.[16]

Full participation in modern industrial society requires the imparting, through the socialization process, of a substantial body of information, skills, and motivational dispositions.[17] This substantial body of information, skills, and motivational dispositions can be fully integrated only when the child's first years of life have provided him with the ability to learn from his experience, with a readiness for the discovery of meaning in his life. There is so much to know before comprehension of one's world is possible, that we must take a new look at the early years and their importance for later competence.

Looking more closely at the consequences of poverty and deprivation has shown us the importance of readiness for learning. We are now more aware that the child must begin to attain a wide range of perceptual, cognitive, linguistic, and social-emotional skills well before the years of formal education begin. Even if the years of formal education are short, the degree to which the person can control his own life depends squarely upon his ability to find his experience meaningful and significant to further growth and effectiveness. The ability to use language, to use concepts to understand experience, to generalize to new experience, affects not only mastery of facts and figures but the ability to perceive, manage, and use the underlying understandings in the total range of human responses. The sense of competence derived from the ability to find one's world intelligible is a key component of a sound self-image.

The recent vast expansion of research and rethinking with regard to the effect of early experience on the functioning of young children has placed great emphasis on the hidden curriculum in the middle class home,[18] which provides the kind of stimulating, enriched, and guided environment that enable children to learn how to learn. The typical middle class child is motivated to reach out to new experience, to delay gratification of his impulses long enough to involve himself in new situations, to deal with the tools of learning because they have been a part of his experience. The middle class mother is described as oriented to the individuality of her child, less concerned with obedience, freer to give the child an understanding of the rationale of order and a clear sense of himself as an independent agent able to initiate action, to explore the unfamiliar, and to manipulate his environment freely for his own learning.[19]

The middle class mother is often contrasted to the lower class mother, who may see education as a way to a better life for her child but does not know how to combat the debilitating impact of slum life. She does not see herself with intrinsic integrity, as having power in the home-school relationship. She has realistic awareness that the school will not tolerate outspokenness from her child; she sees his role as passive and nonparticipatory. Thus she does not transmit to him the mental attitude that he is worth being taught and capable of mastery. This freer, more autonomous conceptualization of self is the product of the atmosphere of a middle class home, where achievement and security are realistic expectations. Life therefore has a structure and goals, and parents more clearly see a role in preparing children for it. The concept of time—past, present, and future—has meaning because expectations are realistic and thus must be carefully planned for. Time becomes important because there is so much to be done.

Thus we find that there are many children who arrive at school able to be the center of their own learning, to respond to the whole range of cognitive and affective experience, to integrate new information about themselves and their world in an orderly way, to feel competent and effective, and to want new experiences. There are, on the other hand, many children who find their environment diffuse and unexplainable, who have few rules for ordering the meaning of their experience, whose approaches to coping with new experience are weak and disordered. Although they may have a wide range of competencies for dealing with their immediate home and community lives, when they face the tasks that the school or larger community impose they are ineffective and they experience a deep sense of failure.

There can be no question that our society as a whole must make radical changes in its fabric to provide a more nurturing world for many, if not most, of its people. There can be no question that the schools have an urgent task in reaching children at a deeper level, in the student's own terms. But there are certain universal prerequisite skills that every child must develop if he is to achieve any level of personal freedom within our present complex society. Those skills are bound up essentially in the ability to make sense out of one's experience, whatever the social context or value system. Those skills are intrinsically related to the role the parents play in mediating between the child and his experience, and although our understanding of the nature of these skills is incomplete, it is possible to conclude that parental competence in these skills can be enhanced through education.

THE NEED FOR INCREASED PARENTAL COMPETENCE

The program for nurturing children's essential learning skills through increasing the competence of parents can be combined with the many approaches to the critical and immediate task of eliminating poverty. We will discuss this further in Chapter 6. But there is much to indicate that all is not well in the child-rearing styles of the more advantaged parents. Senn's [20] sample of middle class parents found an alarming lack of substance in parent-child relationships in the early years—few if any toys, little verbal interaction, disturbed relationships, vague and diffuse direction. Teachers find large numbers of middle class children whose focus is largely on conforming to the expectations of adults. They behave in a constrained manner, are careful to avoid error, and develop great anxiety when asked to take chances. They function poorly without the support of an adult behavioral structure. Hess indicates that the status-oriented family style, commonly associated with low income families, defines the behavior of the members in terms of role expectations, allowing little opportunity for the unique characteristics of the child to influence decision-making processes or the interaction between parent and child.[21] This model is often followed by middle class families whose concern for status and whose perception of their children as extensions of the parents' egos do not allow children to be person-oriented any more than the low income families, whose restricted life has not allowed them to see themselves or their children as worthwhile individuals.

These studies reflect, perhaps, the frantic efforts of middle class parents to push almost hysterically for achievement on the part of their children. There is no place today for a child who underachieves in anything—for slowness of response, for the gradual unfolding of normal development, for individuality in learning.[22] Children are seen as objects to be manipulated into preestablished patterns, pressured through predetermined schedules into preselected colleges and prefabricated careers. There is no time or space for a child to integrate what he learns and determine the meaning of his own experience.

There is, then, a clear need to recognize the dramatic difference between the competencies a child needs if he is to interact effectively and joyously with an increasingly complex world on the one hand, and the frantic push for success that is manipulative and destructive of individual integrity and uniqueness on the other. —There is a need for parents to develop, in relation to their child, that special quality of interaction, possible from the beginning, which will create in him a steady, growing love of learning and a respect for his increasingly effective interaction with the world around him.

Middle class parents are generally well informed about their children's physical, emotional, and social growth needs, and although there may often be snarls in these areas of the parent-child relationship, problems are recognized and guidance is sought. But what is less often recognized is that the parents are the prime teachers of their child, not just in his physical and emotional life, but in the underlying integrative process whereby he learns how to learn from all of his experience. Parents need to understand how their children learn to perceive, to think, and to know; how to get their children ready to learn meaningfully rather than mechanically; and how they can have the joy that comes from guiding this kind of growth. It is perhaps this inability to conceptualize the learning process and to nurture its growth that makes modern parents restless during the preschool years, yearning for the day when the children will be off to school and "learning something, for a change." There is so much exciting learning going on from the day of birth, and the parents play such a key role in making this learning meaningful for the child, that their awareness of this process would open many doors for both parents and child.

If we assume that early experience influences later development, then it follows that the young child's perception of the world as an interesting and safe-to-explore place is important. Opening up vistas of the many-faceted ways in which one can respond to the environment will provide the child with basic patterns of approach that will expand with new experience. If we nurture his curiosity, reduce the mystery and the unknowns, and accustom him to approach the world of physical and social reality with increasing comprehension, we may well provide him with security patterns that have beneficial adaptive effects.[23]

Early childhood educators have placed tremendous emphasis on helping parents understand that play is the child's work, interpreting the physical, social, and emotional learnings that come as children explore their environment and themselves. We can now place equal emphasis on helping parents understand what these early experiences also mean for children's cognitive functioning, as the process that integrates all experience and determines its meaning to the child. This emphasis may provide the kind of competence that would enable readiness, not for achievement in the status sense, but for the kind of fully developed self-realization, openness to change, and commitment to others our society so desperately needs.

A broad definition of a disadvantaged child helps us view development more clearly: *"Any child from any circumstances who has been deprived of a substantial portion of the variety of stimuli which he is maturationally capable of responding to, is likely to be deficient in the equipment required for learning."* [24] This definition applies to many so-called advantaged children. There is a great deal of learning inherent in the structure and content of the privileged home that is either never realized or is short-circuited by the parents' attempts to manipulate their children's behavior with a view to adult comfort or to the achievement of certain "acceptable" standards of behavior.

We have only recently become aware of the full implications of all this for the parents' role of guiding learning—bringing meaning to the child's experience, increasing his competence to deal with and make sense of his environment and experience. We will explore these areas further in Chapter 2. The point here is that these processes are operational within the parent-child interaction systems, parts of the automatic teaching role many parents assume. Greater consciousness of the process, and thus increasing competence in the task of child-rearing, is teachable and may well serve as a broad base for parent education.

A NEW LOOK AT THE IMPORTANCE OF VALUING

Rapid societal changes and the resulting confusion of values are both great sources of the present instability of the American family and the reappraisal it is undergoing. The world is changing so fast that people do not always have the time—nor do they perceive the need—to make conscious decisions about how much of the new ways they really want to absorb, how much of the old ways they feel are still valid, what they really believe in. Advantaged parents too often lose their personal identity in the struggle for material achievement, and in the rejection of past patterns they have not reconstructed a clear set of values. Disadvantaged parents have too often found little or no personal identity within the conditions of poverty; or they find that the values that derive from their environment preclude their participation in the general society.

THE NEED FOR FAMILY VALUE SYSTEMS

At the same time, we are becoming increasingly aware that a sturdy structure of family values is fundamental to the sound growth of children. The parents' value orientations, whether consciously or not, play a central role in their every act as parents. Child-rearing practices reflect what the parent values, and although techniques may reinforce or modify what the child learns to value, it is the underlying value premise that the child absorbs into his own perception of himself and the world. Parents who know what they believe in and who maintain a consistency between responses to daily interaction provide both guidelines for the child's early growth and something solid against which the maturing child can assess his own experience. Parents who do not know what they want to ask of their children, or who swing with every passing pressure, confuse the child's picture of the world and blunt his capacity for judgment and self-determination.

Our youth have been reared by a generation of parents who are themselves confused—who have been and are unsure about what is right and wrong; and rather than making wrong decisions, many parents have chosen to let their children determine their own set of values. Thus our present generation is said to be "other directed" rather than "inner directed." That is, our youth look to their peers who have as little experience as they, in order to find their sense of values rather than looking within themselves to a set of standards that has been internalized.[25]

Many young people have rebelled against this lack of direction from their parents and are seeking their own path through the confusion. It is difficult for them to understand why parents are finding the sorting process so painful. They raise cogent questions: Why do parents expect their children to trust them when they don't usually trust their children? Why are parents so concerned with what other people think of their children's every action? Why are parents so competitive about everything, including their own children? Why are parents more concerned with some proof of accomplishment (grades, awards, diplomas) than with talking out their learning with their children? Why do parents give their children examples of what other children do to follow? Could this be a way of shirking their own disciplinary problems? Why don't parents trust themselves more instead of relying on the Jones's? Why do parents feel that youth's sole task is to stoically carry on parental values? [26]

But the confusion parents experience does not originate in personal problems, it originates in social problems.

Mankind has never, in all his history, been caught in the forces of such violent, rapid social change as we have. We are caught by the pressure to conform, to stand pat and preserve the status quo, to hang on to whatever stability we can and not rock the boat; and on the other hand, we are caught by the pressure to change, to move, to grow, to question, to seek, to use our freedom—to keep up with scientific and industrial advance.[27]

Families find, on the one hand, a pull toward the values of being, knowing, caring, loving, unconditionally committing oneself, and on the other, a demand for achievement, efficiency, success, material self-betterment.[28] These values are essentially incompatible. Although in the abstract, parents may value intellectual curiosity, considerateness, happiness, and self-control, there is often deep ambivalence with respect to the living of these values. The "good words" are mouthed, but the old emotional responses determine the nature of daily parent-child decisions. The parent hears the expert talk about a child's growing sense of independence and need for self-expression and assents intellectually, but at the point of immediate decision he becomes aware of an inner need demanding obedience to his parental authority. The parent verbalizes the value of honesty, but inwardly he feels that dishonesty is a fact of life with which he must often compromise in his own life dealings. The parent intellectually recognizes the right of the child to be "what he is," but under the pressure of what other people say (and as a reflection of his own lack of autonomy) he finds his children easier to love and to handle when their behavior conforms to set patterns. The parent may be aware of the meaning of individual difference, but deep inside he is more comfortable raising a child whom everybody "likes," or who won't "get into trouble." The parents are perhaps aware of the need to extend the reach of the child into a living concern for others, but they are unable to resist making the home into a self-contained (and often empty) fortress against the world. Frequently parent knows he should be secure enough in his own value system not to be threatened by differences, but in reality he is more comfortable when his children's experiences—their choice of playmates, perhaps—do not call that shaky structure into question. The parent may know in some vague way that an emotional attitude in which there is too much hate and anger may incapacitate the child who absorbs it for future constructive commitment to the world and to change, but he cannot untangle these emotions from the attitudes he transmits in thousands of unconscious ways.

CONSIDERING ESSENTIAL VALUES

There are certain values which are inherently essential to the continuation of the highly complex society in which we live: a commitment to personal integrity, to the full use of oneself in a contributive way, to rationality, to abstract learning for its own sake, to an active and effective coping with an environment one sees as masterable, to self-restraint in recognition of the needs of others. These are values which have been labeled middle class, but when we view them within the perspective of our present-day social needs they are seen as prerequisite orientations to the ordering of modern society and to individual fulfillment in it. It is because society does not provide, for so many of its people, the conditions which nurture these values that it is in trouble. The social ills of materialism, the pressure toward conformity, and anxiety which are manifested in the mainstream and the stunted growth, hopelessness, and despair which characterize the alienated portion of the population are side effects of a central cause: the failure of society as a whole clearly to define where it is and what it believes in.

We are increasingly aware of the social pressures that our expanding society places on people and of their impact on person-

ality development. We are also increasingly aware of the urgent
need for a generation of people who can define their direction and
cope with change. It then becomes incumbent on this generation
of parents to recognize the impact of their values on their children's
capacity for growth, to become involved in the valuing process, to
consciously determine those values which most clearly reflect what
they want for themselves and their children.

THE PROCESS OF VALUING IS LEARNED

Valuing is knowing: knowing what one's life is for and what
is worth working for. The valuing process is not a simple one that
can easily sort out what is right and wrong. Values evolve and mature as experiences evolve and mature. The conditions under which
behavior is guided, in which values work, typically involve conflicting demands, a weighing and balancing, and finally an action
that reflects a multitude of forces. This is a complicated process;
experience shapes and tests our judgments. Values result from ham-
mering out a life style in a particular milieu and specific conditions.
After enough experience in testing, certain patterns of evaluating
and behaving tend to develop. Certain concepts, attitudes, and responses are seen as right, or desirable and important. These tend
to become our values.[29] Most of us live with a dual set of values;
those we cherish and believe in and those that dictate the way we
respond to immediate situations. The degree of awareness of this
duality and of conscious effort to bring belief and action into harmony is the degree to which we find our lives meaningful and significant. Children desperately need to know that their parents find
life meaningful and significant, even though they may eventually
choose to live their own lives in other ways. They need to know
why a parent makes the judgments he does, and how that judgment
relates to this direction in life. In order to make sense of his experience, the child needs not only the skills for receiving, storing, and
retrieving all that he experiences and the capacity to discern the
range of alternatives in solving his problems; he also needs the skills
involved in choosing from among alternatives, and these skills are
dependent upon his experience in valuing.

Parents need competence in coping with their uncertainty.
The existence of contradictions and paradoxes in values is the key

to exploring this question. The fact that for every value our culture presents, its opposite exists and a choice must be made, is one that must be faced and accepted before thoughtful, conscious selection of values can occur. Awareness of the conflict that often arises between verbalized values and daily behavior and the blurring impact of this conflict on the learning process of children is a prerequisite for value choice. Recognition of a child's need for a steady view of the world and his place in it as the cornerstone for developing self-determination is an integral part of being a competent parent. Parents need a framework within which they can decide what is important to them, what kinds of guidelines they find meaningful for their children. Parent education programs, whatever their base, can provide a place where parents can think these questions through, in dialogue with other parents and with leadership to insure consideration of the widest range of alternatives and their consequences for daily life. The capacity for conscious choice that proceeds from the center of oneself is a valid goal for adult education.

A SHARPENED FOCUS FOR PARENT EDUCATION

The quality of the parent-child relationship hinges on mutual love and respect. Whatever the family life style, or life situation, the parent who somehow manages to love and respect the individuality of his child provides the groundwork for the development of an effective adult. But if parents cannot now do this, can they be taught? The skills involved in loving and respecting are not easily isolated for our consideration from the fabric of individual lives. Many parents have difficulty dealing with abstract concepts—i.e., self-image, identity, motivation, personality. Even if they can deal with them intellectually, they often cannot translate that knowledge into consistent behavior. Parent educators have long struggled to find what is really teachable, particularly when they have been faced with the pendulum swings of theory, conflicting trends in research, and varying views of just what relation seems to exist between certain parental behaviors and certain personality tendencies and how all this applies to parents who differ broadly in the many ways in which they view the task of parenthood.

WHAT IS "TEACHABLE"?

New understandings may enable us to take a different tack on the question of content in parent education programs. If in their early years children need to develop certain skills on which depends the effectiveness of all further interaction with their environment, and if parents teach these skills through their interaction with the child, then we can take what we know about this process and make the knowledge available. If it is true that children need a sturdy system of family values on which to base and to evaluate their own experience, and if parents impart values in every act of their parenthood, then we can take what we know about the valuing process and provide a place where parents can practice, sort, and choose.

GOAL: PARENTAL COMPETENCE

Parental competence can then be seen as a measure of the parent's conscious awareness and acceptance of the teaching role he plays in the life of his children, and the desire to increase his skill in guiding his children's growth. The increase in competence holds within it the cyclical effect of deeper levels of relationship between parent and child, both growing and constantly learning from their interaction. Mutual love and respect can be the effect as well as the cause of joyful mastery in interaction.

The challenge of parenthood today, then, can no longer be the carrying on of traditional forms. Parents must bring to bear what we know about how children grow and learn, and this within a framework of consciously chosen values. Parents need a set of problem-solving and growth-nurturing concepts and skills that will decrease their general uneasiness in the face of the overwhelming complexity of life and their sense of powerlessness in the modern world. They need concepts and skills that foster the growth of children who see themselves and others as worthwhile, who have a zest to invest in new experience, and who move into the community with skills that make creative and meaningful use of their lives possible, and with the commitment to changing those conditions that inhibit maximum personal and societal growth.

IMPLICATIONS FOR PARENT EDUCATION PROGRAMS

All this seems to contradict the age-old belief that parenthood is a matter of instinct and not of learning. Parents generally want to be successful, but in the face of change they have lost the old criteria for judging their own competence. The tasks they face in effective family functioning today are the tasks for which they have had the least preparation. The many-faceted field of parent education has developed in response to a widespread confusion and a reaching out for guidance primarily by middle class families who are grappling with the impact of cultural change on traditional patterns of behavior; but a recognition of the vital need to include lower class parents in the enrichment process of compensatory programs has brought heartening response from lower class parents who also want to know how to help their children.

If being a parent does not automatically confer the knowledge and skills for perceptive guidance of children's growth, then education and mental health agencies must accept responsibility for organizing this knowledge and making it readily available on an ongoing basis and within a workable structure. Along with the many other economic, social, and educational needs of people today, parents of young children need to develop competence in their teaching role. This need can be met through a broad program of education that is relevant regardless of the parents' economic status, class, or ethnic identification. A concept of parent education as education enabling competence in nurturing the learning and valuing processes essential to children's growth embraces all family patterns at all levels and within all subcultures. It provides skills for enhancing the learning process whatever the milieu; it insures maximum individual value selection whatever the choice. The investigation of the way the child learns to think and to value is a content universally applicable, regardless of the starting point of the individual and/or the group, or the life styles or family patterns they reflect.

The modus operandi of parent education must involve providing a safe enabling structure within which the individual parent, in the light of an extended range of alternatives provided by the parent educator and a wider scope of experience provided by the group, can sharpen his own skills, explore his own values, and make his own decisions.

If being successful parents has a specific meaning in terms of today's world and its challenges, then the accumulating understanding of skills for parental competence can be developed into a body of knowledge. If there is a body of universally applicable knowledge, then it can be taught. If it can be taught, the parent educator can function *as* an educator, teaching with maximum individual growth and decision-making as a goal. The knowledge of how children learn and how parents teach can be integrated with a meaningful learning process, focused on helping parents discover their underlying value premises so that immediate decisions have a continuity with long-range goals. This knowledge and process can be seen as the content and structure of a parent education which, beginning with the present situation in which each parent finds himself, can increase his awareness of how he is already teaching and expand the skills with which he may continue to teach. It offers concrete skills that lead to enhanced interaction, gives specific understandings that reflect and prepare the ground for deeper levels of relating.

Parent educators have long been concerned with conceptualizations of a program. There have been wide variances in content, adaptation to differing family patterns, the role of the parent educator, the level of involvement necessary for behavioral change, the nature of the adult learning process, and the remedial approach of programs.

If there is a broad societal need for an increased level of parental competence, then there must be a broad societal approach to educational programs. If planning is to be effective, programs must have certain common denominators that determine their structure and content, so that such vital components as funding, training, supervision, and evaluation are included. In view of this, we see the need for parent education programs that have

1. A "teachable" content that is adaptable within many different agency formats;
2. A content meaningful across a broad range of class, cultural, and subgroup factors;
3. Parent educators who *are* educators, providing for parents the range of alternatives and the process essential to individual decision-making;

4. Flexibility in focus depending upon where people are, but sturdiness in framework and process to enable learning;
5. Concrete and positive programs aimed at extending present capacities rather than at remediating present inadequacies or failures.

We attempt to take the basic tenets of early childhood education and integrate them with new understandings of the pervasive effect on child development of both learning and valuing skills. We attempt to reassess the role of the parent in the light of new conceptions of the impact of his teaching role, define its dimensions, and abstract what is teachable. We hope at least to intrigue the growing number of deeply committed parent educators into considering the potential of this approach for broadening the impact of this field.

SUMMARY

We have explored the impact of social and technological change on the family, and we find that this impact demands a redefinition of the role of the parent in the socialization process. This role is seen more clearly when perceived as a teaching function, rather than as behavioral management per se. Parents are the prime teachers of their children, providing the genesis and direction of their child's capacity to deal effectively with a complex environment and derive meaning from that unique experience. The frame of reference that the child evolves to evaluate his experiences is constructed according to the values he employs to sort them. The confusion in values so characteristic of our times must be confronted by parents, and choices consciously made, in order that children may learn from their experience, perceive alternatives, and recognize the necessity and implications of choice.

Parental competence is seen as a measure of the conscious awareness and acceptance of this teaching role, and the desire to engage in the process of becoming ever more competent in guiding children's development. These are new requisite skills. Previous concepts of the parental role no longer provide guidelines for families. Parents operate in too many varied milieus to find much of the current child-rearing doctrine of value.

Educational efforts to provide direction have yet to solidify into programs integrating a sound philosophical base with teachable content and a workable methodology that is applicable across class and cultural lines. Valid premises emerge from a consideration of the competencies our society demands of its members and a reassessment of the teaching role parents play in their central task—enabling their children to mature into effective and fulfilled adults.

REFERENCES

1. Mario D. Fantini and Gerald Weinstein, *The Disadvantaged.* New York: Harper & Row, 1968. P. 98.
2. Erich Fromm (quoted without reference) in Charles Hobart, "Commitment, Value Conflict and the Future of the American Family," *Marriage and Family Living,* Vol. 25 (November, 1963), p. 407.
3. Robert F. Winch, *Identification and Its Familial Determinants.* Indianapolis: Bobbs-Merrill, 1962. P. 5.
4. Clark Vincent, "Family Spongia: The Adaptive Function," *Journal of Marriage and the Family,* Vol. 28 (February, 1966), p. 10.
5. Otto Pollak, "The Outlook for the American Family," *Journal of Marriage and the Family,* Vol. 29 (August, 1967).
6. John H. Edwards, "The Future of the Family Revisited," *Journal of Marriage and the Family,* Vol. 29 (August, 1967), pp. 505–511.
7. Charles Hobart, "Commitment, Value Conflict and the Future of the American Family," *Marriage and Family Living,* Vol. 25 (November, 1963), p. 410.
8. John A. Clausen, "Family Structure, Socialization and Personality." In Lois W. Hoffman and Martin L. Hoffman (Eds.), *Review of Child Development Research,* Vol. II. New York: Russell Sage Foundation, 1966. P. 46.
9. Alex Inkeles, "Social Structure and the Socialization of Competence," *Harvard Educational Review,* Vol. 36 (Summer, 1966), pp. 280–281.
10. *Ibid.*
11. Hobart, "Commitment," p. 410.
12. Ruth Useem, "Changing Cultural Concepts in Women's Lives." In H. Peters and James Hansen (Eds.), *Vocational Guidance and Career Development.* New York: Macmillan, 1966. P. 63.
13. *Ibid.*
14. Jerome Bruner, "The Growth of Mind." In Judy F. Rosenblith and

W. Allensmith, *The Causes of Behavior,* Vol. II. Boston: Allyn and Bacon, 1966. P. 528.

15. *Ibid.*

16. Paul Woodring, "Freedom—Not License," *Saturday Review,* February 18, 1967, p. 97.

17. Clausen, "Family Structure."

18. Fred Strodtbeck, "The Hidden Curriculum in the Middle Class Home." In C. W. Hunnicutt (Ed.), *Urban Education and Cultural Deprivation.* Syracuse: Syracuse School of Education, 1964.

19. Robert D. Hess, *Maternal Teaching Styles and the Socialization of Educability,* prepared for the Symposium on the Socialization of Attitudes Toward Learning in Urban Working-Class Families, Meeting of the American Psychological Association, Los Angeles, September 5, 1964.

20. Milton J. E. Senn and Claire Hartford, *The Firstborn: Experience of Eight American Families.* Cambridge, Mass.: Harvard University Press, 1968.

21. Robert Hess, "Educability and Rehabilitation: The Future of the Welfare Class," *Journal of Marriage and the Family,* Vol. 26 (November, 1964), pp. 422–429.

22. Donald McNassor, "This Frantic Pace in Education," address to the Long Beach City Schools Counselors Association and Psychological Services Administration Staff (Long Beach, California, October 3, 1966), p. 2. (Mimeo.)

23. Irving Sigel, "Developmental Considerations of the Nursery School Experience." In Peter Neubauer (Ed.), *Concepts of Development in Early Childhood.* Springfield, Ill.: Charles C Thomas, 1965. P. 97.

24. Martin Deutsch, "Disadvantaged Children and the Learning Process." In Martin Deutsch and associates, *The Disadvantaged Child.* New York: Basic Books, 1967. P. 44.

25. Eleanore Braun Luckey, "Family Goals in a Democratic Society," *Journal of Marriage and the Family,* Vol. 26 (August, 1964), p. 275.

26. Sally Liberman, *A Child's Guide to a Parent's Mind.* New York: Henry Schuman, 1951.

27. Luckey, "Family Goals," p. 276.

28. Hobart, "Commitment," p. 407.

29. Louis E. Raths, Merrill Harmin, and Sidney B. Simon, *Values and Teaching.* Columbus, Ohio: Merrill, 1966. P. 27.

2

The Learning-Valuing Process:
A Teachable Content for
Parent Education Programs

In the first chapter, we discussed the impact of social change on the traditional teaching role of parents. The changes have been so profound that parents are no longer certain what the world is like, what it will be like for their children, or what to teach them that will have meaning a decade hence.

We focused on two aspects of this highly complex problem that may be relevant to developing programs to meet the needs of today's parents:

1. The constantly accumulating wealth of knowledge and the resultant impact on every dimension of living pose a many-faceted challenge to parents. The concept of the mature person as one able to love, work, and play must be broadened. Today's adult must also understand the world around him, know how to manage knowledge, solve problems, and find new solutions that are at once true to himself and to the needs of society. He must be the ever-deepening center of his own learning in the face of constant change, so that his individuality is not lost. Parents need to perceive their teaching role in a new way, so that those first precious years of a child's life shall lay the groundwork for an adulthood in which can be found significant meaning in life in a rapidly changing world;

2. The prevalent value confusion, in the face of world-shaking conflict between peoples and countries, also demands urgent inspection. It calls upon agencies to find ways to help parents come to grips with the conflict in values and social attitudes. Parents need this clarification for their own personal direction. Children need to know what their parents believe in, to give their growth meaning. It challenges parents to engage in the valuing process, to understand how values and attitudes are transmitted, and to carry this understanding into their daily interaction with their children.

These are the tasks for which parents are often the least prepared. The content of parent education programs has been as variable as the range of agencies conducting them—each agency with a different focus, different premises regarding child-rearing behaviors, different methods of education. The pendulum swings of theory, the spate of (often conflicting) data from the behavioral sciences, the many different lenses through which behavior is observed (with differences of interpretation as a consequence) overwhelm the agency seeking to work with parents. Long-held theories falter under contradictory research. Family structure and function vary greatly from one context to another. Programs that were built on the needs of middle class parents seem misdirected in low income settings. We do not really know what the most desirable attributes of family functioning are; and even if we did, parent educators have run into many snarls in teaching people "what they should be."

Somehow we need to search out the universals, the common dimensions of growth that *all* children whatever their origin require if they are to find meaning and value in their lives, and to determine whether the parent can acquire greater competence in facilitating that growth, whatever his life setting.

As we noted in Chapter 1, our great need is to develop programs containing the following elements: a teachable content readily adaptable to the formats of a variety of different agencies and to the needs of a broad range of parents differing with respect to class, cultural, and subgroup factors; parent educators who are really educators, capable of providing for parents the full range of alternatives and the structure within which the making of free personal decisions is possible; a flexibility in the focus of the program, making it responsive to the present needs of parents, but sufficient sturdiness in the framework to enable learning; concrete and positive approaches which focus on extending the parents' capabilities rather than remediating their present failures.

We need to explore current trends in the behavioral sciences to see if they give us tools for this task. We need to look at new understandings about how children learn to think, feel, and value; what they need for this learning; how parents teach and what they need for teaching; and what this might mean for program development.

HOW CHILDREN LEARN

NEW IDEAS THAT GIVE US TOOLS

We Can Modify Development

We used to think that the sequence and rate of a child's development was fixed. It unfolded as the child matured. Parents could only foster or fail to foster whatever potential the child had inherited, but never really change it.

With the growth of science and research, this concept has changed. We have seen modifications in physical development through better prenatal care, nutrition habits, immunization, and medical care. Children are, as a result, reaching stages in their motor development sooner than ever before.[1] We have seen modifications in intellectual, social, and emotional development when the environment and the nature of the child's experiences are changed. Research on the effect of poverty on the young child shows that a child's experiences can impair his capacities for growth. By contrast, enriched experiences can evoke greater depth and range of development, and an enhanced capacity to deal with life.

The process of maturation makes new behavior possible. But whether or not a child is ready to produce new behavior seems to depend just as much on his previous experience, what he was able to learn from it and whether he has learned *how* to learn from his experience.

The position that development is modifiable makes a difference to parents. The parent then has more than the passive role of nurturing what the child inherited. If the child's growth is inextricably tied to the quantity and quality of his experience, then the parent has an active role in determining that quantity and quality. This does not take us back to the old concept that the child is a ball of clay to be molded. It takes us forward to the realization that the child's own uniqueness can be enhanced by a deeper awareness of the potential for learning within his environment, whatever it might be.

Learning Starts at Birth

We used to see the brain as a telephone switchboard. A stimulus was plugged in and a response elicited; but this stimulus did not make any essential change in the system. Now we see that the brain acts much like a computer. A stimulus goes to a particular center, but, in computer language, the brain is also scanned for any similar data previously stored. This means that with each new piece of information, patterns of thought are reorganized and accommodated to the new information.[2]

Thus, from birth, the infant learns from every stimulus that reaches him. If his environment offers him enough safety, variety, repetition, and clarification, he gradually learns to define these impressions and put them in some order. If he can put them in some order and label them with words, he can register and store information, hold onto it over time, and retrieve it when he needs it. The earlier he begins this process, the greater his capacity for further learning becomes, and the greater his facility for meaningful organization in the face of new experience.

The child must learn to handle all manner of impressions, not just what he hears, tastes, sees, smells, and feels. He must process the vast array of language and thought patterns, intonations, feelings, attitudes, values, and desires that are implicit in more concrete stimuli. Through this, he learns his way into the culture.[3] Through this process, he builds a picture of himself—who he is and what he can do. A sense of self, a capacity to love and be loved, independence, social competence—are integral parts of what a child learns from interacting with his environment. "We see development of intelligence, not as coldly rational information-processing, but as a capacity—in addition—for warm, feeling-laden, sensitive, relativistic, imaginative thinking." [4] The development of both the mind and human capacities depends, then, largely on learning. How they develop depends on how the child comes to perceive and make sense out of his experience. How the child learns to make sense out of his experience depends upon what that experience is like and, often, the degree to which an adult has mediated between the child and his experience and clarified its meaning.

Much has been written about the differences often found between the experiences of middle class and slum children. This statement on the nature of the middle class parent-child interaction system is a succinct summary:

The child in many middle-class homes is given a great deal of instruction about the world he lives in, to use language to fix aspects of this world in his memory, and to think about similarities, differences and relationships in this very complex environment. Such instruction is individual and is timed in relation to the experiences, actions and questions of the child. Parents make great efforts to motivate the child, to reward him, and to reinforce desired responses. The child is read to, spoken to, and is constantly subjected to a stimulating set of experiences in a very complex environment. In short, he "learns to learn" very early. He comes to view the world as something he can master through learning. In fact, much of the approval he gets is because of his rapid and accurate responses to this informal instruction in the home.[5]

In impoverished settings, sensory impressions are often either severely limited or so overwhelming as to defy ordering. The child's freedom to interact, to explore at his own pace, is greatly restricted by the nature of his situation. Adults do not see that they have a role in mediating his experience other than to ward off further problems. Parental instruction is limited to unelaborated demands; language is not used specifically enough to enable discrimination and define relationships. The child is not seen in terms of his own individuality, nor is he rewarded for the efforts he makes toward forming concepts. Frequently, therefore, he does not learn how to learn, nor does he perceive the world as something he can master.

We have polarized the argument. There is, in fact, between the advantaged parent's often conscious, perceptive teaching role, on the one hand, and the impoverished parent's inability to conceptualize any dimension of a teaching role from within the hopelessness of slum life, on the other, a vast range of degrees in the structure and content of the parent-child interaction system. We have carried each position to its logical extreme in order to emphasize that the natural processes of cognition, which determine the extent to which the individual will find his total experience relevant and productive of growth, are dramatically affected by the circumstances of his early life.

The discovery that the skills of perceiving, thinking, and knowing integrate all behavior and experience makes a difference to parents. The knowledge that these learning skills can fully develop only when certain experiences are provided also makes a difference. If we see that what the child becomes, in all aspects of his development, depends on his ability to make sense out of his experience, then parents have a real role in helping the child develop the skills that allow him to do this effectively.

Learning Comes Naturally

We once thought that a child reached out to new experience because some basic instinct needed to be satisfied; this unsatisfied need engendered anxiety, and the child was driven into the experience in order to reduce that anxiety. Today the will to learn is seen as part of the child's nature. The child, from birth, actively interacts with his environment; he reaches out for experience. If encouraged, he engages in a wide range of activities that seem to satisfy no other need than the drive to deal effectively with his environment, to master it. His increasing competence in these transactions is its own reward.

Therefore there is a competence motivation as well as competence in its more familiar sense of achieved capacity. The behavior that leads to the building up of effective grasping, exploring, crawling and walking, attention and perception, language and thinking, manipulating and changing the environment is directed, selective and persistent, and is continued not because it serves primary drives, which indeed it cannot serve until it is almost perfected, but because it satisfies an intrinsic need to deal with this environment.[6]

The concept of competence as motivation is important for parent education, because motivation produces behavior that leads to learning, and learning leads to growth and change. If we see the parent as inherently motivated by desire for competence, then we can stimulate that desire, even in spite of heretofore insurmountable parental defenses. Parent educators are concerned about parents who do not seem motivated to seek new insights into their parent role, at least through the ways we have thus far provided. Perhaps the assessment of motivation is a faulty starting point. Perhaps we can focus on what there is to be learned; define, clarify, and present it; and make effective interaction with this knowledge available. If this process provides tools for greater competence, then the parent's motivation for further learning and his concept of his own increasing competence will follow. With an increasing sense of competence may well come greater spontaneity and emotional expression between parent and child, which is after all one of our most precious goals. When any dimension of life becomes intelligible and more manageable, it strengthens one's total grip on his life situation.

Parents, too, are concerned about their children's motivation. But if we see the child as inherently motivated by a desire to deal with his environment effectively, then part of our attempt to encourage or discourage certain experiences can be abandoned. Within each parent's capacity, the meaning of "achievement" can be more clearly defined; he can accept the uniqueness of the child and focus on the experience he can provide that will nurture his child's natural striving for mastery.

Learning Happens Best When Guided

We used to think that all we had to do was tell children what the world was like and they would know. Then we realized that the child, from the very beginning, learns through his own involvement with concrete objects, people, and events. He looks, touches, tastes, smells, lifts, holds, arranges, and sorts until he begins to attain insight into a sense of order and to define the reality of himself and his environment. But experience alone, with no opportunity to attach meaning to it through the acquisition and increasingly skillful use of language, with no one mediating between the experience and the child, is limited experience; it is insufficient to promote the child's development and often incapacitates him for further learning. We are now beginning to see that children learn best when clarification accompanies their concrete experience.[7]

There is much evidence that children are learning to think logically sooner than they ever were before. In their play, they struggle at an early age with the processes of thinking and reasoning, trying to put ideas together. But without adult guidance they often form incorrect conclusions that stand in the way of more accurate perceptions of reality, and they need guidance in sorting information so that their experiences will be educative rather than miseducative.[8] Today so much more learning is abstract, requiring extensive cognitive and linguistic skill for its mastery, demanding the grasping of broad ideas, that adults must find ways to encourage and develop the habit and ability to reason, to think, to make inferences, to generalize.[9] There is no reason to believe that a discovery is more meaningful if a child has to flounder aimlessly for a period before he makes it,[10] or that the process of discovery has to be itself discovered.

This principle of guided learning does not only apply to the child's discovery of basic scientific concepts through his daily interaction with such phenomena as evaporation, weight, balance, or absorption. It also applies to the concepts of self-esteem, social values, skills, and attitudes that are implicit in his everyday life. These latter concepts too, if the parent guides and mediates the child's experiences with them, enhance the child's awareness of what is happening to him, what he is learning, and how it all relates to other experiences he has had. He begins to see where he is heading in his learning and has some idea of how to get there. The meaning of the parent's role in mediating experience is lucidly illustrated in studies of migrant children, who have traveled far more than most middle class children, but who are unable to evidence any level of awareness or learning from such "broadening" experience because no one made the learning "visible" to them. No one assumed a teaching role.

There is evidence that children learn best from a combination of being given explanations and stimulation to derive understanding from their own experience. This indicates that the parent might well assume the question-asking role formerly assigned exclusively to the child. If we provide a learning environment, are aware of the nature of the child's unique interaction with it, *and* recognize the potential of learning in that situation, then we see the growth-enabling function of asking questions as well as answering them. A child questions: through questions of our own we may determine what ideas the child has about the topic of his questions. With this information, we are able to respond in a way that is appropriate to the child's level of understanding. We are less likely to baffle him with too much information, or to misinterpret his question. Moreover, raising questions that help him extend his own thinking is perhaps as important as answering.

The idea that learning happens best when it is guided and clarified is an important concept for parent education. Parents, whatever their background, know a lot more than children do, but they often do not see their essential role in bringing this knowledge to their children. Enabling parents to weave their knowledge effectively into the child's growing concept of himself and his world is an appropriate focus for parent education. Helping parents to perceive their mediating role and acquire skills in this interaction process is an effective framework for dealing with parents because it stresses what the parent already knows and builds upon it.

We can approach any given situation with the questions: What do you value here? What is the child learning? What do you want him to learn? What does he need in order to learn that? What are the steps, the experiences, that can help him get there? How can we use his spontaneous experiences to help him see the learning process for himself? How do we ask the kinds of questions that get him thinking on his own? This approach serves to take the situation out of the often blocking, emotion-laden areas of parent-child interaction and provides perspective for the parent. Focusing on the mediating role contains the inherent values of seeing the child as unique, worthwhile, and needing guidance—the kind of guidance requiring skills that can be taught to parents.

Before carrying it into a wider range of areas of parental concern, let us review the new ideas that underlie this approach and then discuss some of the current understandings of how children learn and what they need for learning.

Our framework rests on certain concepts:

1. We no longer think a parent's job is simply to nurture the potential the child inherits. Development is modifiable. What a child becomes depends in large part on the nature of his experience. Parents, then, have an active role in determining the quantity and quality of that experience.

2. We no longer think that learning is the automatic coupling of a response with a stimulus, with no learning taking place in the face of new experience. Learning begins at birth, and the young child continually strives to reorder his impressions of the world around him so that they will make sense to him. The development of both his mind and his feelings depends on how he learns to do this, which in turn depends on what kinds of experiences he has. Parents can play a key role in guiding the growth of skills that enable the child to find increasing meaning in his own experience.

3. We no longer think a child takes action simply to reduce the anxiety generated by primitive drives. He has an inherent will to learn. He reaches out to new experience for the sheer joy of learning how to cope with it. Parents, too, are motivated by a desire for competence, and recognizing this in themselves and their children clarifies their concept of their role. Increasing parental competence will have a positive effect on how parents feel about themselves and their children.

4. We no longer think that either just telling children things without providing concrete experience or providing experience alone without clarification is enough for effective learning. We know the vital role of play as the child's way of exploring himself and his world. Parents can learn a great deal from an increased awareness of the many dimensions of learning that are inherent in their children's play. If children learn best when parents mediate between them and their experience, enabling them to see what they are learning and use that insight for further learning, then parents can acquire skill from their own experience in this mediating process.

A LOOK AT READINESS FOR FORMAL LEARNING

"Readiness for school" is a concept generated by social change. The common body of knowledge that must be mastered before full participation in today's world is possible demands early acquisition of learning skills. Thus, the point of school entry becomes a point of assessment of the degree to which these skills have been acquired.

What Is Readiness for School?

What do we mean when we say children are ready for formal learning in the primary grades? Do we mean that the child entering school can read, spell, and add? or that he will conform to the mold—sit still, keep quiet and out of trouble? or that he can receive and regurgitate adult-centered material sufficiently well to get high marks? Are these the attributes of the child who is the center of his own learning? Hardly.

What we mean by readiness for formal learning is that the child has a range of skills, concepts, generalizations, and understandings about the world around him that tune him in to the content of the curriculum. He has begun to grasp of that broad common base of knowledge because his family has given him that foundation through their relations with him since his birth. He can make sense of the content of school because that content is related to his previous experience, which has enough in common with that of other children to provide a core of shared experience. It is the task of the school to convert knowledge into teachable form, to define the basic concepts that underlie knowledge and to teach them in a way which harmonizes with the child's experience. It is the child's task to derive and use the full meaning of the school's content and relate it to his total life experience. He should find the process increasingly meaningful and satisfying. To do this, he needs to learn how to learn.

What are the dimensions of learning how to learn? What skills, concepts, understandings, are implied in readiness? At the age of five or six, a child needs a vast accumulation of skills that make formal learning possible. He needs to know how to pay attention; he must desire to listen. He needs a sense of his own body, how it works and responds, how he functions in relation to his environment. He must understand the language the teacher uses. He needs words to let her know what he understands and to ask questions when he doesn't. He must have some basic ability to express his ideas in thought units and in an appropriate and growing vocabulary. He should be able to participate in conversations with both peers and adults. He needs to recognize and identify sounds, objects, feelings, and events and to see when they are different and when they are the same. He must have an awareness that and view them from a position of positive nurturance. We *are* all the objects and events he perceives can be ordered, and be able to use that inner awareness of order to discover the meaning of new experience. He needs to understand simple quantitative relationships and deal with a wide range of basic concepts of time, space, size, and distance. He must have begun to grasp number concepts, the distinction between cardinal and ordinal numbers, and have a growing number vocabulary. He needs to understand simple thoughts, to be able to interpret his own or vicarious experience, to recognize main ideas, and to put events into simple sequence. He needs to see motives and feelings in some of the behavior of people around him, and to have some understanding of causality. He must be able to remember things with some accuracy and to recall his past experience to find meaning in his present reality. He should have some concept of what it means to plan—and to execute his plans—at his own level. He needs beginning skills in solving some of the problems that arise in his everyday life, and to have the idea that there are other alternatives he can consider when something doesn't work. He needs to see himself as a worthwhile person, with the privilege of error, and capable of new growth. He should be able to tolerate delays in gratification in a few situations. He should be able to play freely and enter with enthusiasm into many different play situations. He should seek interaction with his peers, when he wishes to, and find it generally satisfying. He needs to see the teacher as a supporting, information-giving, and interpreting person. He should be able to understand the necessity for structure and order if it is child-centered in its origin. He needs to trust the teacher and the school and receive them as enabling his continuing growth of competence.

This would seem to be a description of an ideal child, and indeed it is. But all these skills and understandings, to varying degrees, must be considered in any discussion of the child's readiness. We are certainly aware that no matter how ideal the early environment, children enter school with varying degrees of readiness. Levels of readiness vary both within any one group and within any individual child, and any group of children will evidence differences in capacities as well as in approaches to learning. We are not concerned here with all the factors that make each child unique, although the school must be aware of children's differences concerned with the kinds of understandings, attitudes, and skills that seem to be universally essential for deriving maximum meaning from a well-planned curriculum, or indeed from the child's total life experience. If he is missing any of these underlying tools for learning, the good school adjusts and uses remedial techniques. This is the role of the kindergarten, but it, too, assumes that much of this learning is well underway.

HOW READINESS HAPPENS *

Let's look at these dimensions of readiness in a brief overview of why the child needs these skills and some educated guesses as to how they develop. Thorough comprehension of how children learn is a long way off. But we owe a good deal to the demands of the poor, which spurred researchers to explore more deeply the factors that may account for differential development. Inferences can be drawn from data on differences in parent-child interaction systems and family life styles about those factors which seem to nurture or inhibit essential learning. However, understanding why learnings do not happen is perhaps less important for our purposes than the awareness that they do happen; that they constitute essential skills for effective, full living; that the parent has a prime role in their development, and that perhaps the skills of this role can be taught, in varying degrees, to parents.

We will look at learning-how-to-learn skills and their development in terms of the larger categories of (1) attention learning; (2) perceptual-motor learning; (3) cognitive learning; (4) language learning; (5) learning about self and others; and (6) learning to value. These skills are inseparably interrelated and are categorized here for simplification purposes only. We will consider their development briefly, indicate some aspects of the parental role in their development, and draw some implications for using a learning-valuing focus in program planning for parent education.

---

* The reader is asked to bear with the oversimplification of this section and urged to use the accompanying bibliographies and other references to amplify his understanding of specific areas.

LEARNING TO ATTEND

Function and development. The child *learns* how to pay attention and to want to listen. To learn from any experience, the child has to pay attention to it. There are many situations in which, out of the many stimuli that assail him, the child must be able to focus on only those that pertain to the task at hand. He needs to do this often enough to incorporate new information and find it meaningful. Part of being able to pay attention, of course, is related to the "match" between the new experience and what he already knows. Whatever requires attending to must somehow intrigue him, and that intrigue seems to be more often stimulated when something in the new experience relates to what he has already mastered. Voluntary attending—and it makes sense only if it *is* voluntary—depends in part on how the child has learned to attend in his early years.

The child learns to pay attention to things from infancy, when he begins to fix his eyes on certain objects and seems to ignore others. His attention is held mainly by change and vividness, but as he grows he begins to sort out the things that happen often enough to demand his further attention. When he can freely explore a varied environment, he becomes involved with things that require attention in order that movement shall take place. He then becomes more concerned with that sequence of activity than with the variety in time, space, color, and so on, around him. *What* he becomes interested in may be more a function of his uniqueness and the substance of his particular milieu then one of learning. *How* he learns to gain satisfaction from attending is more a function of learning. Although there is a wide variance in the dimension of impulsivity-reflectivity as we assess children's ability to attend to a task, a child's capacity for reflective task-approach seems to be a matter of learning.

Role of parents. This learning has a great deal to do with how and to what his parents respond, how they hold the child's attention pleasurably through their interaction with him, provide materials that stimulate periods of exploration. When they nurture in him this freedom to become involved, indicate that there is a sequence to be attended to, interpret to him through their own attention patterns that sometimes one pays more attention to some things than to others, the child's skill grows.

The value of listening becomes apparent. There is good reason for listening when the child knows how good it feels to be listened to, when parents take the time to explain, interpret, clarify. There is much he can learn by listening, and the child sees listening as a way to enlarge his experience.

When a parent relates in a close, consciously intimate way to his child, he nurtures the child's ability to attend to specific things. It is in the one-to-one relationship that this skill develops. Otherwise, life can be merely a million fleeting, formless impressions that are seldom separated from one another, with nothing defined or graded in its importance. Learning to attend is clearly related to the quantity and quality of the frequency, intensity, duration, and relationship of stimuli. A child's "tuning out" may well be a survival technique in the face of a too overpowering babel of sound and impression that he cannot sort out by himself. The attention span lengthens when there are long, unstructured times during which the child can reach out to what interests him. Barring neurological problems, a child's short attention span may well be the result of his being closed off from this kind of experience because his reaching out causes problems for the adults around him. The natural drive to explore becomes dissipated in the failure to find, or to be allowed to find, satisfaction in paying attention to something.

Parents who take a teaching role with their children get involved in the kind of one-to-one activity that fosters much learning, including the ability to attend. A typical activity is reading to the very young child. While the parent's motives may range all the way from a deep desire to instill love for books to an equally deep desire to lull a recalcitrant child to sleep, there are many obvious learnings for the child in the process. The nearness and concern of the parent, the stimulation of pictures of known and unknown things, the growing idea that those squiggles on the page have meaning, the sequence of action that becomes clear through repetition, and much more, come from the simple act of reading to a child.

Many educated parents place high value on this kind of activity. They enjoy it; they know how to use a library; they are aware of the meaning of the experience to the child. They look ahead to realizable goals for him and see his familiarity with books and reading as movement toward these goals. The lower class parent is often weary and harassed, often nearly illiterate; he may have met only failure in his own school experience. He may never have been to a library. He doesn't foresee that his child's life will be any different from his own impoverished existence. He doesn't perceive a role in his child's life other than that of control, and thus doesn't function with his child in this one-to-one way.

Teachability. Again, we have carried the argument to its logical extremes. Between the poles of "advantaged" and "disadvantaged," as the conditions of life affect the individual child-rearing style, there is obviously a wide range of parental responses to any one behavior. Yet, even at the poles, there is something for us to teach. If we focus on the learning implicit in the activity for the child—of which reading to him is an example—rather than on the one-to-one relationship (which may or may not already exist), then perhaps we shall have easier access to a broader range of parents. Whatever form it has taken, the substance of the message we have been sending parents is that good parents read to their children; and the consequence has been guilt on the part of those who don't or who can't, or reading through clenched teeth by a parent doing what he "should be doing" according to the current expert. Now if we change our tack and focus on the learning involved, what we shall say to the parent who can't read is "just sitting with the child and talking about the pictures gives him some of the skills you want him to have for learning, and that's something you really know how to do." We can say to the more advantaged parent, "did you know all the learning that goes on when you read to your child, what it means to him now, how it builds skills and attitudes for future learning? That really makes the whole process more exciting, no matter how much (or little) time you are able to spend."

We know that learning to attend is an essential skill. We have some idea of how it develops. We see something of the role of the parent. We know, too, that parents have a wide range of feelings toward their children which may or may not be amenable to education. However, greater understanding of the impact of guided experience on the child's developing learning skills may lead the parent to become more involved in interaction with his child. The child's response to this more skillful involvement may lead the parent to a greater sense of his own competence. Greater consciousness of his effectiveness may lead to deeper enjoyment in the parent role—and deeper enjoyment may lead to an enhanced parent-child relationship. All of this growth would then derive from the parent's own experience, launched through a positive focus on increased insight into his teaching role, rather than through a negative focus on questioning the parent's capacity to relate to his child.

PERCEPTUAL-MOTOR LEARNING

Function and development. Perception is the ability to really *know* what one is seeing (hearing, feeling, etc.), to attend to it, and to relate it to previous experience. In order to understand his world, the child needs to be able to recognize and identify sounds, objects, feelings, and events. Through his senses, he has to perceive form and shape, size and weight, texture and color, in the mass of things around him. He has to perceive likenesses and differences among them before he can label them and place them in some order. Formal learning requires that he know whether something is whole or in parts, for instance, before he can deal with the most basic mathematical concepts. He must be able to distinguish between figure and ground (what is and what is not to be attended to in any one experience). He must be able to interpret the meaning of pictures as cues to the words he is learning; he must be able to perceive all the attributes of any one object in order to differentiate, classify, and order it. He needs to be able to clearly distinguish between such similar symbols as *o* and *c,* if he is to learn the alphabet. In other words, his senses must feed him accurate and discrete information.

Perception develops through both maturation and learning. Learning to perceive often depends upon eyes, ears, and hands working together. Recognition of form, for example, demands that the eyes and/or hands actively trace visual contours of different forms over and over again until the child can recognize different forms instantly, without conscious effort. The baby needs to perceive depth and distance very early so that he can reach an object and manipulate it: this is essential to his learning about his world. This reaching and handling involves his eyes and sharpens their functioning, so that through this interaction he learns about the permanence of objects—one of the first big ideas he needs in order to think about his experience. When he can discriminate—see the differences and similarities—among forms, colors, distances, sizes, or orientations, he will develop ideas about them. These ideas help him order his experience in a way that gives new experience meaning because it expands something he has previously known rather than just adding to a welter of meaningless impressions.

Role of parents. Early intellectual development is dependent upon adequate perceptual-motor learning. Much of this learning takes place in a nonspecific way as the child freely explores his environment.[11] He distinguishes the differences in sound, weight, and size, for instance, when he plays freely with common objects in the home—such as assorted pots and pans, canned goods, or blocks. He sees, feels, tastes the differences that occur when he spills water on dirt or sand. He recognizes differences in meaning in the different levels of vocal sounds around him. Thus, the environment can provide a wide range of experiences that are basic to his growth.

Severe deficiencies in perceptual skills are seen in children from very low income areas. In early infancy, the circumstances of the slum environment may in fact provide a great deal of stimulation, but the role of the parent in ordering the stimuli in a child-centered manner and bringing them within range of the child's awareness and involvement with them may well be missing. Certainly when the child becomes mobile in a crowded, difficult life situation, his mobility is seen as a burden to already burdened adults rather than as a factor enabling far greater involvement with experience for the child. Exploration, then, is restricted on the one hand, while a welter of stimulation is not mediated on the other, and the organization underlying the barrage of sensations, is not exposed to him for learning.

Teachability. There is a teachable content, perhaps, no matter what the parent's circumstances or degree of conscious involvement in the child's development. Where the parent is open to consideration of a better life for the child, great amount of equipment, time, or energy may not be as essential as the parent's awareness of the learning potential for the child embedded in specific experiences. Providing the lower class mother with demonstrations of simple, inexpensive, and easy-to-make materials that can be used to enhance the child's understanding of his experiences, along with provision of a deepening understanding of why the child needs the experiences, might be a beginning towards helping such mothers foster their children's development. In addition, as such a person aids her child, her sense of competence as a person and a parent may be enhanced. She sees what her child learns from what he does, and she begins to gain satisfaction, in at least this one area of her unsatisfying life, from her own mastery.

Even in more advantaged homes, the learning potential in the child's spontaneous activity may not be perceived by the parent. This is relatively new information, not yet incorporated in the "conventional wisdom" about child growth and development. Although there is a good deal of teaching going on—i.e., naming body parts, counting, alphabet, etc.—much of it is directed toward the child's learning "facts," but is not part of a continuing program aimed at gradual learning to learn. Sharpening the parent's awareness of what he is already providing, what the child is learning from it, and its exciting potential for growth, may increase the parent's skill in making the world comprehensible to his child, and make the whole process of child-rearing more rewarding.

COGNITIVE LEARNING

Function and development. In order to absorb the mass of impressions he is receiving, the child develops a set of cognitive skills. We have briefly described our current understanding about the child's developing ability to attend to and perceive objects and situations. In addition, the child must develop skills that will allow him to register and store information, to restructure his perceptions in the face of new information, to retain perceptions over time and retrieve them when he needs them in a new situation, to develop concepts that explain his experience. Concept formation does not await the appearance of names or labels provided by language development. Language facilitates a process that has already begun on a nonsymbolic level.

In the process of trying to make sense out of the chaos of primitive impressions of sound, light, taste, odor, pressure, movement, etc., the very young child begins to structure his universe. In a stable environment, he gradually becomes aware that objects and situations have specific identities; they have many properties that can be differentiated, categorized, and classified. He learns to group things according to specific features—i.e., color, form, weight, or function. He gradually sees that objects, images, feelings, can be ordered on the basis of their gradations within one dimension, and in ever finer gradations from small to large, light to dark, happy to sad. From sufficient experience with the components of his environment over time he begins to draw inferences about their appearance and behavior, so that he can generalize and predict in new situations. He develops a vocabulary of symbols—words, numbers, sounds, images—that enable him to hold on to his past experience when the concrete objects or events are no longer in front of him, and use that memory to understand new experience. He learns to conduct an inner dialogue with himself that enables this kind of assessment of experience. He moves from his experience with the concrete to the understanding that a picture represents his concrete experience. Finally he needs only a symbol to recall the meaning his experience has given to a specific object, event, or idea.

Role of parents. The child can learn only from the experience he finds in his immediate environment. He needs sufficient *variety* in these stimuli so that all the dimensions of perception are challenged, so that he can observe the many properties of objects and events that he needs to develop ideas about. This means that his environment should provide a wide range of impressions.

The child also needs the opportunity for *repetition*—objects present around him long enough to be explored repeatedly and consistently, so that their properties can be absorbed through his senses and seen in new ways as he uses them over and over again. He needs the same people around him consistently enough to interact with them, observe their responses, and learn to predict their behavior. These people also need to be content with what may seem like half-learnings on behalf of the child, because they know that whole learnings come only through practice with many partial learnings.

The child needs *safety*, a deep sense that as he explores, he will be protected from danger by a parent concerned both for his physical well-being and his growing competence in dealing with his environment. He needs *time* for the freedom to explore. He needs the *freedom to make mistakes,* because that, too, is an integral part of the learning process. He needs *clarification,* an ongoing mediation between himself and his experience, geared to his present level of awareness, so that what he knows becomes more available to him and a conscious part of how he reaches out to and absorbs new experience.

This does not mean that the parent sets about with a daily teaching schedule, with lesson plans and specific goals for achievement. It does mean that the parent sees the child's early years as years of intense interaction, crowded with vital learning that can be deepened by the safety, variety, repetition, time, freedom to make mistakes, and clarification the parent provides for the child's own unique involvement in his experience.

The child's perceptions are made more real to him if the parent interacts in a way that provides the structure and content for meaningful exploration, and then provides labels for what the child is seeing, for the attributes of what the child is exploring. The child grows to understand simple quantitative relationships more effectively if the parent makes his immediate perceptions more real by spelling out such concepts as large–small, few–many, some–none, a lot–a little, enough–not enough as they emerge naturally in the environment. If the parent is aware of the concepts children need to place meaning in their experience, then he is far more conscious of the many situations that bit-by-bit build these understandings, and how the child transfers these understandings to a wider context.

The child begins to understand cardinal and ordinal meanings of numbers if the parent gradually helps him define his own experience with the "oneness" of one, that "two" is adding one more; using number concepts in the myriad daily experiences in the home, helping him slowly to distinguish between first, second, third, last, until the ideas stand for his concrete experience. The child learns to deal with a wide range of basic time concepts when parents, using the child's own immediate experience, talk about now–later, yesterday–today–tomorrow, before–after, next, etc., and sees some of the learning inherent in the order of daily life. The child learns about space more accurately if his own involvement with space is labeled in terms of the dimensions of in–out, over–on–

under, in front–behind, left–right, up–down, high–low, here–there, too big–too little, etc., and he learns the specific meanings of these essential qualifying terms. He learns about weight from his own experience with what is too heavy to move, too light to sink, etc., but these impressions can be given more usable form through parental definition. The child can more clearly discriminate size and shape and learn to order his observations when parents provide experience and talk about it, differentiating big–little, long–short, round–square, small–smaller–smallest in natural daily dialogue. He learns about distance from his own speed in getting places, gradually perceiving the meaning of far–near, too far, right over there, slow–fast; these ideas are often crystallized through parental interaction.

The child becomes aware that he can attach labels to those different textures he feels with symbols like rough–smooth, soft–hard. He learns that an object can be rough, hard, red, and square all at the same time, and that another object that is rough, hard, red, and round is both the same and different. Gradually, then, he can think about an experience without the concrete object or event before him. His parents have sharpened his perception and range of concepts by specific labeling, defining, classifying, and generalizing the child's familiar experiences. They do not do this didactically but by the use of spontaneous occurrences and by consciously providing those experiences that foster involvement and discovery.

The young child can better understand simple thoughts, interpret his personal or vicarious experience, recognize main ideas, and put events into sequence when the parent explains and relates past experiences so that they have relevance in the present and future. "Tell me about. . . . What happened next? . . . That's a good idea. . . . Did you like that?" The child can infer motives and feelings in events because his parents have made his experiences personal, have elaborated the underlying causes for behavior, have qualified and extended the single event into both cognitive and affective dimensions. "She hit you because she was very angry about. . . ." "That's hard to do when you're tired. Why don't you try it after your nap?" Parents often mediate between a child and his feelings, but not often with an awareness of the essential conceptual learning taking place, of how much more than "feelings" they are teaching.

The child can predict events and understand cause-and-effect relationships because he has been allowed to experience a wide variety of stimuli and events and his own growing sense of consequences has been clarified by the parent's willingness to discuss the why and how of things. "What happened when you pushed that too hard?" "Will that block roll like your ball?" The child learns to remember accurately and use his past experience to make present reality more meaningful when parents give him a chance to think about, talk about, what happened yesterday, or last time, or aid him in a determination of what was different or the same in this situation.

He begins to plan and execute his own ideas more efficiently if parents value initiative, help him sort out the specific components of a task into manageable sequence, and reward him for his effort, no matter how inept by adult standards. "What do you need to do first? If you pick up those blocks one by one, maybe it will be easier to put them on the shelf. That was a good try." He learns to solve problems that arise in his daily experience if parents help him apply his past experience, accept and help him learn from his mistakes, enlarge his range of alternatives and skills for dealing with his problems. "Last time you tried to put that big block on top, it fell down. This time you propped it up. Did it help?" "Yesterday Harry went home when you hit him. Maybe today you can use words and tell him what you don't like." This is something more than the specific teaching of social skills. It is, in a broader sense, seeing one's parental role in terms of enabling the child to learn more adequately from his own experience and deal with it in terms of the underlying concepts.

Teachability. Throughout this overview of some of the dimensions of cognitive learning in the early years, the stress has been on the parent and the role he plays in mediating the child's experience. This level of involvement is predicated on many affective components of a parent-child relationship that lead to the desire to take this kind of role. It is the authors' contention that these skills are perhaps more teachable—if the increments of learning are adjusted to the parent's capacities—than the more abstract and complex dimensions involved in the educational goal of increasing the parent's capacity for "tender loving care." The latter goal may well be more meaningfully achieved through increasing a parent's sense of competence in this teaching role.

LANGUAGE LEARNING

Function and development. The very young child moves from the awareness of objects and situations to being able to identify them and their properties, to recognize their similarities and differences, and to discover their relationships. He does this through interaction with his immediate world, through observation and manipulation. But without language, without word symbols to represent his vast array of discrete experiences, he cannot conduct the internal dialogue essential to relating his past experience to present events. He has no sorting and storing mechanisms with which to hold onto his learnings.

Motor exploration may be managed by the child on his own. Even in the most impoverished communities, if there is some open space in which to play children come to school with reasonably well-developed gross motor skills. But if the infant is to learn the skill of language, he needs to be talked to. He needs the opportunity to hear simple labels repetitively. The corrective feedback offered to the much-listened-to child gives him the chance to evoke, respond to, absorb, and experiment with the rules of language behavior. He learns under what circumstances people listen to him and how he can attract attention and hold it.[12]

The words a child is given to label objects, persons, or properties not only serve to make his sensations explicit for him but shape the way in which he perceives the varied aspects of his world. Spoken language powerfully conditions what is learned and how it is learned, and therefore profoundly influences future learning. This means that the meaning given specific objects and events in any one home is determined not only by the dictionary meaning of the word but also by the connotations this particular socioeconomic and cultural context assigns to it.[13]

The work of Bernstein [14] is extensively quoted in the literature on language development, particularly as it relates to the influence of the parent. His theory of elaborate and restricted language codes has added depth to our understanding of the role of language in the development of cognitive processes. An elaborate linguistic code is characterized not only by an extensive vocabulary, which facilitates labeling of a vast range of discriminations, but also by a richer syntax, which facilitates a high level of qualifying, concept-enriching discussion. A restricted language code is characterized by rigid syntax and limited vocabulary, thus the verbal tools for making discriminations, qualifying events, or widening the listener's concept of his experience are lacking.

Role of parents. The child brought up in a home where language is elaborate in structure and content can more often see his life and his experience with greater breadth and depth. He is given the verbal symbols for an ever-widening number of aspects of what he deals with; his tools for internal dialogue as he meets new experiences are constantly increased. He can become aware of the existence of objects and events that he has not yet experienced. Because he understands what he has lived through, he wants to understand more. Because he has made sense of what he has seen, he is eager to explore further.

The child raised in a home where language is restricted often lives in an ill-defined world, with perceptions unlabeled and unrelated, and has enough to cope with in his present bewilderment without seeking new experience.[15] He does not develop a clear awareness of his own behavior in relation to other persons and objects if the language he hears is confined to "Stop that." He does not perceive any alternative behaviors if all that he hears is "Don't do that," and if he is continually restrained from doing. He cannot derive any rules for guiding his future behavior out of "Shut up" —other than to learn to avoid that which elicited the rebuke. "Don't bother me," when it is a frequent, generalized, and undifferentiated command, does not promote ability to discriminate among situations. He cannot really know his own feelings, or develop ways to handle them well, if they are never verbalized or discussed. He cannot deal with the bewildering abstract concepts of life, death, love, sex, or violence, if parents do not have words to define the ideas in ways he can understand, or if they use a barrage of words to change the subject, or use a few words which they universally apply to all events.

The child grows facile with language when parents respond to his first sounds, listen, speak to him, monitor his expressions, feed back and continually expand the range of his language, define and delineate the aspects of his experience. The child can use words and ask questions more effectively when parents encourage verbalization and curiosity and give him a sense of his own worth. He is motivated to question because he can expect feedback and reward for his effort. He can express ideas in thought units more skillfully when his parents speak to him in thought units that are related to his immediate experience and contain the elements of a system he can then incorporate to extend his understanding. His vocabulary expands when parents accept his beginning efforts, and in their response to single words or simple phrases use additional words to probe and extend the possibilities he sees in the situation but didn't have the words for. He can participate in conversations with both peers and adults more fully when parents relate to him in a way that provides the verbal tools, the chance for practice, the experiences that give him something to talk about, and the sense of self that motivates self-expression.

Teachability. There is much material and meaning for parental exploration of the function of language, regardless of the parent's own linguistic code. The language parents use not only enables the child to develop his learning skills but reflects the way in which the parents view the world, and their place in it, the values they hold for themselves and their children, the attitudes they have, and their style of life. On the other hand, parents can sharpen their mediating skills by being aware of how language is learned, as this process is now understood, and why children need words to attach to their experience. This would help parents to make fuller use of what they can already put into words, no matter what their code. On the other hand, parents can take a new look at the many other implications in what they say to children as they impart meaning in attitudes, values, and action. Thinking through and conceptualizing values clearly and consciously, enables parents to express in words what they feel is important for their children to learn. In our experience, middle class parents with an elaborate linguistic code gain many insights into the hidden messages they communicate to their children by closely examining the nuances of meaning in the words they choose. Parents with a restricted linguistic code also gain from increased awareness of their own language. When discussions with parents are oriented to language, parents can be brought to understand the need for words that clarify the attributes of their environment. If we take an approach of expanding upon resources already available to parents, they can become more conscious of the power of language and more skillful in using words to help their children learn to learn.

LEARNING ABOUT SELF AND OTHERS

Function and development. How a child learns to feel about himself and other people, how he learns to value himself and his place in his world, how he learns to care first about his "significant others" and then the more generalized others, is really the core of concern in parent education. The essential concepts of self (trust, autonomy, independence) are learned. A child's image of himself as valued and worthwhile is learned. These self-concepts affect how he perceives his experience and its meaning to him. Our information about how children grow is the basis of early childhood education methods. The use of this knowledge can be extended to be the foundation of sense of self and others from the first moment of a child's life. Concepts of self and others arise out of social interaction. The child builds a concept of himself from awareness of himself, of others to him; similarly, he comes to understand others and their roles well enough to "play" those roles and feel what they are like.

Role of parents. A child learns to see himself as a worthwhile person more easily when his parents see him as the center of his learning and his experiences as the arena for this learning. The child can be helped to tolerate delayed gratification if parents recognize that such tolerance has to be learned, and if they help him see which situations warrant postponing gratification and for what purpose. The child more readily learns how to play and to place himself in imaginary situations when parents realize that play is the medium through which he explores, extends his capacity to cope with the world, for putting it under some measure of control. In play he learns to handle emotions in a safe way. He experiments, trying on roles and attitudes and behaviors to see how they feel. He may place himself in situations he is not yet ready to handle in real life. And in play he may practice his coping skills. Much of later learning involves the ability to place himself in situations with which he is completely unfamiliar. This ability also, is developed in the free, unstructured play of early childhood, especially when the parents are aware of the functions of play. The young child will seek interaction with other children with greater ease if parents understand the learnings involved when children play together, provide the child with the opportunities and the climate for developing satisfying social skills, and respect his need to refrain from interaction at times.

The child learns to accept differences in other children when parents sharpen his awareness of what *he* is like as a worthwhile person, and show him that others who are different add spice to life and are not a threat to him. He will more readily identify with other people if parents show him that any particular color, life style, belief, or personality trait is not more desirable than any other, and if they reinforce exploration and welcome variety. The child will grow to see adults generally as supporting, information-giving, and interpreting people when the parent plays this role for the child, provides a model for the child's expectations of other adults, and mediates the child's responses to a broad range of differences in people and behavior. Children will understand the need for realistic structure and order when their daily experience provides a sense of inner security.

Teachability. Parent educators have always encountered problems in using their knowledge about how parents nurture or inhibit learning. Differential personality traits do seem to result from differential components of parental permissiveness or restrictiveness, acceptance or rejection. Extensive research bears on this issue. But it is extremely difficult to generalize from the unique combinations of qualities found in any one family. Each parent works out his own style according to his background; his experience, personality, and values; the socioeconomic context; and his own parents' style. A parent can rarely be made to shift from one end of the spectrum to another, even if research demonstrated unequivocally that one approach is more effective than another, or if we were certain what we meant by "effective."

We *are* seeing, however, that permissiveness without the active nurturing of the learning process, without the positive encouragement of growth, may serve to limit the child's ability to learn. Thus, the permissive parent may need to learn to stimulate fuller growth. On the other end of the continuum, restrictiveness may also come from the failure to perceive the nature and function of the parental teaching role. Thus, the restrictive parent may be able to learn to relax his rigid limits on the child when he understands more about what children learn from free exploration. The parent's concept of himself as a teacher in the life of his child seems paramount in parental competence today, in the sense in which we use it here. This understanding may enable permissiveness to be given structure and depth, and establish reasonable boundary lines for restrictiveness, providing a more creative role for love and diminishing the reasons for rejection, insofar as these factors are amenable to education. *Intro.*

A child's growing sense of trust in others to care for and protect him, his developing sense of competence in coping with his world, his deepening awareness that he is the core of his own action and learning are *learned* from the nature of his experience and his parents' participation in that experience. A greater awareness of how this learning happens can assist parents to bring learnings about self and others into sharper focus. With this awareness, the use of daily experience can be made consistent, that parents can feel more competent to deal with daily events in a way that helps children to derive new insights and discover relationships they had not seen before. This is very different from the kind of parental attitude that is judgmental. Parental judgments of "good" or "bad" have little or no meaning for the child. If the parents have some information about what the child needs to learn in order to be a competent person, about how far the child has developed thus far, what experiences will help him learn the next step, and what kind of mediating role the parents should play, then life is no longer a power struggle between parent and child, but an exciting growth process in which they are both engaged.

A learning focus on parent-child interaction may be an effective place to start with a broad range of parents who vary greatly in the ways in which they relate to their children, in how they see their role, in what they mean by loving their children. When a program for parents starts with what the young child needs to learn, increasing the quantity and quality of the parent's interactive skills has a vital impact on the quality of their relationship. The parent who sees his role in helping the child sort out his experiences will see new purpose in interaction. As a simple example, when the parent sees the value of asking the child, "Do you want to wear your red or your blue shirt?" as a way of helping him use his own experience to learn important concepts, he is also telling his child many other things. The parent is also saying, "I care enough about you to ask; I feel you are big enough to make up your own mind; I will respect your decision; your growth is important to me." The child's positive response to these many messages has a cyclical effect that the parent begins to feel. The greater response of the child to the parent, who is focusing on his mediating skills, deepens the parent's sense of competence in a role parents often find bewildering.

LEARNING TO VALUE

Function and development.   It is important to look at how the young child learns values and how he learns to value some things over others. The infant is true to his own values, according to Rogers.[16] He values food when he is hungry, but not when he is full. He values security and rest, but will reject them for new experience. This seems to be an organismic process within himself— he chooses whatever will be self-actualizing at the moment. He then begins to learn what is important to other people, to those he depends upon for security and love. Through the process of reward and punishment, he learns from the responses of his parents, whether they encourage or inhibit, smile or scold, hug or slap him for what he does. As he grows, he tries to identify with and imitate the value patterns of those closest to him; he begins to perceive the generally accepted patterns of the family and community as well as what is not acceptable. Depending upon the degree to which he is the center of his own learning, he develops the ability to consider alternatives, imagine their various consequences in terms of his past experience, and choose the one he thinks most appropriate to the situation.

Role of parents.   Values are an integral part of the learning process and determine to a great extent what a person, whether child or adult, does with his learned skills and concepts. Thinking may be understood as a method of inquiry directed toward understanding; it helps us see the relevant alternatives. Values are criteria by which we choose from among those alternatives. While thinking may help us to anticipate a variety of consequences associated with the alternatives we consider, valuing leads us to make a choice.[17]

A clear-cut set of values is essential to sturdy emotional and intellectual growth. The parents' relative security in what they believe, or their conscious rethinking of their values in terms of their goals for their child, are integral to the child's successful search for meaning, which he finds first in the life of his family. While the child's values may change as he matures in a changing world, the experience he gains from the model of a parent who functions from a core of observable values gives him essential tools for self-determination.

Teachability. It is the *process* of valuing that is teachable. Based on an assessment of today's reality, parent educators need to place primary emphasis on the need for value clarification in their definition of role and function. Adult education is an open system, based on voluntary participation. This is not to say that parent educators are not responsible for having clear aims and value judgments. In an open system, there is as much need for a sense of direction as in a closed system. The difference is that in one the choices are made by the participants, and in the other they are imposed by the authorities.[18]

A LEARNING-VALUING FOCUS: TEACHABLE CONTENT

STARTING WITH A LEARNING FOCUS

The thrust of parent education programs can be learning-centered rather than problem-centered. A learning-centered program has a learning focus. Rather than focusing on existing problems and current failures, the educator can show parents a new conceptualization of their role. He can help the parents see the interrelationship of learning and the capacity to understand one's experience. He can help parents explore the kinds of experiences children need to perceive the meaning of their world and find their place in it. He can clarify the parents' role in providing relevant experiences and help parents gain skills in mediating between the child and his experiences so that information becomes visible to the child and thus available for use in new learning situations. He can help parents see how much they already know that is the substance of this interactive process and enable them to find new satisfactions and a sense of competence in the parental task.

Whether they are working with parents individually or in groups, parent educators can begin their task with the expectant parent or the planning-to-be-expectant parent. Discussion may center on the kinds of experiences parents can provide and why, presented concretely or abstractly, as the situation demands. Programs may follow the development of the young child, taking their direction from the actual parent-child experience, with a view to awareness of the learning potential in that experience, providing skills, and increasing competence.

Even the parent who is already well-grounded in the role of mediating growth can learn much about children's learning. For example, a child may ask a question: "Mommy is it raining?" The mother, willing to answer her child's questions at almost any time, sees that the sun is shining and replies warmly, "No, dear, it is not." End of discussion.

For example, let us look at this exchange between a child and a mother who sees her teaching role more clearly:

Child: Mommy, is it raining?
Mother: What do you think?
Child: Well. . . . Yes, I think it is.
Mother: Why do you think it's raining?
Child: That lady is carrying an umbrella.
Mother: The last time it rained, what did you see?
Child: The streets were wet.
Mother: What else?
Child: The cars were wet. The streets got sloshy.
Mother: Anything else you noticed about the cars?
Child: Ah . . . er . . . their wipers were going.
Mother: Mmmhmm . . . are any of those things happening now?
Child: Noooo. . . .
Mother: Then is it raining?
Child: I guess not.
         (A moment of silence)
Child: Then why is the lady carrying an umbrella?

Mother: Why do you think she is?
 Child: Maybe the sun is too hot for her.
Mother: That's good thinking.

In this mediating role, the mother first probed to find the point the child had reached in thinking about what he observed. The child's first conclusion was that because the lady was carrying an umbrella, it must be raining. He was relating some of his past experience to the new situation in order to understand it. But his conclusion was wrong. The mother didn't stifle his curiosity by telling him he was wrong, but asked him a question that helped him bring more of his own information to bear on the problem he was trying to solve. He found, to his delight, that he could recall a good many attributes of a rainy day from his own memory. The mother helped him use that recall in order to determine whether the current situation was the same or different. If it were different, it needed to be seen in a new way. She gave him time to integrate his growing awareness that this situation was indeed different. By recalling what it is like when it rains he can then turn to thinking about what it is like when it is not raining and then figure out that the lady with the umbrella must be adoptig this rainy-day behavior for a reason other than the child first assumed. He searched for that reason and found it himself. His mother told him he was doing something valuable—he was thinking for himself, and she valued that behavior.

The mother needed no scientific information about precipitation—that was not the question in the child's mind. (Knowledge of a scientific kind will, of course, serve to extend the child's grasp of nature when that question does arise.) She was simply aware that the child's spontaneous question, arising from his own observation, could be a delightful source of dialogue that could have meaning for them both. She saw her role as deepening the meaning the child was deriving from his experience by defining and extending his conclusions, guiding him to draw on his own capacities to reach a clearer conceptualization of what he observed and a deeper sense of his own competence as a person who can figure things out. She had the understanding that she had enriched his awareness of the world a little further. She knew that merely to have made the observation that sometimes people carry umbrellas to keep off the sun at some other time, when he was not involved in this particular experience, would not have any such effects as it was having now, within the context of his immediate interest. She also knew that to have answered his question with "no, dear, it isn't raining" would have been a failure to use the potential for learning that lies in the thousands of incidents in daily life. It was a brief discussion; in fact, the only conversation they'd had in a very busy day. But they both felt very good about it.

With this focus on extending the child's responses to his own experience, the values parents are teaching are implicit in the ways in which they relate to their children. When we add to the parent educator's approach the additional focus of clarifying the valuing process, we strengthen the framework within which the educator and parent can deal with many aspects of the parent-child relationship.

AIDING THE VALUING PROCESS

We have stressed the urgent need for parents to learn how to develop their standards of value, to sort out from the welter of contradictions and paradoxes those values which are meaningful to them—feel right to them—and give structure and substance to the way in which they relate to their children. To have validity, values must grow from conscious choices among alternatives that are clearly seen. They evolve out of the experience of the individual and the nature of his interaction with that experience.

If this is true, then educators can no more impose values than they can determine what experiences people will have. They can, however, provide a setting within which a parent can (1) become aware of how often his values are unconsciously reflected in the daily judgments he makes in relation to his children; (2) consciously consider whether these values, once seen, are indeed in line with his own life philosophy and with what he wants for his children; (3) perceive the role he plays in his children's value learning and (4) find some degree of use for the process of valuing, both in his own daily life and in helping his children to incorporate the valuing process into their own cognitive system.

A learning-valuing focus can place behavior problems, the

core of much parental concern, into a more objective framework that gives parents some aids that derive from their own assessment. If the parent educator has faith in man's capacity for intelligent, self-directed behavior, then he creates the conditions that give parents the chance to explore their values if they choose to do so. If he has faith that there are universal values—human dignity, for example, and the desire to live the kind of life which contributes to the well-being of others—he places merit in the process that promotes movement toward these values. If he is fully aware of the impact of experience on value systems and of the multiple forces that have engendered the present value confusion, then he does not sit in judgment as parents struggle with their confusion. There can be no predetermined answers. He therefore both values the meaning of individual choice and accepts the wide range of possible choices, including the choice not to choose. He sees that a clear-cut set of values is a basic strength of family life in that it enables the growing child to have a sturdy structure against which to carve out his own values. If the parent educator uses his own value system in this way, then it also serves as factor of strong support for parents as they sharpen their own concepts of value—accept, reject, clarify the value guidelines that have meaning for them. His values are clearly labeled as his; the climate he establishes gives parents the freedom to view his values as critically as they do their own. He questions those who agree with him with as much concern for thorough examination as he questions those whose view he personally cannot hold. This desire to assure that a parent's choice of alternatives shall be as true to his deeper tendencies as the parent wishes is part of the parent educator's total approach to his task.

The educator avoids moralizing, criticizing, giving advice, and evaluating. He puts on the parents the responsibility of using the information given them to promote their children's learning potential in the way suggested, or to examine their own behavior or ideas independently and think and decide for themselves what they want to do. As a teacher, the parent educator entertains the possibility that the parent will look at some parts of the situation and not others, or will choose not to look, decide, or think at all. He does not aim to make drastic changes, but to provoke thought and create a climate. This climate does not involve the intensive, probing effort of therapy; it is a steady, relaxed atmosphere in which the raising of questions and the giving of relevant information provides a constant stimulus.

Special focus on social values.   The parent educator should be committed to the responsibility for influencing and participating in the processes of social change. Inherent in this process is the recognition of the urgent need for parents to look at their social attitudes and behaviors in the light of the severe people-to-people conflicts that rock the country and the world. Parent education needs to confront its role in fostering the kind of attitude change that will contribute to solutions rather than reinforce the problems. Parent educators must consider their responsibility in demonstrating to parents the presence of values that inhibit or nurture in their children the growth of a strong sense of commitment to others. The educator must indicate clearly the consequences of inhibiting values and present alternatives that are realistic "next steps" for the parents with whom he deals. But he must do this in a way that clearly leaves the decision to the individual. He must be willing to handle the intense emotional content in these attitudes and to help the individual and/or the group deal with conflict as a vital factor for growth. He must leave all doors open for dialogue and preserve individual integrity if the group condemns. Through the process of dealing with conflict, he draws people closer to problem-solving skills in their own lives, and to the ability to tolerate the temporary discomfort that rethinking values entails.

Methods in the valuing process.   There are differences in the way the parent educator functions with a valuing focus in relation to structure; that is, whether he is working with an individual or a group. His basic tool is what Rath calls "the clarifying response," [19] which can be far more personalized when one is working with an individual. In the one-to-one setting (i.e., the parent-teacher conference) or in the "one-legged conference" [20] (intermittent, sporadic contact with parents as they are involved in the preschool, etc.) the educator has the chance to raise the kinds of questions that serve to move that individual toward clarifying his own thinking in a more personal way. In response to a parent's comment or question, he may ask, "Is that something really important to you?" "How did you feel when that happened?" "Did you consider any alternatives?" "Have you felt that way for some time?" "Would you choose that solution again?"—questions that gently prod the parent to examine his thinking, his actions, his ideas, in the hope that his choices will come closer to what he truly feels is right for him.[21]

In the group, the clarifying response needs to be generalized. "Do some of us find this is true?" "What are some of the other ways people feel about this?" "Can we draw a continuum that gives us the full range of possible ways of thinking about this?" "Is it hard to see that point of view?" "Can we see that values emerge differently from different experiences?" When the process of valuing becomes the property of the group, it loses some of its impact, in one sense; but it is nevertheless effective, and perhaps easier for adults, whose self-image makes recognition of the confusion in their own values more difficult.

There is much that is learned by parents in the process of becoming aware of the wide range of solutions to problems they had previously considered insoluble. When the underlying values that determine these alternatives are made more apparent, parents are better equipped to choose meaningfully, not just in terms of immediate practicality but in terms of their own long-range learning goals for their children.

How does the parent educator use a learning-valuing focus for approaching the concerns of parents?

Example: A parent group raises the problem of the four-year-old who steals. The direction and content of the discussion will be determined in large part by the questions the parent educator raises. The questions the parent educator raises will be determined by his conceptualization of his role. If he sees this role as increasing the parents' competence in helping the child derive full meaning from his experience, within the framework of what the parent consciously values, the following questions might be raised:

What do we know about young children and temptation? What do you remember from your own experience? What do you want the child to learn? There are contradictions in regard to the value of honesty that he sees around him. What are some of them? If we struggle with honesty in our own lives, does this make it harder for him? If we value his being able to "make it" in this world, then what do we want him to learn? If we want him to learn that everybody steals or cheats sometimes, then how would we handle his present behavior? If we want him to be a trusted person, then what do we want him to learn? If we know he needs to learn through his own experience, how do we clarify those experiences for him so that through his own involvement and his own mistakes, he begins to see the value of certain behavior? Children usually grow out of this kind of behavior by nine or ten, but how much do you think parental guidance has to do with this learning? If parents did not use their values in clarifying the child's experience, do you feel this learning would take place? Doesn't what other people think often trouble us here? If we know that learning must center in the child, and that it takes time, practice, and nurture, does this affect how you feel about yourself and your child when incidents like this happen?

Once you know what *you* think about honesty and what you want your child to learn about it, then you can use what we know about *how* children learn to help you set some direction and deal with spontaneous incidents—the increments of learning.

There are many directions in which such a discussion can go. The illustration only serves to indicate that focusing on behavior as learned, the nature of the learning process and the vital role of the individual parent's value base can provide a structure with which a wide range of parent educators, proceeding from an equally wide range of differential backgrounds, can deal effectively with a large spectrum of parental concerns.

Example: "My child always becomes very demanding of my attention when I'm on the phone."

This kind of behavior may derive simply from the young child's inability to share his mother's attention or to understand that she cannot attend to two things at once. It may be symptomatic of his resentment of her use of this convenient device for getting away from the drudgery she finds in her everyday life, her desire to be in touch with other adults, her need to play a role in the community, etc. It is often hard to find a place to start thinking about this kind of question that will not raise defensive barriers to the parent's ability to think it through.

Suppose we approach it from a learning-valuing focus. The parent educator asks the parents to consider: What do you want the child to learn here? There are values in this question. What are they? That you have a right to your own time is indeed a value you may want him to learn as he develops concepts about himself in relation to others. How is he going to learn this idea? Will he learn it just from being told? We know children learn from their own experience. What kinds of experiences will he need to learn about people's right to their own time? From his own experiencing of what "own time" means? How? And he doesn't learn from just one experience. How do we give him practice with this idea? Every mother pushes a child away from an important phone call and sharply demands quiet in some way or other. We all say "Keep quiet" or "Get outta here." What does he learn from that to help him handle this kind of situation the next time? What does he need to make sense out of this experience? Does he need to know that there is some reason and some time factor involved so that he can predict when his needs will be met? What else can we add? Does "Keep quiet until I finish" tell him more, that there will be an end to the waiting, that you find him important enough to explain to, that your limits on him have some reasonable basis?

Again, this kind of discussion can go many different ways. But we are not at this point digging for the mother's specific motivation, although we might explore it more deeply if the mother and/or the group were ready to discuss feelings that might be involved. We start with the learning for the child in the situation and ask for a look at the underlying values that are being taught here. We define the conditions in which children learn most effectively and ask what kinds of experiences the child might need to gradually grasp the ideas involved. We recognize that this is a common experience and relate it to other problems. We look at the language we use, not in terms of properness or grammar, but with regard to how we can use words that give children more clues for their own thinking. We give the mother some tools, based on her own experience, for handling a situation she finds exasperating, and in a way that gives her a larger picture of her child's learning process and her role in it. We hope that this focus gradually gives her a method of approaching other problems that concern her, and we do this in a safe, supporting setting. The educator is saying only that behavior is learned and we need to explore what and why we want the child to learn in order to help him learn that better.

Example: "My child just won't share his toys."

It is important for parents to know that the literature on child behavior tells us that sharing is hard for young children; a long time passes before someone else's feelings are more important to them than their own. Sharing is also realistically dependent upon what there is to share. But if sharing is learned behavior, what are the steps we take, the experiences we provide, the ways in which we use spontaneous experience as meaningful increments of learning such difficult behavior as sharing? What do we value here: the child's conformity to our demands or his coming to his own inward understanding that sharing can make playing with friends work better, or make someone happy, and that is important? If we value conformity to our demands, then what is the child learning? That we value our feelings over his? Sometimes we do. Is this one of them? What about other times? Can we let him learn through being rejected by his friends until he submits to sharing? Or can we give him the job of learning through having some control over his own life? Do *we* only share with some people and not others? Do *we* share everything we have? Does he have a choice? What does he learn through parents who value learning to share and who are willing to help him learn how to do it until he can handle it on his own? Does it help a child to learn when we verbalize goals and reinforce any movement toward that goal? We know lecturing doesn't help much without the experience, and the experience can get all tangled up without talking about it. What can we do with the next experience that ends unhappily because he wouldn't share, when his feelings are at a peak for learning?

When the parent (1) sees the problem, (2) clarifies her own values, (3) defines the learning task against a background of understanding how children learn, (4) knows that the child needs experience defined so that he can use it to see his own growth, and (5) knows that the child needs room to make mistakes and repeated times to practice new learning, then she can see a direction for herself and her child. The problem is not seen as a power struggle, and the parent doesn't get bogged down in probing for deep emotional meanings. The problem is viewed within a conceptual framework where tools for coping with it are more readily available for use—within the framework of seeing the parent as a mediator of his child's experience and learning to help him use his experience to make further learning possible.

SUMMARY

A learning-valuing focus for parent education is an initial attempt to take the tenets of early childhood education and integrate them with new understandings of the permeating effect on child development of both learning and valuing skills. It attempts to reassess the role of the parent in the light of new conceptions of the impact of his teaching role, define dimensions of this role, and abstract what might be teachable.

When the parent educator focuses on the learning inherent in the situation, helps the parent clarify what he wants the child to learn, and provides tools for greater competence in the parental teaching role, parent education becomes something more than a piecemeal, problem-by-problem, supplying of emotional Band-aids or ready-made procedures. It avoids the old guilt-producing bogey of the "You should feel . . ." approach. It starts where the parent is, sharpens his awareness of his own skills, nurtures his own decision-making ability and provides ways in which he can proceed in self-determined directions. The learning-valuing focus of the parent educator gradually becomes the lens through which the parent sees immediate concerns and provides him with a process by which he can place those immediate concerns within the context of long-range goals he has clarified for himself.

REFERENCES

1. Ira J. Gordon, New Conceptions of Children's Learning and Development. In Walter B. Waetjen (Ed.), *Learning and Mental Health in the Schools*. Washington, D.C.: Association for Supervision and Curriculum Development, 1966. P. 51.
2. *Ibid.,* p. 63.
3. Fannie R. Shaftel and George Shaftel, *Role Playing for Social Values*. Englewood Cliffs, N.J.: Prentice-Hall, 1967.
4. Joseph Church and Joseph Stone, *Childhood and Adolescence* (2d ed.). New York: Random House, 1968. P. 183.
5. B. S. Bloom, Allison Davis, and Robert Hess, *Compensatory Education*

for Cultural Deprivation. New York: Holt, Rinehart and Winston, 1965. P. 15.

6. Robert White, Motivation Reconsidered: The Concept of Competence. *Psychological Review,* 66:5 (September, 1959), p. 317.

7. Margaret Faust, What Is A Good Program for Economically Deprived Young Children?, *California Journal for Instructional Improvement,* 8:4 (December, 1965), p. 28.

8. Annemarie Roeper and Irving Sigel, Finding the Clue to Children's Thought Processes. *Young Children,* 26:6 (September, 1966), pp. 335–349.

9. Kenneth D. Wann, Miriam Dorn, and Elizabeth Little, *Fostering Intellectual Development in Young Children.* New York: Teachers College Press, 1962. P. 35.

10. Milly Almy with Edward Chittendon and Paula Miller, *Young Children's Thinking.* New York: Teachers College Press, 1966. P. 139.

11. J. McV. Hunt, *Intelligence and Experience.* New York: Ronald Press, 1961. Pp. 258–259.

12. Vera P. John, Intellectual Development of Slum Children. *American Journal of Orthopsychiatry,* 33 (1963), 813–822.

13. Mario D. Fantini and Gerald Weinstein, *The Disadvantaged.* New York: Harper and Row, 1968. Pp. 96–122.

14. Basil Bernstein, Social Class and Linguistic Development: A Theory of Social Learning. In A. H. Halsey, Jean Floud, and C. A. Anderson (Eds.), *Education, Economy and Society.* Glencoe, Ill.: Free Press, 1961.

15. Fantini and Weinstein, *The Disadvantaged.*

16. Carl R. Rogers, Toward a Modern Approach to Values: The Valuing Process in the Mature Person. *Journal of Abnormal and Social Psychology,* 68:2 (1964), 160–167.

17. Louis E. Rath, Merrill Harmin, and Sidney B. Simon, *Values and Teaching.* Columbus, Ohio: Merrill, 1966. P. 201.

18. Malcolm S. Knowles, Tensions and Gaps from Philosophical Differences. In *Seeking Common Grounds in Adult Education.* Washington, D.C.: Adult Education Association Monographs, 1958. P. 86.

19. Rath, Harmin, and Simon, *Values and Teaching,* p. 53.

20. *Ibid.,* p. 71.

21. *Ibid.*

3

The Decision-Making Process:
A Workable Methodology

Despite a long history of varied attempts to influence parent behavior and to give parents understanding and skills in child-rearing, parent education has not gained a clear-cut identity nor universal acceptance. Here we briefly discuss the different parent education approaches that have been taken, their strengths and limitations, and how the field might benefit from greater specificity and a sharpened focus.

ASSESSING CURRENT METHODS
IN PARENT EDUCATION

Brim's analysis of existing parent education programs is the basis of this consideration. He states:

The primary objectives of those parent education programs acknowledged as successful and outstanding in quality is to make the parent more autonomous and creative, to improve his independent judgment, to increase the rationality of the parent's role performance.[1]

In a broad sense, any advice to parents is parent education or at least an attempt to influence parent behavior. Many organizations and agencies have been interested in influencing child-rearing practices. Few books on child development fail to stress the importance of the relationship of the parent to the child. Most parents are influenced to some extent, at some time, by some form of these efforts.

MASS MEDIA APPROACH

The mass media have had numerous and varied effects on parents and their choice of child-rearing methods. The general effect has been to make many parents self-conscious about their child-rearing practices, with both positive and negative results. The term mass media is used to include books, pamphlets, radio, television, and lectures, all of which are addressed to an audience of anonymous individuals of varied motivations, understanding, and desire to pursue content. These methods appear to have the advantage of economic dissemination of information, but until there is further research (difficult to obtain) on the impact, the economy remains questionable. In the absence of information regarding audiences reached, decisions made about mass media continue to be regulated by matters of cost, expediency, and personal conviction.[2]

Television is increasingly used as a medium of communication in connection with a wide variety of current parental concerns and problems. It lends itself to a varied set of presenting approaches and has great impact. Public service time on commercial stations is not given to a topic unless there is sufficient general interest to attract many viewers. Information can be presented, expert and parent opinions expressed, and questions posed that provide alternatives for parents to consider, but television viewing cannot approximate a setting wherein there is give and take, consideration, and feedback to determine response.

Many newspapers and magazines engage specialists to write columns or articles in response to public interest and demand. Such specialists vary widely in education, experience, and philosophy. The writer bases his content on his own assumptions regarding parental needs and problems. He may answer questions he receives from parents, however, this approach gives little opportunity for exploration of the meaning of the question to the questioner. Although this exchange adds to the questioner's store of information and expands his range of alternatives, it is not likely that it makes the questioner more autonomous. The experience is isolated and brief.

A parent may turn to the vast supply of books and pamphlets to discover the answer to his question of the moment. He may become a serious but solitary student of the changing literature on child development, and read extensively. He is faced with the problem of selection and will find many questions and ambiguities. He studies alone, without guidance. Unless he obtains a carefully selected bibliography, his choice is random and his chore never-ending. It is unlikely that he would study any other subject in this disorganized fashion. As one young mother entering a parent education class said, "I became so confused and disturbed by reading what appeared to be contradictory advice that I simply quit reading."

The mass media provides no place for interaction between the communication source and the seeker. It may arouse anxiety, but there is no place for verbalization or the reassurance that comes from awareness of conflicting theories. There is little stress on individual decision-making as the primary goal of parent education. There is no opportunity for weighing and testing, no consideration of alternatives, no recognition of the fact that the alternative must be suited to the individual. Such approaches attempt to persuade the parent to a particular point of view, frequently based on a single frame of reference. This is advice-giving rather than education. Education presents a range of evidence, values, and attitudes from which the parent may select those meaningful to him and thus increase his skill in rational autonomous problem-solving.

INDIVIDUAL COUNSELING

The use of individual counseling as a parent education method may occur as a primary or as a secondary function of other professional services. As a primary service, it is far less available than in its adjunctive role. Individual counseling when done by a well-trained professional person avoids the problems of anonymity and mere advice-giving. Generally the advantage of this method lies in the fact that the person seeking assistance, either with a specific problem, or a more general desire to sharpen parental skills, is already well motivated.

As an ancillary service, parent education is likely to become limited by the special emphasis of the particular professional group consulted. For instance, much parent education is done by the medical profession, with a primary emphasis on physical care and health practices. Methods range from individual consultation to the handing out of printed materials of an advisory and informational nature. The pediatrician is an authority to whom the parent often turns for an answer to his question. Frequently, there is little opportunity for questioning the answer. The busy pediatrician may say "don't worry" and be wholly correct in his assessment, in terms of the child's physical health, but not be able to take the time from his primary function to tune in on the parent's underlying concerns. It is a rare pediatrician, indeed, who has the time, training, and skill to see his role as enabling the parent to enhance his own problem-solving skills rather than continuing the advice-seeking pattern when problems arise.

Each community service with its own special interest and competence influences a segment of the child's life—but each is dependent on the parent. The doctor cannot successfully treat the baby if the mother will not administer the medicine unless, of course, the child is hospitalized and that, too, requires parental consent. The teacher is limited in educating the child if the parents do not provide interest and encouragement as well as a place to study. The school is limited when it accepts a child who has not had prior experiences that enable him to develop the prerequisite skills.

Social agencies and professions that fulfill the role of official helpers of the family feel a pressing need to "educate" parents. When the child does not succeed, or when the behavioral problem persists, the cause of failure or lack of success is often attributed to lack of parental competence or failure to cooperate.

PARENT EDUCATION THROUGH DISCUSSION

The primary long-range goal of parent education must be to make the parent role-conscious and autonomous. The method that provides the greatest potential for achieving this goal is the discussion group, because it allows for the kind of guided interaction that nurtures learning. The "parent group education" process is described and utilized by the Child Study Association of America as "one form of parent education to help parents increase their com-

petence as parents and develop effective methods of child care." [3]
The need for parent education is based on the belief that something
can be done about the confusion relative to the large body of
knowledge about child development, family relations, and the psy-
chodynamics of human behavior. Auerbach states:

In the experience of the Child Study Association of America, the type of
group education that comes closest to achieving these goals (knowledge
and clarification of role) is the small continuous discussion group made
up of approximately 15 members who meet together for a series of eight to
twelve weekly sessions under skilled leadership. [4]

Approaches to the introduction and determination of content vary among the agencies and organizations using the discussion method. On one hand, Child Study Association of America
stresses the introduction of content as parent-initiated and arising
from the parents' immediate concerns and interests. On the other
hand, the content approach of the program, *Parenthood in a Free
Nation,* is essentially predetermined through the use of a manual
outlining areas of consideration. [5] The National Parent Teacher
Association has long been a sponsor of discussion groups and pub-
lishes topical outlines for study groups. Conceptions of the leader's
role strongly affect process in discussion groups. The lay-versus-
professional leadership controversy is one of long standing. CSAA
consistently makes the case for professional leadership by persons
knowledgeable in the fields of child development, family relations,
and the skills of parent group education. However, lay leadership
has had its proponents in many programs. The *Parenthood in a
Free Nation* program gives specific training to lay leaders in discussion methodology related to precise content. In other programs
leadership ranges from no training at all to varying degrees of
preparation.

Lay leaders may have discussion method skills and no professional background. The "professional" may have knowledge in
relevant areas but no specific skills in group leadership. Too many
assume the advice-giving stance. They are the experts: if the parent
will only follow their advice, all will be well. This approach often
has a guilt-producing and repelling effect. It does not enable parents
to become more autonomous and creative. More often it drains off
the spontaneity essential to warm family relations. This kind of

experience drives many adults away from parent education opportunities.

Leadership may range from the leader as an expert to the
leader as moderator whose function is only to equalize participation, from the task-oriented leader using an outline of content to
the leader who sees any introduction of content as imposition. The
approach to leadership that lies between the didactic and mere
group management has been described by Brim.

To use persons of professional background who elicit by their leadership
the knowledge and experience of the group members, who seek to involve
the members in the problem and to bring to bear on the solution their
own personal data, who encourage the parents' own problem-solving, but
who supply information as needed to fill gaps in parent experience.[6]

Even this definition appears to preclude the introduction of content by the leader. To say that information is provided only when
it is needed seems to imply that leader-introduced content would
rule out or inhibit freedom of discussion and the achievement of
problem-solving skills by the parent. While the need for a leader
with knowledge is recognized, there is the implication that to have
specific goals and assume an active role in introducing content will
have a negative impact on individual growth. Hereford's study [7]
(one of the few on the discussion method used in parent education)
specifically contends that only the lay leader with no knowledge
can achieve free discussion. This research, however, did not test
the use of the professionally trained parent education leader.

It is our contention that there is no dichotomy inherent in
the situation. If guided interaction is the key to effective learning,
then a knowledgeable educator, skilled in group process, is needed
for maximum individual learning. This point will be elaborated in
a later section.

GOALS DEFINE CONTENT IN PARENT
EDUCATION PROGRAMS

Brim categorizes seven types of goals for parent education
programs; [8] goals based on assumptions as to what the good parent
is. Briefly stated, these "good parents" may be the rule follower, the

loving and accepting parent, the one with knowledge about child development norms and sequences, the parent who understands the effects of his behavior on his children, the problem-solver, the home-manager, and the comfortable and relaxed parent.

Programs directed at making parents "rule followers" have faded into the past. Experience in working with parents and increasing knowledge of parent-child interaction point to the limitations of such a narrow goal even when it might be achieved. Furthermore, it is generally unacceptable to the parent himself, even when he might come asking for prescriptions.

The "loving and accepting parent" cannot be produced by educational methods. Parent education programs having this as a primary goal may produce guilt feelings on the part of parents who cannot achieve it. Not enough is known about the effect on children of total acceptance without setting direction, without some insistence on growth. To hold such a specific behavioral pattern as a goal conflicts with the philosophy of self-determination and choice of values by the parent. It presumes a cause and effect premise based on insufficient data.

The limitations of a program based solely on parent knowledge about developmental norms are readily apparent. When used as the only framework for viewing child growth and development, it raises problems for the parent educator and the parent. For some parents such knowledge relieves anxiety while for others it creates it. Because Johnny does not tie his shoes at the expected age level, Johnny's mother is alarmed, while at the same time, Mary's mother may be developing a false set of expectations for Mary because she tied her shoes six months "early." Mary's mother may become troubled later when Mary fails to show her genius potential relative to another behavior development. Parental anxiety is aroused by age-level expectations, and we don't really know the significance of achievement of a particular skill at a particular age.

Even when developmental norms are not the explicit content of a parent education program, the theory inserts itself and becomes content. The general awareness of these norms creates problems for the parent educator. Brim has called this the "Gesselian dilemma" and most parent educators have had to deal with it by pointing out the tentative nature of the data on which the conclusions were made, the homogeneous socioeconomic level of the children observed, as well as the inapplicability to individual children at all times. More to the point in parent education is the necessity to deal with parental reaction. To do so requires knowledge on the part of the educator about the research itself, its limitations, conflicting studies, and causes of parental reaction of this sort.

Another conception of the good parent is one who understands the effects of his own behavior upon his child. Here the usual possible guilt-producing effects must be considered, as well as the fact that there are only general conclusions about how parent behaviors affect the child's development and that there are no specific cause and effect relationships validated by research. There is no recognition of the active role the individual child plays in determining parental response.

Insofar as the multiple causation theory of personality determinants is included, some guilt is probably relieved. To make the assumption that parents are one determinant in personality development does have general validity. Every small act does not irreparably affect the child; parents can be helped to face themselves as one of the forces in personality development and find constructive ways to assist the child in his understanding of the world around him. Instead of a negative approach we turn it around and say, "Look how you are enabling the child. Here is new information to help you do this more effectively." Even without specific prescription parents can chart a general course of action for themselves, based on what we do know at this time. The denial of the parent as a force among many forces in child development does not add to the strengths of those parents who know of this theory. For those who do not see themselves as influential in the child's development, discussing it makes no difference. Facing responsibility and tackling problems with information and support from the parent educator and other parents brings a possibility of growth in self-determination and decision-making.

Another instrumental goal described by Brim is that of the parent as a problem-solver. Programs with this as their aim attempt, through education, to enable the parent to utilize the best information available as a basis for his daily decisions about child-rearing and to integrate and apply it creatively. This is accomplished through a consideration of varying life situations as well as learning the problem-solving process. Brim states that few parent educators would disagree with the desirability of this as a working goal but that it is a realistic objective for a limited group only.[9] We would differ with the conclusion that it is practical for only a limited number of people, if one thinks of such a goal as one of several and if one measures even partial success as success. Full and complete use is often limited; but partial, occasional use is possible for most people and carries potentials for further development in this direction. This method of parent education can carry the ever-present possibility of the parent making choices based on a broadened conception of the meaning and nature of the problem. For example, parents present a common concern about sibling rivalry and an expressed wish to know how to deal with it. They may start with the expression of their concern in as simple terms as "the kids fight, it drives me crazy, what do I do about it?" This example has been seen as a concern of mothers ranging from the lowest to the highest socioeconomic and educational levels. The teacher response will determine what the parents do with the learning opportunity as it arises from immediate and recognized needs. The teacher who is lacking in awareness of the tremendous learning potentials might simply tell them some things to do. If he has the courage of ignorance, he tries to provide a rule for the parent to follow. Some may fall into line, but many won't. And what if the rule does not work in the next situation?

When a teacher, committed to the development of problem-solving ability, asks that the group think about why brothers and sisters fight, he starts a process of problem-solving. Participation is invited, involvement encouraged, credence given to the idea that parents know something. Because the teacher has knowledge beyond their experience he will provide a focus. Teacher and students are now working together. The teacher brings something to the situation, as the students had expected he could and hoped he would. From here, they can move to the next step—what are some ways of handling the situation and what are the effective results as well as the cognitive potentials of the various proposed parental actions and reactions.

If the teacher keeps in mind his values and goals for the parent, he will lead the group to consider some of the specific implications in this situation for value selection and teaching opportunities and methods. What kind of a child and, later, adult does each parent want? What opportunities does this situation provide for demonstrating her values? What and how can she teach her child within the context of the behavior which is presenting difficulties to her? If a mother values individual differences, how does she communicate this? If she values seeing the other fellow's point of view, does her behavior indicate this? Does she believe that a first step in understanding our relationships with others is to understand our own motivations and, if so, can she help the child frame questions to himself which will help him understand himself and aid him in his interaction with others? To say that at this point every parent happily and confidently makes his own diagnosis and prescribes his own treatment is to be unrealistic. Some do; some will be considering the matter for some time and others may see nothing that applies to them or may quickly reject possibilities that are too painful to face. Some parents, even though content and method seem inapplicable, stay to consider another day. Some may withdraw as did one mother in one of our groups, for as she expressed it, "If I stay here, I'm going to change my mind."

In varying degrees, then, problem-solving demonstrated and participated in, has an effect. We object to the belief that this approach works only for a highly intelligent and selected group. It has been implied that the poor cannot use this as a method because they wouldn't be in the position they are in if they had such skills. This is to deny the reality of the poverty cycle. It also denies the impressive coping powers many lower class persons demonstrate in the face of what to others seem to be impossible barriers to any achievement. Recognizing these strengths of the parent can and does give additional motivation. A teaching-learning opportunity where knowledge and a chance for participation are offered the learner is an enabling process wherein the parent may increase his awareness of alternatives and the necessity for choice.

Those programs that have as their goal the increase in home management skills with resulting environmental changes affecting the child, teach specific skills. They have been criticized as being limited and not tackling the important areas of personal relationships. This need not be true. Either having or not having these skills may in some way affect the environment of the growing child. Sometimes a simple management skill can have an effect on a mother's attitude toward herself, on her reaction to her children.

To stop here, however, is to seriously limit the educational program and deny the potential of learning in a broader sense. We would teach a home management skill when it appears related to need and interest, and when the lack of this skill is standing in the way of long term goals. We would use it as a technique rather than content as an end in itself. The teacher then needs to know resources for such skills, be able to help the mother see the role she plays in providing the environment of her children, and at times make practical suggestions for the more effective management of this environment.

Home management content may be applicable at times depending on student needs and their perception of these needs. If a group of mothers have reached the conclusion that they need more time to spend with their children in their newly perceived teaching role, they may bring up the question "How can I manage more efficiently in order to have more time?" The home management content might come from a pooling of suggestions by group members, from suggestions by the teacher, or by the use of an outside resource person—a specialist in the field. The teacher need not rule it out as inappropriate content when it is seen as contributing to the central purpose of parental competence. The degree of use and usability of the content depends on the individual parent. The objective remains one of bringing knowledge and a choice of alternatives based on values as perceived by the individual.

If the goal is the confident and relaxed parent, Brim points out that there is no content. Such a goal was probably adopted as a reaction to the evident anxiety aroused by the "expert" advice to parents. This new advice to relax did not relieve that anxiety, but more likely created a vacuum, a withdrawal of the offer to help in the face of parental expectation. Having indicated there were things known about children and about parent-child relationships, to tell parents to do what is natural for them did not perform the magic hoped for by anxious parent educators. Even without parent educators, parents have problems and questions relative to their children. Society itself will not allow child battering, for instance, even if it is what comes naturally to the parent. This approach, in addition to having no content, does not achieve its implied goal of relieving anxiety. It merely constitutes an abdication of the responsibility to assist and a denial of the learning available. This conception of the good parent may have lessened the guilt of some parent educators but it is doubtful that it did as much for most parents.

PROBLEMS OF EVALUATION

Up to now we have indicated some of the values and limitations of parent education programs currently in existence. There are very real difficulties all parent educators face in determining the effects of programs. Ten years after the publication of Brim's study, the evidence for social science research regarding the efficacy of parent education programs is still inadequate and inconclusive. Existing studies are limited in scope, subjects, goals, control groups, and contrasting methods. They are characterized by short-term study, do not include the variety of learning experiences such as observation, participation, group discussion, and content being introduced by the parent educator and by the students.

If parent education is assessed in terms of changes in knowledge and attitudes, there still remains the question of effect on the child. Longitudinal studies have not been done. Controversy still revolves around the basic assumptions on which programs are based. Goals of programs are vaguely stated and hard to measure. Conclusions are quickly seen to ignore countless variables. Little research assesses change in performance of either parent or child. No effective instruments have been developed for measurement of behavioral change. Some of those issues are the genetic-versus-environmental determinants of a child's behavior, the importance of the parent in contrast to other environmental influences, what aspects of parent behavior, actions, and/or attitudes, are most conducive to the child's mental health, the potency of the single act, permanency and durability of parental influence, the problem of contradictory child-development theories.

Research evaluating the effects of different group methods is almost nonexistent and the research on consequences does not permit one to choose between the several variations on a scientific basis.[10] Research that has been done on the effectiveness of the group process is not within the context of the parent education group but rather training in group dynamics. Here the purpose is to make the participants conscious of the roles they are playing within the group rather than a focus on an increased competence of the individual to deal with his life.

Perhaps a more precise statement of goals with a clearer focus on direction and method would be helpful in meeting some of the problems of evaluation. Measuring change in the parent is difficult enough and the second step of assessing the impact on the child makes the problem even more difficult.

The learning-focused approach we are suggesting may more easily lend itself to evaluation. More specific goals with observable changes in behavior may more objectively lend themselves to measurement. When parents see themselves as a teacher of their child with specific tasks that lead to their engagement in the parent-child interactions that promote learning, the performance of such tasks may indicate the parents have moved in the direction of program goals. We may be able to measure decision-making behaviors—a parent's increased facility for problm-solving in his daily interaction with his child. When program goals are discussion of parents' problems, what happens as a result of the discussion? What is supposed to happen? "Feeling better about" and "changed attitudes toward children" are nonspecific and leave the question "from here to where?" unanswered. Of course there are dangers in the search for specificity in that the obvious and insignificant may be used for measurement simply because they are readily observable. Because an act or behavior is observable and thus measurable cannot be the sole criterion.

There are specific behavioral tasks, the performance of which indicate whether or not a mother or father understands the importance of his role as a teacher of his child, has accepted that responsibility, can state the reasons for his significance. As a result of this understanding, the parent behaves differently. If he tells us, or we observe, that he listens when a child speaks and truly becomes engaged in a conversation with him, attempting to understand the meaning of the situation to him, feeding back both questions and information, then this is significant and measurable behavior. When he has accepted the role of assisting the child in the valuing process, he illustrates the understanding and acceptance of the role by relating his own actions to the child, by helping him view alternatives and explore consequences. The way in which the parent participates in the group problem-solving process indicates movement or lack of movement. He views situations with new understandings of the causes of child behavior, of the meaning of parental behaviors to the child, of his possible reactions and responses. He selects his own behaviors as a result of the problem-solving process in which he has been engaged.

The goals are the acquisition of knowledge and understanding upon which new behaviors are patterned and the transfer of processes used in the group to daily living. This is significant behavior, observable and measurable.

Measurement is essential. Parent education efforts have been severely criticized for functioning with little scientific base to their premises, little sound research on method and effect. We hope that with a sounder content rationale, a more specified educative process, and a delineated leadership function—all focused on fostering individual choice—the resultant behavioral change or participating of parents will be observable and measurable.

PROBLEMS OF CONFLICTING THEORY

While theories of parent-child relationships and the educability of parents are logical determinants of specific working goals, the parent educator must squarely face the fact that our knowledge of parent-child relationships will always, because of its continued growth, have unintegrated and contradictory segments; that these segments may endure side by side for decades; and that he, the parent educator, must learn to live with this situation and neither seek a single master theory nor reject science because it cannot provide that theory.[11]

Thus parent educators must continue on the "basis of theoretical allegations as to merit" in the absence of research.

If one accepts the general belief that parent education is important and necessary, those involved in action programs must proceed with what information is at hand and develop and modify practice on the basis of experience. The practitioner in the field, therefore, can only make asumptions based on what little is available, continue to refine his goals, base his experimentation on empirical evidence gained from practice, and hope that the social scientists will be motivated toward research in this field. Perhaps experimentation will provide the stimulus for research.

In the face of conflicting research, there is a need to develop a basic approach to knowledge that has more universal application. We need to select a method to generate this content. Working with parents in anticipation of their learning, we need to base our approach on what is known about how adults learn.

ADULT LEARNING

The principles of adult learning are basic and important to any parent education program design. Role learning, and specifically the parental role, must be viewed as adult education in whatever setting it takes place. Until effective education for parenthood is an integral part of the secondary curriculum, with appropriate experience-centered learning, education for this role needs to be made available to adults. Even with preparenthood education, today's knowledge demands a total lifespan to absorb. Constant change requires continual reassessment in the face of new information. Each new set of understandings leads to the realization that some of the most significant learning experiences take place in adult life. The obvious conclusion is that adults need the opportunity to acquire this learning in a systematic and organized manner. It behooves education and mental health agencies committed to reaching parents to view their task more sharply within the larger framework of adult education. Current thinking in the field of adult education and into the nature of how adults learn becomes pertinent.

ADULT EDUCATION APPROACH TO GOAL AND VALUE CHOICE

Today more than ever it is important to understand the best methods of focusing adults' attention on their responsibilities in a free society and of equipping adults, through education, to assume these responsibilities.

The degree to which adult education should "prescribe goals and values" to serve as content has long been a matter of debate. To what extent can we agree on ultimate values and criteria for validation, or perhaps, more importantly, is it essential to the establishment of valid programs that basic agreement take place? In areas where content and method are concrete, i.e., typing and auto mechanics, certain performance standards are essential requisites to mastery. However, in areas where performance is intensely personal and independent choice is the medium for learning, i.e., marriage, family living and parent education, the task of the adult educator becomes the provision of a framework within which deliberation and choice can take place. The fostering of the systematic and disciplined process of inquiry, then, is the task of the adult educator. Rather than look for validation of program effectiveness in terms of resultant behavioral change, "can we rather assert that the quest for validity is a basically human quest and that the informing, and disciplining of those processes through which men make the quest is a major claim upon all adult education effort?" [12]

The challenge of today must be met with openness rather than the drive for uniformity. There are many points where society is in conflict about what is true and what is valuable. Benne makes a strong case for effective choice as the focal concern:

It is in the processes of *choice* that men, individually and collectively, bridge the gap between thought and action. It is in choosing and deciding that requirements of sensitive and valid thought must come to terms with the requirements of committed and effective action. Were one to take "choosing" as the distinctive human function, and excellence in choice as the overall goal of general education effort, perhaps the claims of thinking and action could both be taken into just account within the planning and execution of educational programs.[13]

The ideal of continuous growth does not rule out the pursuit of specific aims, but suggests that the educator, in helping clients to achieve their aims, to go forward from where they are, enables that growth.[14] Even though the parent comes with specific aims, parent education has the potential of enabling adults to define the value base of their judgments and to think through the implications of those judgments to an understanding of the practical consequences. On the basis of more lucid conceptualization, they may then decide to strengthen or alter their behavior as parents. Perhaps this perception of the task of adult education is the most meaningful as it relates to education for parental competence, "that it takes place within a setting that is neither pupil-directed, nor teacher-directed, nor subject-directed.' [15] It is rather process-directed, which means that problem-solving is properly analyzed and none of its component parts ignored.

As parents search for guidance in their parenting task, they find little in the offerings of adult education specifically focused on their concerns. Education for family and personal competence, although available in a great variety of voluntary, community, and health and welfare agencies, is disparate and rarely offered in a comprehensive manner in any community. There is a dearth of program planning, facility development, and teacher training to support those institutions that are attuned to the differential learning process of adults and the needs and challenges which they face. "A philosophy of adult education which places final responsibility for determining the form and content of adult education on the learners, also places heavy responsibility on the adult educators to provide maximum learning opportunities and a high level of educational counseling." [16]

CHARACTERISTICS OF THE ADULT LEARNER

Even though our knowledge of personality development of adults is limited mainly to clinical data, the adult personality is accepted as different from that of the child or adolescent. An important psychological characteristic of the adult is his concept of self; he has come to regard himself as a certain kind of person.

Paramount among adult needs is success as a parent. The society demands it, even though it can no longer clearly define just what it means. Status needs in the parental role are often as strong as the areas of economic and vocational achievement. White [17] points to the intrinsic motivation to competence. Erikson [18] labels it a generativity drive, the interest in and wish to nurture and guide the young. Most adults have learned to conform and to act out their roles in line with their concept of society's expectations.

Although considerable research validates the ability of the adult to learn new behaviors, he may need assistance to succeed because of past failures or blocks to learning. He has a tendency to underestimate his own ability.

Brunner [19] points out that although adult learning may be slower than that of the child or youth, it is probably more accurate when interest and motivation remain high. Adult learning takes place faster with adequate motivation and when the desire to learn is aroused by adequate teaching. The adult needs positive reinforcement of his strengths as well as recognition of his important role. Based on this knowledge, good teaching calls for an approach that says, "Look at what you are already doing effectively as a parent. Here are some ways to enhance this competence."

When considering adult motivation it is necessary to keep in mind that the learner has "growth-expansion motives which are translated into a succession of goals" while at the same time he has developed "protective defense maneuvers." [20] Those growth-expansion motives are favorable to learning when experiences of an appropriate nature are provided. They contribute to the continuation of learning as well as affecting new motivations, an inherent part of the educational responsibility. Negative results may have positive effects on the amount learned by children. This may be because children have no alternative but to remain in the learning situation, whereas the adult does. When negative reactions prevail with adults, they may withdraw. There is a high degree of personal reference and sensitivity to the material that makes reinforcing experiences essential. Here we find implications for program planning and method selection. To which of these two forces will program communication and method appeal?

An adult's general sense of competence will often carry him into a new experience, but if met with frustration the adult student withdraws.[21] Even with the need to achieve present, there may be independent and dependent needs to be met within the same individual at the same time. This requires not only awareness on the part of the teacher but clarity as to immediate and long range goals —his and the students. The teacher must meet the immediate needs of a dependent nature, in a nurturing fashion, without losing sight of the goal of independent judgment for the students, without robbing them of their opportunities to achieve new independence and competence.

The presence of growth-expansion motives can be used to enable learning. What counts in adulthood is not the level of a particular ability but what the individual himself interprets the condition to be and what he wants to make of his ability.[22]

It is essential to consider the information we have about the adult learner and make some assumptions about him even when the data are limited. For example, McKeachie theorizes that adults tend to be

. . . higher in authoritarianism, rigidity, achievement motivation, affiliation motivation, and power motivation. From the studies of the three motives and from Beach's study of sociability one would guess that for both attitudinal and higher cognitive outcomes a friendly permissive teaching style would be most effective for adults. However, this must be balanced against the greater authoritarianism and rigidity of older students which would suggest that abrupt shifts to new teaching methods would be difficult for the students to accept and adjust to. It thus appears, as in most teaching situations, that the teacher cannot follow any general rule of thumb but must adjust his approach as he sizes up each class, and receives feedback from them.[23]

If it is true that the majority of adult students are high in rigidity and authoritarianism, while simultaneously they seek close associations and opportunities to satisfy the power motive, what approaches do we choose? Persons high in rigidity and authoritarianism may learn better in a highly structured, traditional information-giving situation. These same persons, however, may have motives that can best be served by participation in the group process.

Adult students, then, have conflicting desires and needs. Organization for learning can provide an environment that meets these conflicting needs. The parent expects knowledge and some is provided, while at the same time the stage is set for interaction based on the student's own experiences and for guidance toward the goal of individual decision-making.

Before engaging in an educational process, the adult must recognize the positive value of education for solving problems and must relate education to success and happiness.[24] Some persons, because of their situational experiences, have not seen education as goal-serving, particularly outside of the vocational obligations. In reaching out then, goals must be clearly defined, closely related to action, and congruent with some perceptions people have of their own desires. Interest must be stimulated in order to motivate students to seek further information.

In our attempts to reach low-income groups, goals were specifically defined. We hazarded a guess that parents were interested in helping their children succeed in school. This message was communicated along with the message that the parents were important, that there were things to learn, and that the school was seeking a partnership with the all-important home. The response was strong. Without seeing structured parent education programs as a panacea for every parent, there is growing indication that parent education, when focused on parental concern for their children's school success, has a deep appeal to low-income families.

From poverty programs has come a great deal of knowledge, particularly in terms of the need for clearly stated goals that jibe with parental conceptions about learning. Certainly the concept of the parent as a teacher has been markedly sharpened by research into the learning sources and processes of the preschool child.

PRINCIPLES OF ADULT LEARNING

Organization for effective learning evolves from a full awareness of adult needs. Adult educators have been advised to focus attention upon the importance of self and those elements in the personality which involve choice, self-direction, and the manipulation of outcomes.

Motivation influences the intensity or frequency of the individual in exposing himself to the learning experience, and the adult comes to regard himself as the instrument for achieving his goals. The adult is concerned with selection, regulation, and integration of behavior; with the growth of competence and mastery, with the control of outcomes; with the growing awareness of the self as the instrument for achieving one's aims.[25]

The provision of a structure within which parents can analyze the experiences in their parental role, and evolve a systematic and coherent integration between belief and behavior, should incorporate what is known about how adults learn. Here we have drawn from the works of Knowles, de Brunner, Sillers, Kuhlen, and others in an attempt to describe those characteristics of a parent education program most likely to have meaning to the participants.

To be meaningful to the learner, the content must be experience-centered, and the adult must be free to look at the experience. The most effective learning situation requires the individual to be set for it, in terms of general attitude, previous knowledge, and immediate orientation. This reemphasizes our contention that clarity of goals is an essential element, in terms of both attracting the learner and the subsequent involvement in the learning process. The more active the intent to learn, the greater the likelihood of success. One must be able to anticipate certain successes even before he experiences them, and this requires some awareness about the program's approach. With this stimulus, he becomes concerned enough to seek further knowledge. All too often program goals have been so vague that the learner does not see their relation to his own goals nor the possible usefulness of the experience. A direct message of importance as a teacher of his children—that there are ways in which he can teach his child the processes of learning, valuing, and relating—make apparent both needs and usefulness.

Adult learning must be appropriate to known needs and clearly related to action. Our approach incorporates these aspects of adult learning. Goals are clearly stated as providing a learning process wherein the parents adds to his skills as a teacher of his child. Role definition is clearly established. The parent's present experience is looked at in terms of what he is already doing, thus giving satisfaction through recognition of success. He becomes involved in determining ways in which his values have been thoughtfully and individually determined.

The goals are set and the search organized by the learner, but within a setting that provides a structure, stimulus material, and freedom to evaluate and to make personal reference. Here he can weigh the merits of numerous ideas and practices; he can see how they work in practice; he can adopt or not as he sees fit. He achieves greater perception of his parent role and a deeper sense of competence in it.

To facilitate learning, the teacher presents material that is meaningfully organized, with the relationships clearly established, with content appropriate to the learner's established needs and attitudes and most likely to be absorbed and incorporated. The educator knows that repetition is part of the learning process. There is frequent reiteration of important points in different contexts so both concepts and their applications become strongly associated. Frequently summing up, an effective learning tool, provides the learner with rewarding awareness of his own gains in knowledge and insight. There is constant reinforcement of the learner as a person, unique and self-determining, through acceptance of what he is, his contributions, problems, and potentials. There is continuing feedback about his own progress.

The process we suggest has defined goals. The teacher functions as a model of the competent parent. The parent learns a process through experiencing that process, and transfers it to his daily life. The parent experiences the mediating adult who provides an enriched learning environment, labels and clarifies his responses to it, defines the range of alternatives, and recognizes his movement in just the way he may learn to approach his child.

The needs of parents are many and varied, yet the majority of parents do not engage in parent education of any formal nature. This may be due in large part to the lack of communication about what can be learned. Programs of parent education need to be more readily available and clearly understood as a societal provision for increasing competence in this vital life role—a task accepted as important by both the individual and society.

None of this fits with the all-too-frequently accepted stereotype of adult education. It is not the academic-intellectual approach —the information-giving picture—that so many persons have of education as a whole. Neither does it fit in with the format of education that provides information only on request. In our concept of parent education as role learning, immediate goals are attended to as parents attempt to understand the reactions of their children and their own feelings and attitudes, but long-range goals and total understandings are kept clearly in mind.

THE DISCUSSION METHOD

Adults can learn. What and how they are to learn are determining factors in organizing the learning situation. In the usual parent education class, interest in learning more about children is the common focal point. Parents who come want to know more about children. Through the process of growth and effective teaching, they see the relationship between this and knowing more about themselves and their own behavior. Most parents come to be told something about children, but a healthy determination to make their own decisions often underlies their initial motivation.

Lectures are prevalent. However, lecturing does not lend itself to the development of concepts and problem-solving skills because there is little feedback and involvement of the learner in the development of generalizations that can be useful and available for application to a variety of situations.

When the long range goal is the enhancement of problem-solving skills, the process most likely to achieve this end is the group discussion method. As the key to any educational process lies in a clear delineation of the role of the educator, we start our analysis of the group method with a look at the leader and leadership.

LEADERSHIP AS IT AFFECTS GROUP DISCUSSION

The teacher plays a major role in affecting the nature of the educational experience, the effectiveness of the process, as well as the final accomplishments. The total learning experience will be influenced by each teacher's basic philosophy, knowledge, teaching skills, and most importantly, goals. The validity and effectiveness of each part of the total effort can be tested when measured against final goals. To build an action program without goals is impossible; to build a philosophy without clarity of purpose is equally impossible.

Clarity of goals is a prerequisite to building structure and direction in the group process. Implicit in such goals is the concept of others as basically self-directing and responsible. The teacher can't be responsible *for* others, but he can be responsible for his own behavior when working with others, and this responsibility includes defining goals clearly.

Each teacher engaged in parent education has some philosophy although it may vary greatly from one teacher to another. There are certain concepts and principles, however, with which few experienced parent educators would argue. Most basic of all is the belief that each person is an individual and has the right to make his own decisions. Unless this concept is firmly held and the principle of respecting the right to decision is clearly communicated through the techniques used in the educative process, the goals as stated can never be reached. When this concept is a solid part of the professional's philosophy, it is the core of his practice and serves as a yardstick against which to measure every technique used. It is the first and most important principle on which parent education should be founded. With the incorporation of the right of self-determination into one's teaching, it is impossible to impose one's will upon the class members, to be didactic, to restrict a student's potential for growth in the direction of intelligent decision-making.

The degree to which the right of decision is communicated probably depends largely on the extent of the teacher's self-awareness and self-acceptance. Basic to the achievement of a professional self is acceptance of self, not as a static and achieved condition, but with attempted full use of present competence, recognition of present limitations, and a belief in one's own ability to grow and change. To accept others with all of their needs and limitations requires understanding of both self and others and "a teacher's understanding can only be as deep as the wisdom he possesses as he looks inward upon himself." [26]

Deficiencies of self-awareness may lead to unknowing over-emphasis or omissions arising out of the teacher's own emotional needs. The acceptance of limitations makes possible commitment without compulsion and controls the setting of unrealistic goals that stifle growth. The ability to face failure in ourselves as teachers allows the same freedom for those we purport to help.

The background knowledge of the leader affects the group process, not simply in the consideration of whether the content is introduced by the teacher or the group. There are the participants' expectations that the teacher knows something they do not know and that they have come to find out. For the teacher to deny the giving of any information as inappropriate to his function as a parent educator would lead to frustration and irritation on the part of the participants who came with such expectations. For the teacher to withhold knowledge until called upon to divulge it by the group neither guarantees freedom of choice and responsible decision-making nor precludes them. To give some information can meet a need or desire. For the parent educator to give first can set the stage for future giving and sharing on the part of all.

The parent educator often introduces material from his own knowledge background that stimulates parent students to think in new areas they might not otherwise have explored. He broadens their horizons without imposing. A leader with knowledge provides the possibility of expanded learning and carries an educational responsibility for stimulus and guidance.

The task of the parent educator is to help parents view knowledge and develop skills in its use. Having a lay leader with no more knowledge than the group members makes for interaction, but perhaps not education. Self-education can take place in such a process, of course, but it is different from parent education taught by a knowledgeable, trained, professional parent educator.

Use of research findings is an example of the educator's role. The teacher's acceptance of responsible use of research is inevitable. Even when the parent educator is explicitly called upon to bring information to bear on the problem under consideration, the extent or limits of his knowledge has an effect. The parent educator serves as an interpreter of research, translating it into understandable and usable terms for the parent. His ability to make it meaningful to the group has an effect on group process and progress.

In addition to the extent of the teacher's knowledge, there are the more subtle influences of his own beliefs and values that affect what he presents. He may strive for complete coverage, but cannot have total information or bring every study to the group. This is not only impossible but inefficient. To be abreast of current research and thinking, however, is essential and has great implications for the availability of in-service training programs for parent education staff.

Perhaps a realistic approach is to strive for awareness of what is happening in child study, and to develop student awareness provided by any new information material for problem-solving. The teacher admits to his own beliefs and biases (they probably show anyway), his own limitations of knowledge, and by so doing, implies acceptance of these factors in his student's concept of self. The group process will be affected by the parent educator's ability to say "I don't know," or "I feel strongly about . . . ," or "within the limits of my knowledge."

The educator's special competencies and interests in subject matter areas also affect his role. Because he comes to parent education from other related fields—social work, psychology, nursing, or teaching in another area—he is likely to have more knowledge as well as a stronger interest in his own particular specialty. To deny that this affects group process and content is to be unrealistic. It should not and need not exclude other considerations of content. It merely makes one area a bit richer perhaps than some others.

All parent educators should have a working familiarity with certain areas of knowledge. The extent of the teacher's knowledge about how adults learn will have a direct bearing on selection and techniques. He modifies and adapts his knowledge skills to the special needs of parents.

How then does this conceptualization of leadership affect operative decisions, such as selection, group member involvement, and process?

GROUP STRUCTURE

Criteria for selective participants can be determined by agency personnel as a screening process: these may be factors of location, purpose, teacher reputation, or the expressed or presumed needs of parents. For the parent educator these factors raise a barrage of questions: Who are the participants, and why have they come? When do you clearly state goals and methods; whose goals; how do you know when to modify method? Is it possible to derive a set of common goals and a method of approach that will meet the needs of individual members? Can you change initial motivation and what is your responsibility in this regard? What are the parent educator's responsibilities in the face of these questions? How can he gain knowledge of the people with whom he is dealing? When he has this knowledge, what does he do with it?

The belief that homogeneity is valuable leads some program planners to develop admission policies delimiting the nature of the group. Usually, this is done by focusing on children in a particular age group. Invitations or publicity indicate this emphasis and constitute the first process of selection. The message may include interpretations of purpose, some delineation of what the parent group could hope to obtain from such a program or a list of topics of possible interest to potential parents. Parental interpretation of these communications continues the selection process.

A variety of selective factors are present even in the face of the most carefully thought out approaches to the problem of recruitment. A constant process of self-selection and elimination takes place.

There are inumerable ways as well as a variety of motives involved in the choice to attend a study group. One parent wants help with questions he has about his child-rearing practices and will inquire about the availability of such opportunities. He might be described as being highly motivated, but he may not necessarily be motivated for what that particular group has to offer. Another person may want to know more about child growth and development; he has studied for skill in other activities, why not this one? Still another parent may find herself in a parent education class when all she was looking for was an opportunity to give her child a guided play experience with other children. This often happens in the child observation class or cooperative nursery school having a well-developed plan for parent involvement and education. Inevitably the process of natural selection goes on. Even among mothers of preschool children who have a high level of understanding of goals and methods, some discover that the effort is too great. Others find they really don't want to be involved in a learning process, that they wanted ready answers to immediate problems. Still others recognize a need for individual assistance with serious problems before they can use this type of service.

Thus even during the exploratory process before the experience is clearly defined natural selection continues to take place. Almost always some people decide not to return. The dropout is much discussed and analyzed in adult education literature. Losing members this way is a natural and inevitable phenomenon. Leaving may represent a healthier action for some than staying on in a situation they find uncomfortable.

The educator dislikes losing a potential student and sometimes attributes this loss to his own inadequacies. In some instances this may be true but by no means is it always so. One woman may find the idea of so much flexibility, with its implied personal responsibilities, overwhelming. Sometimes the emotionally disturbed parent uses her natural protective devices to shield her from what could constitute too threatening an experience. Awareness of this personal shield can be reassuring to the educator still struggling with a delineation of the differences between education and therapy.

Another mother with a limited store of energy may find the effort too great for the potential perceived. This does not exempt the educator from all responsibility. Errors in practice do cause loss of students. Educators do cause dropping out by failing to make students feel welcome, or to make the first meeting meaningful, or to give the whole experience a direction from the start. Anyone working with adults should be sensitive to and aware of all of the causes for the withdrawal of adult students.

Another differential factor in terms of the size of groups becomes markedly evident in working with low income families. Classes can be large and still be effective in areas where middle class women have organizational know-how and have steadily taken advantage of study opportunities. However in low income areas, where they are new and relatively unknown, classes need to be smaller to be comfortable. Brim [27] points out that in spite of contentions about class size, no research has been done to validate these assertions. Appropriate size depends on factors such as previous group experience of members and their consequent ability to work effectively in groups. Repeatedly, we have seen classes start with an enrollment larger than the members or the teacher could tolerate and then drop to a smaller number that stabilized itself. Once again, the characteristics of the group members and their needs appear to influence selection. No matter how motivated a parent might have been to participate, many reality factors operate in low income communities. Money for transportation alone have kept some away. This is a graphic example of location as a selective factor.

The teacher needs to adjust to conflicting needs in groups as well as those within the individual with whom he is working. This calls for knowledge, flexibility, and adaptability, and an awareness that he cannot preconceive his students' characteristics or predetermine choice of method.

Finally, the agency conducting parent education using the group discussion method will influence the composition of groups. In some instances the opportunity may depend on invitation, in others it may be mandatory. In a public school adult education program such as ours there can be no screening to determine suitability for membership; it is legally mandated that all such classes be open to the public as long as space is available. Agency goals then need to be clearly stated in the beginning and the method of approach described. The teacher describes program goals and defines the focus that will be the group tools for approaching group based content. Needs will vary from person to person and will not remain static. Any area of concern can provide fruitful exercises for clarifying the learning-valuing approach. With this climate of freedom to explore, with this sharing of responsibility for decision-making, the teacher sets the stage for the possibility of a truly creative learning experience.

SETTING THE STAGE FOR LEARNING

Parents need to know from the start that this class will not provide prescriptions for action, pat answers to all problems, decision-making *for* the parent. On the other hand, the teacher will carry his responsibility to provide knowledge. Students are seeking new information to extend their awareness. If the teacher refuses to accept this responsibility, or does not see this function as inherent to the task, then the students rightfully question why this person is acting in this role. We once heard a lecturer, painfully conscious of the criticism directed at didactic parent education techniques, contend repeatedly to his audience that he knew nothing they didn't know. Finally a woman asked a most pointed and appropriate question, "then why am I here?" This is not to make the case for expertise or advice, but rather for one of recognition that there is something to be learned here, in whatever way the individual decides to use it.

Among parent educators there has been much anxiety about imposing goals, much discussion regarding the ethics of doing so, as well as much searching for approaches that avoid such imposition. To say that an educator is completely neutral is to avoid reality. Enthusiasm for the potentials of study alone may suggest possibilities heretofore unknown to the person affected. This is basic to good teaching. It constitutes a commitment to the process of becoming rather than imposition of goals and values. It is the responsibility of the professional educator both to define his approach and to insure the participant the freedom to accept or reject.

Parent education *is* a program of influence and one of its tools is to make others aware of the potential values of such study.

CARL A. RUDISILL LIBRARY
LENOIR RHYNE COLLEGE

The mother has come with one purpose in mind; the professional educator seizes an opportunity to provide knowledge that extends this purpose. Their goals may then become similar in this respect. There is a responsibility in such an accidental encounter to point the way to new goals. A good teacher has always been one who communicates enthusiasm in such a manner that the student sees the possibilities and is free to pursue new values with an increase in knowledge.

Initial motivation does change; we have seen it happen repeatedly. Teachers, for their own guidance, often ask the beginning group members to write down their reasons for joining and their expectations of the class. At the end (usually at the close of the school year), they are again asked to write an evaluative statement about what they may have gained and how the experience measured up to expectations. For the continuing participant there is almost universally a broadened view of values gained in contrast to expectations, and an expression of satisfaction with the learning experience. This is particularly true of the mother who comes to provide her child with a play experience and finds a bonus in unanticipated rewards for herself in terms of greater understanding of her child, herself, and her role as a wife, mother, and individual. "I came for my child, but I benefited more for myself." Initial motivation then is subject to change, and the goal of the parent educator to make the parent role conscious, thoughtful, and knowledgeable has become the goal of the parent.

Since 1963 we have been working with parents in low income areas, parents who had not been reached by parent education before. From this experience a fairly well-established fact has emerged: parents respond to a simple and direct message that they are important to their child's learning. In a variety of ways we have tried to communicate to parents the concept that they are important to their children's success in school and that they and the school can work together to achieve that success. The recruiting emphasis repeatedly stressed this one central idea of enabling children's success in school. This was our primary goal. This made sense to parents. The message was carried by many cooperating school personnel and other agencies. Parents did respond. The idea of a simple, direct message of purpose, rather than a conglomeration of potentials proved to be a most effective approach for these parents who had not been reached before. As the groups progressed, related and reinforcing goals evolved as students envisioned the larger problems and the greater potentialities for study.

THE PROCESS OF DEALING WITH CONTENT

This section deals with content; how it is selected, introduced, treated, and emphasized. These questions are considered as they relate to the group discussion method. Content—or curriculum —as we have used the term, consists of a wide range of subject matter. Here content is referred to as a total entity and in a broad sense.

Content may be derived from a variety of sources and each proponent can make a case for that source. Content may be introduced from several sources—from the teacher, from response to needs of group members, or from the group members themselves. A course outline may be present but it is never used slavishly or rigidly. It is used as an aid to the teacher in seeing multiple possibilities and interrelatedness of subject matter with a consistent focus on goals.

Each person has a goal no matter how vaguely it may be defined in his own thinking. The student often has conflicting wishes to be told and to decide for himself. How then does the parent educator decide which need to meet, where to start, how to proceed?

Experience enhances a teacher's sensitivity to group members' expectations and conceptions of how things should proceed. One mother may want an immediate answer on toilet training. Another, arriving with a note book, is prepared to put down all of this new knowledge she anticipates, following the pattern of past school experiences. Still another is there because she needs the company of other adults after the many hours spent alone with little children, but she doubts that there is anything anyone can tell her and she has no intention of letting someone else make her decisions.

A clear statement of the wide range of possibilities for study must be made at the first session. This would include a delineation of the teacher's focus on the underlying process of learning, suggested class goals—as possible but amenable to change, some clarification of how knowledge about children can be useful and applied, and of course, the ever present need to deny this setting as a source of prescription. This is not only an honest approach but one that can highlight the possibilities and direction as well as prevent misconceptions and false hope. For the mother wanting direction there are small useful suggestions that can be made while at the same time setting the tone for a future experimental and selective approach to the solutions of child-rearing. For those resisting direction in the didactic sense, it is made clear that this is a place for choice and self-direction. For those just looking, and not knowing what to expect, an overview of content and approach can be clarifying and stimulating. An inventory of topics in which individuals are interested and which they wish to explore enables the group, as well as the teacher, to become a source of content. To limit content to that coming only from the group is constricting and wasteful of the educational potential. To limit the teacher to the moderator role negates the education process.

One very important skill required of the educator is the ability to recognize readiness for learning on the part of class members. Readiness for learning manifests itself in a variety of ways and bears a relationship to subject content and motivation. A group coming together for the expressed purpose of learning to help their children learn how to learn, and to become active partners in the education of their children, will wish to start here. This is not to say that they will stay here. They will encounter blocks to the accomplishment of this purpose that will move them to extend their concern to other dimensions of parent-child interaction. Learning related to a specific circumstance is applicable beyond the immediate situation.

Discussing a relatively value-free topic such as suitable toys for young children quickly makes sense to mothers and provides opportunity for the development of positive relationships and trust between teacher and group as well as among members of the group. For this reason it may be a good starting point. Certain topics such as sex education may be deferred until later when comfort, trust, and mutual respect have been established in the group. We do not move rapidly into emotionally loaded areas that often involve conflict, self-doubt, and social and cultural taboos. Brief encounters with a subject will occur, sometimes long before readiness to adequately explore it. The experienced teacher will help the group to handle this material at their present level of readiness and insure that it comes up again when the climate is more conducive to deeper exploration.

All the group members do not achieve readiness for a particular topic at the same time. An interesting phenomenon observed repeatedly is the individual who does not "hear" those things he is not ready to tackle with conscious consideration. A mother may say, "I know you talked about masturbation last year but I guess I didn't pay much attention as I hadn't seen this behavior in my child. Now this subject is very important to me." Was she wasting her time last year on that particular day? On the contrary, the stage was being set for future receptivity to knowledge, while at the same time, the operative principle was that of the greatest learning taking place when there is a perceived need. Repeated observation of this kind of learning taking place is reassuring to parent educators when they conjecture about the introduction of material that may be too threatening to certain members of the group. The self-protective devices of the individual appear to screen them out.

An urgent need may arise; for example, a case of child molesting in a neighborhood. A group with an established relationship demands immediate mobilization of their resources to analyze the problem and think together about action (either individual or group) that will intelligently guide their own actions and reactions of their children to the problem. This calls for an appropriate reaction by the teacher, that is, responding to the group need taking this as content, even though the previous week the group had made careful plans to explore another subject. To stick to a predetermined plan at a time like this would waste a valuable opportunity for learning. Flexibility must be used when selecting content, determining the manner of its presentation, and timing its introduction.

We maintain an eclectic position combining approaches and methods, taking the most usable and effective aspects of each. This approach is a synthesis.

The choice of method is clearly related to content. Use of the group discussion method does not exclude the use of mass media nor role playing techniques, nor observation. Rather it incorporates several approaches and provides unity. There are skills which are essentially part of the discussion method, and other concomitant techniques which strengthen the group discussion process.

USE OF QUESTIONS

The teacher uses questions as a technique to stimulate thinking and bring out valuable experiences and ideas that illustrate the common nature of problems. There are multiple reasons for behavior and a variety of ways of responding to it. When the group is called upon to think about "why," they contribute from their own experiences. The problem-solving approach is demonstrated, students are enriched by the ideas of others, and the goal of mutual support served. The sensitive teacher poses questions that cause the learner to carry on his own dialogue, ask questions, and seek answers that will affect his own behavior. The teacher exerts influence as he focuses on a direction and guides discussion in response to the questions raised. As an educator, this is his responsibility. We hope his influence will be used wisely and decision-making will be based on knowledge both of the content and himself.

The teacher guides the learners to see the gaps in their perception of the problem. The skillfully placed question is a technique enabling this process. If he can draw from the group their speculations about the variety of possible causes for a particular behavior and expand the range of possible solutions, then individuals may put together their own whole. As this takes place, still other questions are put, such as "What else? Does this relate?" and later "Have you thought of this?" Such questions enlarge the learner's chance of seeing gaps and reaching for information he needs to apply problem-solving techniques to the original question.

If during the process of exploring and eliciting responses, the teacher responds to one answer with greater enthusiasm than to most others, he will defeat his purpose and change the relationship of student to teacher. Individual goals may then come to be giving the answer the teacher wants to hear, making the class something like a quiz program. But what if, in the teacher's opinion, this is the one best answer? Does he have a right to state it as his own opinion? We think so, if it is clearly labeled as his own. The teacher's major goal remains to help parents find ways to solve their own problems. He should provide documented source material students can consider in reaching their own decisions. He is never prescriptive.

A focus on the learning that takes place in any situation can provide a more objective view for both parent and teacher. Here the use of the question is a primary tool. What is the child learning from the situation? What is the parent communicating about his values? What does the child understand as happening here and now? What learning can the child carry over to the next experience? Is the parent valuing what he desires *most* or what he desires *now?* Is he communicating conflicting values? Perhaps the parent can transfer this learning as he experiences it here to his next transaction with his child.

THE PERSONAL QUESTION

New teachers repeatedly ask, "what do I do with the individual and personal question?" There is no single, simple answer to this. It poses multiple questions the teacher must consider. Is the question within the context of the day's discussion; of interest to the group as a whole and at this time? Does the questioner show signs of emotional stress? If under stress, will she reveal more than she intends or say things she will regret later and which may keep her from returning to the group? As a general rule, individuals do not ask emotionally laden questions in their early group experience. Later, the leader will be in a better position to make the sound decision quickly. For the person in need of specialized therapeutic services, the teacher must be able to recognize that need and be skillful in the referral process. There are a variety of reasons for the personal question, all the way from being an attention getting device to a sophisticated awareness of its use to the process as a whole.

If we really believe that clarification of the individual's own experience is the most effective way people learn, then personal questions are essential to the process. With it, the group can go from the specific to the general, draw from the general, provide a framework for consideration of a point which may clearly illustrate and have meaning for all. In the relationship with the group, the leader maintains an awareness of the needs and reactions of individuals while at the same time remembering that this is a group process and that the needs of more than one person must be served. For the professional, accustomed to the one-to-one method, this may present initial difficulties in maintaining the necessary focus.

Individual personal questions arise and to ignore them is neither possible nor appropriate. How then does the teacher serve the needs of the individual and the group at the same time? Sometimes the question needs to be deferred, but more often than not it can be explored in a fashion that provides a learning experience for more than one student. For the most part, questions of this sort have a general interest to groups of parents and can be approached in an exploratory fashion so as to consider some reasons why a particular behavior occurs and what the learning-teaching possibilities are. Now there is practice in problem-solving with each person taking what he can use from the situation.

For the question not of general interest, the teacher may suggest that he and the parent talk about it privately. If the question indicates needs that cannot be met appropriately within his competence and function, he is aware of this. He does not allow the student to involve him in a therapeutic process. The skills required here are diagnostic to the extent that they involve assessment of the need for referral to other sources of assistance. Because a relationship has been established, the teacher is in a strategic position to assist movement toward the use of other resources.

SUMMARIZING

As the use of the question contributes to the development of the problem-solving approach, so the summary provides for clarification and reinforcement. It provides the repetition essential to learning and the opportunity to make relationships apparent. The use of the summary is not confined to a final summing up at the end of a session. There should be small summaries throughout the discussion—these are the points you, the class members, have made; or these points seem to need further consideration. A request that the group make its own summary enhances participation, clarification, and reinforcement.

GROUP INTERACTION

Student interaction is essential. It has value to individuals and the group as a whole. It can be achieved by skillful leadership; group interaction is largely influenced by the attitude of the teacher and his respect for individual contributions. The didactic teacher can never attain the movement of the group to discussion in the form of student to student—only from the student to teacher. Recognition of the value in each contribution fosters student interaction.

Why is student interaction important? There are supportive values stemming from the group for the individual parent. The exploration of mutual concerns based on the commonality of experience appears to lessen the anxiety caused by fear that a child is peculiar or that the parent is incompetent. The parent finds she is no longer alone. Other have problems, others are not perfect, others are trying. She is being helped by others and she helps others; her sense of making a difference to others contributes to her own sense of self-worth and an accompanying healthy acceptance of the limitations of here and now.

In a group, the parent can move in and out of concentration on self. This freedom to dilute the intensity of the situation is less avoidable in the one-to-one relationship. Depending on readiness a parent can set her own time schedule both for introspection or self-revelation. Verbal participation comes with personal readiness rather than demands from without. She has a chance to conduct her own internal dialogue before declaring herself. Not everyone needs this space, but the group setting gives this kind of freedom.

There are specific values in the parent discussion group led by a skilled parent educator. Parent education in a school setting, for instance, does not replace the teacher-parent conference but provides a vehicle whereby parental learning and understanding is enhanced, reinforced, and enlarged. Some well-recognized values are:

1. Group support for the parent.
2. The benefits of knowledge and experience of others.
3. The enlargement of the scope of learning.

4. An opportunity to see the child in relation to others, the entire family, and the community.
5. An opportunity for the parent to gain greater insight into his own feelings, thoughts, and opinions as well as those of others.
6. Exploration of problem areas without the threat of self-revelation.
7. An effective method of building parental self-esteem and developing problem-solving skills.
8. An opportunity for the parent to think for himself and express himself in a group.

SOME OTHER TEACHING TECHNIQUES

Films. The use of the discussion group process in combination with other methods is our considered choice in parent education programs. While a variety of materials and presenting devices are used with discretion and selectivity, the process of group discussion remains the core of the program. Other techniques are used only in combination with discussion. A film may be used to present a problem, a point of view, to spark interest and stimulate thought, but becomes meaningful only when accompanied ·by discussion. We need to ask if this is the most effective way to present this particular subject. Will it stimulate thought and discussion with the most efficient use of time? Will it clear away barriers blocking our considerations? Will it provide information that couldn't be provided more effectively in some other fashion? Will the use of this film generalize the issues in a fashion that will make them less threatening to the discussants? Is the amount of material presented in this film too much to absorb? The answers to these and other questions can determine the validity of any technique.

Sociodrama. The sociodrama has proved to be an excellent technique for stimulating discussion as well as providing the opportunity for parents to play different roles. Members who have previously actively participated little may volunteer to act a part and then in the ensuing discussion find themselves stoutly defending a point of view. This device often enables participation by people who have heretofore not brought forth their own ideas and experiences.

Either this structured type of role-playing, or the unstructured role-playing of a problem situation, may provide the emotional impact necessary to sufficiently involve some persons to enable them to contribute.

The skillful teacher uses a variety of techniques carefully assessed in terms of their purpose and limitations. A limitation of the use of films and sociodramas becomes apparent in working with low-income families—most of them are written for and about middle income living. In turn the majority of middle class parents cannot make the transference to themselves when viewing that excellent film about a poor Puerto Rican family, "Roots of Happiness." This empathic kind of response, the ability to extract the basic meaning and consider the implications for understanding the larger group of others, is a goal worth striving for in the learning process, but the assessment of success or failure in its use must be measured against our awareness of student readiness. Extraneous matters stand in the way of receptivity and responsiveness—even the outmoded clothing in an old film can detract and divert.

Lectures.   The use of resource persons and lectures can provide information and give variety to the methods of presentation. This technique can provide a change of pace, is valued by and usable to many participants, and fills in the ever-present gaps in knowledge for the leader who cannot be all-knowing. There are certain areas in which the teacher does not have knowledge readily available for use. Rather than being a handicap, this can serve as a demonstration of how we all look beyond ourselves in the search for new knowledge to strengthen our own decision-making ability. Before selecting the method, teacher and students explore why they wish to use a particular person to bring them facts and/or a point of view on a particular question. Group members are prepared for the resource person by learning something about him, his position, his background, and his assumed area of competence. The resource person is prepared for the group; what their question or concern is, the length of time allowed for the presentation, if a question and answer period is planned for, significant information, if any, he should have relative to the characteristics of this group. Sometimes, although not always, groups find it more comfortable to discuss later with the teacher the information brought to them by the resource person. Depending on the stage of group development and the characteristics of the visitor, as well as the content, part of the presentation may effectively include discussion.

Panel Discussion.   Another way of bringing information to the group is to use presentations by panels of outside experts or group members themselves. Perhaps the panel of experts bring information from several points of view. If class members are the panelists, they will probably engage in outside study prior to their presentation. The use of the student panel has developmental potential for its members as well as demonstrating to the others the possibilities and values of independent study. It may also enhance group solidarity. Research on group interaction and participation should be familiar to the teacher so that he can bring the findings to bear in his task of selection and evaluation of any particular technique.

Reading.   The use of the literature of child growth and development, parent-child relationships, family relationships, and related topics is inherent in the parent education process. Few teachers would deny their objective of helping parents develop an interest in reading, evaluating literature, and selecting from it what they find useful. Parents are encouraged in a variety of ways to delve into literature and this makes familiarity with the written body of knowledge mandatory for teachers. Encouragement of reading is fostered by quoting from source material—including controversial points of view—by exhibiting selected books and pamphlets, and by encouraging book reviews by parents when the readiness and interest is there. Several purposes are thereby served. Wide use has been made of selected bibliographies both of broad scope and of specific topics. One such general bibliography is the "Skillful Parents Booklist" developed jointly by the parent educators of the Los Angeles Adult Education staff and the Los Angeles City Library. In addition to use in classes, this publication is widely distributed by the library and used by other school personnel in their individual work with parents. Revision of this publication takes place every two years and has been going on since 1939.

Buzz Groups.   Other intragroup techniques often used are buzz groups and small working committees. Their purpose is practice in involvement so that the student develops his sense of competence. As he makes contributions to the total process, his ideas are valued and considered by others, and he is often better able to make his own decisions with confidence.

Selected Materials. Teachers often use mimeographed informational materials. These should be used sparingly and thoughtfully. If handed out before the discussion of a topic, the ideas they express may seem to have the stamp of the expert, and thus they may destroy discussion and creative problem-solving. Preferably they should be distributed after the discussion and then other ideas can be added to the written material. They should be valued as "take home" reminders and perhaps can serve as a stimulus to further discussion between the class members and their spouses.

Observation and Participation are important techniques in a preschool parent education program such as we describe in Chapter 5. The child observation class is based on participation of the mother as a source of learning, and has been termed a laboratory providing an opportunity for observation as well as a place to practice newly acquired skills. To see and work with other people's children and to see her own child in the larger context has specific values to the young mother, intensively concentrating on and concerned about her own child.

From the observation of children's behavior and preschool experience can come discussion of behavior causation, of learning processes, of possible responses, guidance, techniques, and of parental reactions to children's actions and achievements. The middle class mother may have a strong emotional response to her child's lack of participation and success in relating to other children; a lower class mother is more likely to be deeply concerned about whether or not her child "minds the teacher." Knowledge and "thinking through" often reduce anxiety and dispel ignorance and fear. Observation is an excellent way in which to provide relevance to the student's own situation.

Observation without preparation, however, is often meaningless, and knowledgable observation without some discussion has limited values. A most efficient first step may be for the student to look for some one thing until his skills as an observer improve. Teachers may supplement actual observing with discussion of the meanings and implications of sample records done by other observers. It is suggested that specific projects for observation of each session be listed until the group members are experienced enough to observe independently. Understanding what is observed is essential to satisfying and successful participation. One program[28] requires a period of study in a child observation class before mothers are permitted to enroll their children in the cooperative nursery where mothers must assist on a part-time basis.

A LEARNING-VALUING FOCUS AND THE DECISION-MAKING PROCESS

If the parent sees himself as a significant teacher of his child, his acceptance of that responsibility may grow with practice and success in relation to what he may have previously considered insignificant parent-child interactions. The parent understands the meaning of his answer to his child's question. His awareness of something being taught and learned contributes to his understanding and respect for his own role. The parent starts gaining satisfaction from a simple skill in teaching the child, as well as gaining new motivation. As he learns that he is one of the significant teachers, and that there are techniques he can thoughtfully apply to this vital interaction, his self-concept is enhanced. As he gains knowledge of how children learn and some of the tools for effective teaching, he analyzes problems and concerns in a new light. With the realization that he is constantly teaching values, he more carefully examines his own values.

With the learning-focused approach providing a structure for parent and parent educator, each area of interest is looked at in a new way. What is the child learning? What does he need to learn? What are you, the parent, teaching him? What do you want to teach him? Is he ready for this learning at this time? What do you value? What values are you communicating and, therefore, teaching him to value?

Whenever there is parent-child interaction there is a teaching-learning situation. If the parent views it in this light, he can focus on different aspects of each interaction. He can see each situation as an opportunity rather than a power struggle, see it with its various meanings and possibilities for action.

SUMMARY

The discussion method is selected as most appropriate for increasing parental competence and for enabling effective adult learning. From a survey of parent education program goals and methods are drawn those factors helpful in conceptualizing an approach with clearly defined goals. Information about how the adult learns is useful. The approach of discussion method is not entirely unstructured, but neither is it didactic nor solely information giving. The teacher is sensitive to differences in groups and approaches content on the basis of the needs of each group. Purpose, content, and teacher characteristics all influence the determination of methods and goals.

REFERENCES

1. Orville Brim, Jr., *Education for Child Rearing*. New York: The Free Press, 1965. P. 10.
2. *Ibid.,* p. 208.
3. Aline B. Auerbach, *Parents Learn Through Discussion*. New York: Wiley, 1968. P. 3.
4. *Ibid.,* p. 5.
5. Ethel Kawin, *Parenthood in a Free Nation*. Chicago: University of Chicago Press, 1955.
6. Brim, *Education for Child Rearing,* pp. 224–226.
7. Carl S. Hereford, *Changing Parental Attitudes Through Group Discussion*. Austin, Texas: Texas University Press, 1964.
8. Brim, *Education for Child Rearing,* pp. 95–109.
9. *Ibid.,* p. 104.
10. *Ibid.,* p. 215.
11. *Ibid.,* p. 48.
12. Robertson Sillars, *Seeking Common Ground in Adult Education*. Adult Education Monographs, Adult Education Association of the U.S.A., 1958. P. 20.
13. Kenneth D. Benne, "Some Philosophic Issues in Adult Education," *Adult Education,* Vol. VII, No. 2, p. 73.
14. Sillars, *Seeking Common Ground,* pp. 91–92.

15. Harry S. Broudy, "A Philosopher Looks at Adult Education," *Seeking Common Grounds in Adult Education.* Adult Education Monographs, Adult Education Association of the U.S.A., 1958. P. 95.

16. Malcolm S. Knowles, "Philosophical Issues That Confront Adult Educators," *Adult Education,* Vol. VII, No. 4, p. 240.

17. Robert W. White, "Motivation Reconsidered," *Psychological Review,* Vol. 66, No. 5, 1959.

18. Erik H. Erickson, *Childhood and Society* (2nd ed.). New York: Norton, 1963.

19. Brunner, Edmund D., and associates, *An Overview of Adult Education Research.* Chicago: Adult Education Association of the U.S.A., 1959. Pp. 13–14.

20. Raymond G. Kuhlen, "Motivational Changes During the Adult Years," *Psychological Backgrounds of Adult Education.* Chicago: Center for the Study of Liberal Education of Adults, 1963. P. 101.

21. W. J. McKeachie, "Psychological Characteristics of Adults and Instructional Methods in Adult Education." In Raymond G. Kuhlen (Ed.), *Psychological Backgrounds of Adult Education.* Chicago: Center for the Study of Liberal Education of Adults, 1963. P. 116.

22. James E. Birren, "Adult Capacities to Learn." In Kuhlen, *Psychological Backgrounds,* p. 60.

23. McKeachie, "Psychological Characteristics," p. 141.

24. Brunner, *An Overview,* p. 29.

25. Bernice Neugarten, "Personality Changes During the Adult Years." In Kuhlen, *Psychological Backgrounds,* pp. 60–61.

26. Arthur T. Jersild, *When Teachers Face Themselves.* New York: Columbia University, Teachers College, 1965. P. 82.

27. Brim, *Education for Child Rearing,* p. 217.

28. Baltimore City Schools, Adult Education.

4

The Parent Educator:
Selection, Preparation, and Training

Universities and colleges do not yet grant degrees in Parent Education. There are, of course, departments of Family and Child Development, Human Development and Home Economics that touch importantly upon the subject. To date, however, there are few coordinated efforts to integrate the interdisciplinary knowledge related to the parent task, to teach the specific skills required to transmit this knowledge to parents in a usable fashion, or to consider program goals and procedures. More often parent education is viewed as an ancillary service to an agency with other primary functions. Administrators attempting to establish a parent education program find themselves with the question of who shall teach, and many potential programs have not been started for lack of trained personnel.

SELECTION

Until such time as institutions of higher learning offer specific programs for the preparation of parent educators in sufficient numbers to be readily available to agencies staffing programs, the responsibility for the selection of persons potentially capable of performing the task lies with the administrator. Guidelines for such selection presented here are based on a philosophy of parent education and the knowledge and skills considered necessary. With well-defined program goals, adequate training programs, and supervised on-the-job experience, knowledge can be reorganized, gaps assessed, and growth programmed over realistic periods of time. Skills, defined within the context of program philosophy, can be learned.

PHILOSOPHY

When the administrator searches for people with qualities that seem to enhance rather than inhibit the growth of other people, he may find that his most effective personnel selection method is the delineation of program philosophy. If he succeeds in making the value base of the program sufficiently visible to a prospective employee, together they can determine whether or not the program is where this person belongs. The prospective parent educator must know that the purpose of the program is toward enabling the parent's decision-making process rather than pressuring for preferred behavior. This thrust may well separate those who are only comfortable in the "expert" role from those who are very uncomfortable in it, and who would prefer, given the appropriate structure and methodology, to stimulate individual growth through choice.

VALUE PREMISES

How might an administrator spell out the program philosophy? A restatement of what we have been propounding thus far might sound something like this: A valid philosophy of parent education must be based on clearly delineated value premises. Premises that underly the procedures in this program are:

1. People are potentially autonomous;
2. People find meaning in their lives as a result of the choices they make;
3. Rational choice is difficult in a complex, rapidly changing society;
4. Problems often result from a lack of awareness of alternatives and their consequences;
5. Therefore, the purpose of education aimed at improving the quality of family life is to encourage the development of individual autonomy.

These premises provide a framework from which to view the complex role of parents in today's world and the need for a clearly defined education approach. We have emphasized the key teaching role of parents and the recognition that traditional guidelines are no longer valid in the face of great change. Parents have little or no opportunity to select new guidelines or to think through what they want to teach their children and what their children need to learn. A need for a structure within which parents can increase their understanding of the learning and valuing processes in growth and development, and thus their competence in the parent-child teaching-learning interaction, is evident.

A valid parent education program must be based on a philosophy. Its value system must be visible to parents in order that they can experience, judge, and experiment with these ideas. Parent education programs must say, "Here is a system of values that we believe has meaning in terms of the task we face today. Use this framework to assess your own thinking and cherish your own conclusions."

Such a program embraces a few fundamental general values within a structure that accepts change and variety in the ways these values are interpreted. We believe that human qualities are learned and that there are some human qualities more desirable for our society than others. To trust oneself and others is better than to doubt oneself and distrust others. To be aware of one's feelings and those of others is better than being closed off from oneself and insensitive to others. To handle problems rationally and learn from one's own experience is better than to lash out unthinkingly and to rely on external controls. Tolerance of difference, change, and ambiguity is more desirable than rejection of difference, rigidity in the face of change, and demand for absolutes.

If human qualities are learned, and we value some over others, then the way in which parents provide, stress, and mediate experience will increase or decrease the probability of their development. The program would, then, embrace the value of conscious provision of an environment that promotes a respect for individuality and learning through experience rather than rote. Implicit in this approach is the belief that there are some parental behaviors that seem more feasible to educate for than others, namely, those that are arrived at through thoughtful examination.

With this prime educational goal, the parent educator can define his values, present the range of alternatives, and accept the end result of the parent's thoughtful deliberation. Within the framework of these few fundamental values, the parent educator defines the significant ideas and raises the most facilitating questions in order to enable parents to think through their unique experiences.

Some of the key concepts that, once understood, enable more meaningful assessment of experience, fall into a teachable sequence:

1. Behavior is learned.
2. Parents teach.
3. Teaching is a qualitatively different process than "managing behavior."
4. In order to teach effectively, parents need to know
   a. what the child needs to know about himself and the world in order to live effectively and fully;
   b. what the parent himself wants the child to learn (the parent's conscious value choices);
   c. what is known about how children learn;
   d. how to enable that learning while seeing the child as a separate person learning from his own experience.

Parent educators need clearly perceived basic concepts in order to function effectively in a learning-valuing approach. Their teaching needs to be based on the understanding that, in order to learn effectively, parents need (1) to be seen as capable of thoughtful choice; (2) to be in a learning environment that values the choosing rather than specified choices, and (3) to be given the same components of safety, time, variety, freedom to err, repetition, and clarification that children need for learning.

These are the essential components of this approach to the education of parents. An administration's role in the hiring process would focus on determining the degree of the applicant's compatibility with the direction of the program and willingness to function and grow within it.

KNOWLEDGE

The base of knowledge needed by the parent educator is interdisciplinary in nature, drawing its major premises largely from the fields of psychology, sociology, anthropology, education, and social work. Educators sift, sort, and integrate theories and data from the behavioral and social sciences into an approach that is relevant to parents. Tolerance of wide gaps in understanding is essential to this task. The lack of absolute, scientific answers to questions of human relationships and parent-child interaction systems creates a climate for stimulating the process of individual choice.

The parent educator must constantly pose questions. What do the social and behavioral sciences have to offer parents? What is known and not known about the development of human personality? What makes the present social scene "normal behavior" different from what it used to be? What findings about learning are applicable or lend themselves to experimentation in the context of our present experience? Willingness to make the best sense out of what is available and to reevaluate in the face of new information is a key factor in a dynamic program. A solid grasp of human development includes working familiarity with a wide variety of theoretical assumptions, provides a spectrum of lenses for viewing any one question, and a sensitivity for the broad range of unique individual behaviors.

To function effectively, a parent educator needs a working knowledge of the institution of the family and the impact of social change on its function; an awareness of the variability of parenting patterns and of the effect of socioeconomic and cultural factors on attitudes, values, behaviors, and skills; an understanding of the community's role in meeting individual needs and a facility for connecting families with community resources. A knowledge of the history of parent education efforts brings perspective and direction to current programs. A solid understanding of the learning process for both adult and child, of the group process and the function of leadership, of the communication skills that nurture individual growth are all integral parts of the parent educator's knowledge. Part of the task is the capacity to translate sophisticated theory into everyday language that parents can use as they relate it to their own lives and action.

The administrator is faced with the difficult task of determining the nature of the applicant's present knowledge and whether it provides a sufficient base for the beginning; the level of the applicant's motivation for continued development in the direction of the program's goal for its personnel; the capacity for commitment to professional growth.

SKILLS

Skills, in themselves, have little meaning. Facility with the many techniques for presenting content has little or no value unless those techniques clearly reflect an underlying philosophy. An educator may be able to "skilfully" involve a group in discussion, get them to perform in buzz groups, panels, role-playing or sociodrama, but if the end result is not increased autonomy and awareness on the part of the participant, the skill is in manipulation, but not in enabling change.

Parent educators need to be comfortable in the role of mediator rather than expert; at ease in a function aimed at "how to think about it" rather than "what to think about it." They must have deep conviction that learning can happen through the assessment of experience, whether individually or collectively, and clearly see their goal as enabling enlightened individual choice rather than maneuvering parents into the educator's personal belief system. They must see themselves as part of the process, as equal to parents in the sense of being a fellow human being, as similar but different in the role they play and the knowledge they bring.

Parent educators should see their task as providing a model for enabling learning that parents can observe. They illustrate a teaching process that parents can get the feel of and relate to their own parental teaching task. By beginning with each situation and defining the basic ideas that make it work, they help parents to try ideas on for size at whatever point they can, help them to see the range of alternatives, and then to choose. The parent educator fosters learning by spelling out underlying concepts, illustrated in the parent's own experience, reinterpreted in many different settings, tied to what parents already know, and presented in the context of the concerns they bring.

Goals obviously have a vigorous impact on the teaching stance and skills of parent educators. If we are really committed to helping parents in the process of choice, then as educators we can no longer make judgemental responses; i.e., "That's right, Mrs.

Jones," or "That's a good answer, Mr. Smith." That is, if our responses to parents do not reflect our stated premises, we place them in a highly confusing double bind. If we are, on the one hand, saying that the essential goal is the *process* of choice rather than the product, but on the other hand approving of one choice over another, then we reinforce desire for approval rather than the struggle for congruence. We defeat our goal of individual growth. In order for the responses of the parent educator to be consistent with basic premises, we would not make judgemental responses. Rather, we would reinforce parents' expressions that indicate searching, learning, growing clarity of thinking, recognition of basic concepts in everyday situations, problem orientation, and the sense of being able to work things out. Recognition of the need to reach congruity between premises and practices is vital. Many parent educators finding validity in this approach will find they need to consciously retrain themselves in order that they may respond consistently.

Along with skills that clearly reflect program goals, the parent educator needs the skills of relating as a helping person. These skills are based on a consciousness of self, an understanding of one's motivations, needs, desires, strengths, and limitations. The teacher's most important teaching tool is an awareness and use of self, based on acceptance of where he is and a deep sense of his own becoming. Only if he views himself in this dynamic sense can he respond to others in a helping way.

A helping relationship is "any relationship in which one person facilitates the personal growth or development of another, where he helps the other to become more mature, adaptive, integrated, or open to new experience." [1] Empathic understanding, unqualified care, respect, and availability are essential qualities. The capacity to know and appreciate how another person feels while retaining one's own identity, the ability to feel connected while retaining a sense of separateness, the skill of relating to feeling while allowing the other to retain responsibility for his own growth are indications of skillful helping.

Awareness of dynamic forces in the growing process is also part of skillful helping. Understanding the role that anxiety plays in learning and change, knowing what may engender anxiety, how it is evidenced, is important. "Anxiety may arise as a reaction to anything that threatens one's existence as a separate self or that jeopardizes the attitudes one has concerning one's self and one's relations to others." [2] Couple the probability of change, which is anxiety-producing in itself, with the very content of parent education and anxiety is inevitable. It will vary in degree and intensity with individuals and with content areas. It may indicate imminent change or withdrawal, decision not to change or temporary resistance. But if perceived and gauged sensitively, anxiety is a generative force for change and a concomitant part of all movement and growth. The educational task is to accept the inevitability of anxiety, recognize its presence, make it visible to the learner so that it can be dealt with. To advise a parent not to worry evades the educational task at times. To arouse anxiety needlessly and without supportive help during acute stress, as some educators do when they forecast tragic effects on children of certain parent behaviors, can be immobilizing. But to view anxiety as a healthy response to the inner demand for growth and to confront it effectively is part of skillful helping.

Thus, the administrator spells out the process through which learning happens, a process made meaningful because it is anchored firmly in a clarified philosophy and articulated goals. The attitudes, behaviors, and skills that make values operative can be taught in theory and learned in practice, *if* the prospective parent educator sees himself as fitting into this broad framework and is concerned about the development of his unique capacities within it.

THE EDUCATION OF PARENT EDUCATORS

CURRENT STATUS

Who are the trained parent educators today if no university has assumed the responsibility for specific preparation? Partial training is found in other professions. A teacher, social worker, psychologist may have acquired during the course of professional development a body of knowledge appropriate to the content of a parent education program. It is unlikely that he will have thought through the appropriateness of content, developed a philosophy incorporating goals and values related to a program, considered techniques and methods or their suitability in a parent education setting. It is unlikely that these professionals will have had the opportunity to observe or practice in a specifically parent education–oriented program.

When family casework agencies conduct parent group education, it is usually a service supplementing their major agency function. The Child Study Association of America [3] has conducted training programs for the preparation of social workers and public health nurses in the parent group education process. Unfortunately these excellent programs are relatively limited in number. When schools of education deal with the need to work with parents, it is usually in terms of individual counseling or home visitation. There is rarely an attempt to explore objectives and methodology in addition to the many complexities of the process.

For the most part then, the training of parent educators has been left up to those agencies offering such programs. The need for preservice education for those who are to teach parent education was recognized by administrators in the Division of Adult Education of the Los Angeles City Schools and such training has been provided for some years. Responsibility for this training has been that of the subject field supervisor. A comprehensive and well-planned course of study for the preparation of parent educators at a university or community college is the next step. The agency could then carry the responsibility for in-service education and staff development.

The procedure in the Los Angeles school system is to select persons with a professional background that will have provided them, at least in part, with the essential body of knowledge. Highly subjective judgements must then be made by the agency regarding the individual's potentials, personality and attitudes that will determine ability to work with parent groups. The informal training program consists of internship or practice teaching with opportunities for the trainee to assume portions of the actual practice under the supervision of an experienced teacher. Arrangements are made for work with both preschool children in the demonstration portion of the program and with discussion group leadership. In addition, either before or within the first two years of work, the teacher is required to take four units of course work in methods and materials and in the philosophy of adult education. Preferably, the parent educator takes a methods course that deals specifically with the content of parent education.

PROPOSAL FOR TRAINING PROGRAMS

Many professional people in departments of family life, human development, child and family study, and so on have become concerned with the need to develop a specific, sequential, interdisciplinary program geared to the special needs of people who wish to work directly with parents. They have wrestled with the common problems of specifying frame of reference, goals, philosophy, methodology, and skills. Several programs (i.e., the Department of Human Development, University of Hawaii; the Department of Family Life, Seattle Community College) are actively engaged in the process of developing degree programs to train parent educators. The initial delineation of such a degree program submitted for consideration below evolved out of the authors' exploration of this problem in both of the above settings.

GRADUATE LEVEL SEQUENCE

FIRST SEMESTER

Human Development I

Impact of social, cultural, physical, emotional, and intellectual factors on the growth and development of the young child from birth to twelve years, with focus on the effects of parent-child interaction on the learning process. Range of individual responses.

The Family: Structure and Function

Redefining the role of the family in the face of social change; value confusion and the process of valuing as family function; technological change and implications for family functioning.

The Community: Structure, Analysis and Resources

Examination of human needs in today's society; the role of the community in meeting social realities of individuals; role of individual, family and change agent in coordination of needs and community resources.

Adult Learning Process

Sociological and psychological processes pertaining to individual motivation, internal and external forces. Nature of adult learning patterns; the decision-making process.

Seminar: Theoretical Framework for Parent Education

History of parent education: goals, structure and content. Contributions of major premises from behavioral and social sciences to parent education theory and practice. Implications for programming.

SECOND SEMESTER

Human Development II

Impact of social, cultural, physical, emotional, and intellectual factors on the growth and development of the child from twelve years to adulthood, with focus on the nature and process of interaction within the family and the larger community.

Cultural Factors in Child-Rearing and Family Dynamics

Cultural context of socialization: class and ethnic differences and their impact on child-rearing and personality development, with emphasis on assessing effect of subcultures (in community) or family's perception of role and capacity for effective functioning.

Group Process and Leadership

Interpretation of group process, role of leader and individual in terms of goals of parent education, with directed observation in ongoing parent education groups; implications for individual counseling.

Seminar: Areas of Concern for Parent Educators

Function of parent education as adult education for competence in key life role; nature of competencies of parent role. Survey of parent education settings and methods. Assessment of current research.

THIRD SEMESTER

Human Development III

Growth and development in adulthood and old age, with focus on nature of primary relationships and developmental tasks of modern family.

Research Methods and Statistics

Analysis of current relevant research in terms of methodology. Validity of research in areas of behavior and attitude change. Defining research needs in parent education.

Independent Study

Directed research in thesis area.

Practicum

Supervised teaching experience in ongoing community setting, to include conferences with faculty sponsor and supervisory personnel; focus on group process and leadership. Student to have one semester each in middle- and low-income setting.

FOURTH SEMESTER

Socialization of Competence

Review of human developmental processes in terms of competencies essential to effective family development and individual fulfillment in today's world; new understandings re: the role of learning and implications for 'teachability' in parent education programs.

Seminar: The Teaching Process

Translation of the basic premises of parent education programs into visible terms of presentation; development of relevant teaching aids and sequences.

Independent Study

Directed research in thesis area.

Practicum II

Supervised teaching experience in ongoing community setting. Focus on defining goals, process, and limitations of role in dealing with individual parents.

This is an initial effort in the task of integrating the substance of many disciplines into a practicable training sequence for parent education personnel. The combined effort of people, involved in both theoretical and practical dimensions of the field, could produce a more precise translation of the needs into a specific program for training.

SUPERVISION AND IN-SERVICE TRAINING

ADMINISTRATIVE POSITION

The provision of a planned program of staff development is consistent with the belief that growth is a continuous process and that individuals have the potential for change. As a teacher gains experience, he sees gaps, feels reactions, raises questions that he didn't perceive before. Teaching is a lonely job and, if he is concerned about his professional growth, the teacher demands ongoing evaluation.

A program to meet these demands varies in content, because it is based on teacher needs and designed to enhance the growth of those unique individuals who make up the staff. It may range from practical procedural information that facilitates teaching to consideration of relationship areas, i.e. teacher-student interaction, developing relationships with community agencies, etc.

It is not a top-down program, but consciously calls upon the variety of backgrounds within the staff to enrich collective thinking. It is not a totally staff-directed program, because supervisory personnel accept the responsibility for enabling staff growth and providing leadership in areas where particular experiential histories create gaps in understanding.

There is constant concern with increasing competence. The task is so multifaceted that an alert staff is never content with present knowledge and skill. Skillful supervision provides a structure within which common problems can be faced, new approaches evolved and tested, insights shared. Teachers recognize their own needs, see their own problems, and out of their experience are motivated to continued learning. An administrative climate that encourages choice, change, and individual responsibility for growth can give this motivation effective direction. A rigidly imposed curriculum with line-by-line procedural directives, a didactic in-service program that squelches active interaction, an autocratic approach to supervision will not produce teachers who can create an appropriate climate for parental growth.

There may be areas in which the teacher does not make the final decisions. Institutional function and its concomitant rules and operative procedures are often present. Whenever possible they are open for negotiation, responsive to staff assessment. Hopefully they provide a framework that encourages mutual responsibility for program development.

In summary, it is the role of supervisory personnel to assess the needs of staff, to make these needs visible so that they can be dealt with, to set a model for problem-solving that is consistent with program philosophy. Supervision is a resource for teachers use that should enable them to translate this resource-model into their own perception of their role with parents.

KNOWLEDGE: A CONTINUOUS PROCESS

Secure teachers who feel a partnership in their agency constantly seek growth. The task of keeping up with the literature, in this multidisciplinary endeavor, is tremendous in scope and demands full participation of both staff and supervisory personnel. New knowledge cannot merely be reported; all of its implications for program must be explored by the total staff, through the use of their own resources and others in the community, both professional and nonprofessional. It must be sifted, sorted, and tested against program premises. It must be evaluated in terms of its overall validity and implications for parents.

DEEPENING AWARENESS OF SELF: A CONTINUOUS PROCESS

The web of interpersonal reactions in which the parent educator is continually involved is a forever changing one. New confrontations arise, new people interact, new topics are considered, different-from-self parental responses are aroused. The teacher needs help with this dynamic process; he needs increasing clarity in seeing how he acts and reacts. This ongoing analysis can be programmed in a variety of ways.

Dealing with this process in groups is supportive as well as clarifying. Sometimes growth is enhanced more effectively in the one-to-one relationship between teacher and supervisor. Frustration, anger, guilt, anxiety about failure—all of these feelings and more are part of normal responses. Even though controlled, they cannot and should not be eliminated. They can be more adequately dealt with and are less likely to block effectiveness if they are faced. That confrontation need not be a lonely one.

One vital area of concern to parent educators is acceptance of self as an agent of change. The idea of changing someone else is sometimes rejected to such an extent that the concept of change as growth is lost. The reaction to authoritarianism may be so strong that the educational responsibility for providing opportunities for another to change himself may be denied. The parent educator does not change someone but he does enable another to change himself. The parent educator who honestly faces the responsibility and the authority inherent in the situation can deal with it without imposing his will on others.

Another area of deep concern is that of personal failure; that is, in not meeting one's own standards. People with a deep commitment to a task find it difficult to accept the inevitable occasional failure to function exactly according to their own concept of their role. When staff members share experiences of failure and accept it in one another, self-acceptance is encouraged. Facing one's own limitations squarely and accepting them provides a base for the acceptance of others. The search for self-understanding is never-ending; it requires constant self-examination. In-service education should aid this process.

DEALING WITH DIFFERENCE

As programs for the culturally different parent expand, there is a heightened awareness of teachers' reactions to those who are experientially quite different from themselves and of the impact of this difference on the teaching-learning process. Significant insight into this situation resulted from the Los Angeles program through the use of professional consultation (under the Short Doyle Act of California) for a group of parent educators working for the first time in low income communities. The consultant for this group, Dr. Siegel, made the following observations about the concerns and needs of teachers in this setting:

There is initially with all groups or classes for adults where the teacher comes from a different geographical area, even within the same city, the problem of the teacher's feeling of being the outsider. When she is dealing with children, she has lower expectations for being accepted as one of the group. Where there are economic, racial, and cultural distinctions, even the most secure teacher is beset with concerns about being the outsider—the different one. Regardless of the fact that the mothers may not have known each other prior to the beginning of the class, and have little to do with each other after or outside of class, they still have a common bond by virtue of their disadvantaged state—i.e., they don't have the knowledge or the training of the teacher.

The ability to tolerate this state of being "The Outsider" depends to a great degree on the teacher's assurances that she truly has something to offer. Whether one's students consider you valuable is often hard to determine. For example, the most frequently repeated experience has been the teacher's surprise (and delight) in finding, through some overt expression, how important she is to a class member.

Even after the class has been well underway, the teachers' recognition of the value of her enlightened, patient, and persistent interest in the parents and their children can be vulnerable to many forces. The dissenting, demeaning parents who use these techniques to produce guilt and obedience in their children often use the same techniques on the teacher to relieve their anxiety.

Teachers working with low income classes are often sensitive about being more economically fortunate. The tendency is often to feel apologetic or to try to diminish the difference by running themselves down to their students.

Teachers can readily acknowledge and thereby respond to the mothers' and children's wish to be accepted and approved of. But teachers themselves can become more comfortable through the recognition of their own needs to be accepted and approved of. That the desire for approval and acceptance can be shared with a teacher's group visibly relieves tension.

As is natural, teachers tend to choose special parents in each class who are most rewarding to work with, because they provide her with the gratifications of being appreciated. Often they are parents who grasp our concepts quickly, often using our own words and actions as demonstrations. With many others the changes are more subtle and not verbal in form but nonetheless very real—for example, improvement in grooming, or less sense of desperation with themselves and their children.

There are women who are often not active class participants although they are regular attenders. Almost every class has a few of them. The teacher is often hard put to understand why they come; to know whether they are being helped. In truth these women are often completely estranged from their own society and the class provides for them a valuable and unique function—giving them the sense of being part of something even though on a passive level.

One of the most pernicious problems in dealing with poor people (or with old people) is the constant danger of being overwhelmed by the impossible and overlooking the possible. There are many teachers confronted for the first time with child-rearing habits quite alien to what we would consider promoting good future mental health. Severe corporal punishment, shaming, etc. have tradition behind them, and stem from frustration and isolation. The possibilities of other modes of response are not considered or sought by the parents. Teaching these groups is frustrating: what can the teacher offer in the face of these apparently unchangeable behavior patterns. If the teacher can tolerate such frustration without becoming too disappointed or resentful, she can then experience the later pleasures of watching parents learn—through group discussion, from observation of teacher demonstrations of her own handling of children's classroom problems—a new respect and understanding for the children's needs that will make more severe forms of punishment less often necessary.[4]

Here we see a number of affective reactions to the teaching situation and relationship to the students. Many of them are not unknown to other teachers in other situations; perhaps here they are more intense and therefore more evident. All teachers experience emotional reactions to their students, even those who deny them. The act of facing feelings increases the probability of dealing with them constructively and as Dr. Siegel points out, tension is visibly released when facing them within a teacher group. The values of the consultation group have been attested to by the teachers who had this opportunity.

Another group of parent educators working in the traditional middle class setting met with Dr. John Peck, also of Los Angeles. Of particular interest is this comment of Dr. Peck's:

These teachers must be flexible and willing to listen and try to understand value systems and moral standards which may be totally different from

their own. They must be able to accept unsophisticated and even destructive attitudes expressed by the mothers and try to modify them
in a nonpunitive way.[5]

He names emotional integrity and maturity as necessary characteristics of teachers dealing with "extremely fundamental and at times
anxiety-laden psychological situations." Some current literature
contrasting the lower class and middle class child-rearing practices
may tend to stereotype both systems while in actuality there is a
wide range of values and behaviors within each class.

Not all of our staff has had the opportunity of mental health
consultation. Some of these problems are dealt with in teachers'
meetings, though on a less intensive basis. The act of facing one's
own need for acceptance and student recognition is probably more
easily faced in the more protected and intimate setting of mental
health consultation.

Other dimensions of the parent educator's role have been
expanded through a more flexible approach to programming. Home
visits and work in the community, now often a part of the parent
educator's role in low-income areas (see Chapter 6 for a more thorough description of these programs), were not formerly a component of the traditional program. Experience found that parent educators who were formerly social workers were most comfortable and
effective in this phase of work. Thus, the strengths of one group
were used to supplement other staff; teachers who were unclear as
to the purpose and value of home visits and transmitted this confusion to parents were given the clarification of purpose and necessary skills for making this part of their assignment meaningful.

INTERAGENCY COOPERATION

A vital area of staff development is the ability to work with
other agencies and professionals cooperatively, while retaining a
clear grasp of the definition and limits of one's own function. If,
for example, we move toward a format in the preschool where the
preschool teacher and parent educator are working as a team, a
new relationship evolves, whose roles and functions must be defined.
This development must have administrative sanction, planning, and
procedural guidance, based on a realistic awareness of the problems

that will inevitably come and a capacious and patient zest for working them through.

SUMMARY

The delineation of a philosophy, a body of knowledge and the skills that make that philosophy and knowledge available to parents provides a viable basis for selection of potential personnel. The prospective staff member must decide whether this is a framework within which he can work and grow, and he must make this decision with a clear perception of the basis and direction of the program. Once the applicant finds meaning in the philosophy, the administrator then assesses readiness for entry in terms of present knowledge and experience, and determines the degree to which in-service training is needed. In-service training must be set in a climate that nurtures continued growth of knowledge, awareness of self as a teaching-learning helping person, increased competence in the teaching process, and the meeting of individual staff needs. The vital need for specific training programs must be met if parent education programs are to become a significant component of the education of adults in their key life roles.

REFERENCES

1. G. R. Barrett-Lennard, "Significant Aspects of a Helping Relationship," *Canada's Mental Health,* Supplement No. 47, Mental Health Division, Department of National Health and Welfare, Ottawa, Canada (July–August 1965), p. 8.
2. Arthur T. Jersild, *When Teachers Face Themselves.* New York: Columbia University, Teachers College, 1965. P. 27.
3. Aline B. Auerbach, *Parents Learn Through Discussion.* New York: Wiley, 1968. Pp. 222–235.
4. Correspondence with Dr. Donald G. Siegel, Mental Health Consultant, Los Angeles County Department of Mental Health.
5. Correspondence with Dr. John Peck, 1967.

5

Working with Parents
in Advantaged Circumstances:
Parent Education in California

California was one of the first states to incorporate parent education as an integral part of its education system, and remains one of the few states to have done this to date. The development of the California experience, and more specifically the Los Angeles program, reveals some characteristics that have bearing on our task, and is the source of our first hand knowledge and experience. This is not to say that the approach taken in California is the only way to meet the needs of parents, however we believe the principles and methods, as well as the content, are usable in other settings.

Early California programs of parent education were based on sensitivity to "the quantity and quality of education that takes place before children start to school, also that which takes place outside schools after they have entered school." [1] A 1934 California State Department of Education bulletin on objectives and procedures for parent education points out that "organized study by fathers and mothers and teachers is essential to effective articulation of the many phases of education in our lives." [2] Many public school systems in California have maintained programs of parent education since 1926.

Traditionally, parent education has served the educated middle class parent who looks to education as a means of achieving his aims. The middle class person sees education as an approach to enhancing his role function, whatever it may be. He is often accustomed to working in groups, to looking to the specialist for information, to engaging in his own problem-solving on a conscious level. Many parents have used such programs, although by no means the majority.

Goals, method, and content have been influenced by the clientele using the programs. In this case, the recognition by school personnel and parents that there was a need and a value led to the development and continuation of such programs. The guiding premise was that understanding the child and his growth and development, understanding the parents' sense of self, and increasing the parents' problem-solving skills would enhance parental competence and in turn lead to good mental health for the child.

Many parents have rejected traditional child-rearing methods or mores, intellectually if not in practice. What do they substitute for tradition? Their own parents' practices, which they experienced as children, are often the opposite of what they wish to follow now that they are themselves parents. What are they trying to accomplish, what are they worried about? Answers to these questions have been projected from those parents about whom we are able to get some data—those who use communication sources such as the mass media, education programs, doctors, and so on. The belief of parent educators that information and understanding lead to increased skills for child-rearing, and their faith that parents strongly desire to raise their children well, have led to the development of parent education programs.

HISTORICAL BACKGROUND

The history of the parent education movement in California reveals the impressive vision of the pioneers in this effort. Their basic philosophy has undergone little change over the years. Why is the program not more extensive than it is?

A grant from the Laura Spellman Rockefeller Foundation in 1926 to the University of California and the State Department of Education made possible the experimental establishment of an Institute of Child Welfare and a bureau of parent education. In 1931 the State Department of Education was authorized by legislative enactment to assume control and support of the experimental activities already begun, and a bureau of parent education was set up. This bureau and the parent education committee of the California Congress of Parents and Teachers worked cooperatively to promote and coordinate the program.

In 1933, the program's eighth year, Dr. Herbert Stolz of the State Department of Education pointed it out as the only parent education program recognized as an integral part of the public school system. This program displayed certain distinctive traits that set it apart from the programs of other states, and was designed primarily to stimulate parents to solve their own problems rather than turn to the opinions of experts. Also, according to Stolz,

Perhaps the most important characteristic of the California program is the active and constructive part which is being played by the California Congress of Parents and Teachers. The work during the past seven years has been characterized by real cooperation between the State Department of Education, the California Congress of Parents and Teachers and the local school authorities.[3]

Two State Department of Education publications, one written in 1934 and the other in 1935,[4] by Dr. Gertrude Laws, then director of the department, also reflect the program as an established responsibility of public education working in close cooperation with the California Congress of Parents and Teachers. The objectives and suggested procedures for parent education in the 1934 bulletin are the same as those first issued in 1928. The objectives emphasized the following desirable educational achievements for parents:

1. To appreciate the child for his own sake.
2. To develop the habit of sympathetic observation.
3. To develop interest in the study of psychology.
4. To develop the habit of making wise judgements based on facts.
5. To gain an understanding of mental health.
6. To increase one's ability to face facts about oneself.
7. To increase parent interest in school procedures.
8. To develop a method of attack on problems of child adjustment.
9. To learn sources of information about child care.

These original goals are repeated as valid expressions of parental needs in the 1961 California Department of Education publications, *Parent Education—Curriculum, Methods and Materials.*

In 1935 [5] Dr. Laws reported the principles that guided the development of the programs from 1927 on:

1. Parent education is an integral part of the total program of adult education, and must be supported as such.
2. The vitality and continued growth of parent education depends upon the maintenance of an experimental attitude on the part of all leaders.

So long as parent education is in its infancy, it is better not to attempt to start in a community until a man or woman can be found who is reasonably well-prepared both by nature and nurture to do it well. Organized study is too important to be introduced into a school system by a poorly prepared person.[6]

Laws believed that "a truly integrated educational system cannot exist if any important part of it is conducted on a volunteer basis, without requirements for preparation of leadership while other parts are conducted on a paid basis and with more and more exacting demands for preparation."

Although Laws preferred to call parent educators leaders rather than teachers and often referred to them as lay workers, she never denied the need for training nor the assumption of responsibility for this endeavor. She believed that the teacher leader must have knowledge of child development and research findings related to parent-child relationships. Her emphasis appears to have been on content rather than method, although her approach was certainly not that of the professional expert telling the parent what to do. The early bulletins often state that the leadership should come from the groups themselves, but there was no indication that it could be done without training or that it should be left entirely to the volunteer.

A 1946 manual of parent education published by the California Congress of Parents and Teachers states,

Policies of the parent education program in California have remained consistently the same from the beginning of the program. Leaders are trained for study groups; parent education is interpreted as an integral part of the state system of education; leaflets on objectives, methods and suggested procedure and subject matter have been prepared in view of the early experiments conducted. The Bureau of Parent Education in the State Department of Education and the parent education committee of the Congress have worked cooperatively to promote and to coordinate the program. By this cooperative effort the study program has made steady growth with the continued high standards of accomplishments and outstanding achievement.[7]

In this program, then, we see a commitment to trained and paid leadership and institutional provisions for a defined educational need. Many leaders in the field of parent education still maintain that paid leaders cannot be afforded, and that there are not enough people to do the job. Yet paid parent educators, trained in content and method, are the rule in many California communities. The California Congress of Parents and Teachers lists study groups led by credentialed teachers whose salaries are paid by the public schools and others led by lay or volunteer leaders. Many lay leaders pursue their interest and study and become teachers in adult education programs.

The California program is characterized by institutional responsibility, trained and paid leadership, and strong private organizational support from the California Congress of Parents and Teachers. In contrast, a look at the national picture of parent education has led Hendriksen to say, "Basically there have been no clear-cut definitions of parent education, and therefore, as a field it holds no clear-cut status. The present tendency is to view parent and family life education not as fields but as methods and approaches which can be utilized by a large variety of professions." Summing up, she states,

In the historical study, it was found that many activities carried on by the numerous organizations were not well coordinated. There was little evidence in the history that individual agencies had tried to define their operational roles in the field. The pattern seemed to be one of autonomy, each agency carrying on certain types of functions which historically had developed in it whether the functions were appropriate for the agency or not. Therefore, there are many duplications and gaps in services in parent education. Some of the agencies (i.e. the public and higher education institutions) which were well suited to carry on parent education activities were not assuming the responsibility to any great extent in the majority of states.[8]

The 1966 Handbook on Adult Education in California gives the total enrollment in classes in parent education as 28,612. The homemaking field and the forum and lecture series, no doubt, involve some study of parent education, but even so this is a surprisingly small number of persons in view of the way the state positively encouraged the program over the years. Classes are not as broadly available as the original planners hoped they would become. Although California's public adult education program is the largest in the nation, it still suffers from what Clark terms a marginal position within the public school system. Parent education has always had a low priority in the budget, a situation which can hardly be expected to change, considering the present emphasis on vocational and basic education. Budgetary limits are placed on parent education programs even where the demand is present and qualified teachers are available. Administrators remain especially sensitive to the preferences of community groups and a doctrine of immediate needs and a program such as parent education, characterized by future values and not readily understood by many, is not in a good competitive position. Unfortunately the excellent program encouraged by the state is spotty because it is controlled by many decentralized agents, autonomous school systems, and autonomous administrators.

Traditionally parent education has been geared to and used by the middle class. Only since 1963 has there been a reaching out and modification of content and approach as the nation became actively concerned about the underprivilidged. Much has been learned from this work with the poor (see Chapter 6).

PROGRAM FORMS

The Los Angeles program of parent and family life education with which we are most familiar has grown constantly since 1926. The topics offered run the gamut of the urban family's experiences in coping with rapid social and technological change. Courses are designed to meet the needs of families at various points in the life cycle. Interests and study opportunities range from how the child learns to what the school teaches, from understanding the gifted to guiding the handicapped.

The most popular part of the parent education program has been the Child Observation class. This class, not to be confused with the nursery school, is parent education with a children's program serving as a laboratory for adult learning which can be extended into the home. The mother is the adult school student and the purpose is adult education. This is not to say that there are no values for the child—of course there are many. There is a program of planned activities for the child as the participant and the mother as the observer. This constitutes half of the mother's morning during which time she keeps a written record on the activities of her child. The parent has the opportunity (1) to share in her child's initial exposure to formal education; (2) to observe child behavior and parent-child interaction at close range; (3) for an on-the-spot analysis of her observations under the leadership of a skilled teacher. For the young child there is experience in learning to cope with his environment. He has practice in working with materials, in living and learning with his peers, in taking direction from people other than his immediate family, in coping with the social situation of other children. The program is designed to foster physical, social, emotional, and intellectual development. His mother observes and then discusses his needs and how she can practice what she learns at home. The child benefits both directly by class activities and indirectly through his mother's changed attitudes and learning, the kinds of learning that form a firm basis on which to continue in public school. No less important is the mother's increased knowledge of the public school system and her understanding of the relationship between parent and teacher.

Parents earnestly seek guidance on principles and methods of education and in this setting they learn through observation, participation, and discussion. Each adult has a folder of printed instructions and suggestions for observation and recording, as well as directions for carrying out work committee duties. The adult learns the skills of observing and gains knowledge of the meaning of the child's behavior and learning. The adult no longer refers to play as *just* play, and he learns the skills and sensitivities of a teacher to appreciate the full value of play.

Following the observation half of the morning program the remaining hour and a half is devoted to group discussion by the mothers under the teacher's leadership. A basis for discussion is provided by written records kept by the mothers in addition to a wide range of material introduced by the teacher concerning growth and development of the preschool child, family relationships, children's learning, play and play equipment, home management, nutrition, and any number of other typical concerns of the mothers of young children.

A good discussion meeting hinges on the ability of the

teacher to draw the group members into active participation. Teachers are carefully selected and have preservice training, theoretical and practical. In addition to an academic study in the fields of psychology, sociology, anthropology, education, and child growth and development, the teacher is well prepared for work with children and for leadership of effective adult discussion. The parent educator is nonauthoritarian in approach and is accepting and nonjudgmental in relating to class members. She is not prescriptive and has the ability to listen and value student contributions. She teaches problem-solving techniques by exploring the whys of a situation and bringing forth a variety of possible solutions for consideration. She uses questions to stimulate and focus thinking, to bring out valuable experiences and ideas to illustrate the common nature of the problem.

This, of course, is a very brief description of the parent educators approach explored more fully in Chapter 3. Discussion is the major technique although other methods are employed in combination with it, such as films, sociodramas, panels, resource people, and literature. The parent educator has a sound knowledge of group dynamics and is able to help the individuals profit from and contribute to the group learning experience. Students learn from one another, develop a respect for the rights and contributions of others, and are reassured of the commonality of the many problems they face.

The teacher needs to distinguish between problems that are likely to yield to time, maturity, and judicious neglect and those that need clinical service. This demands another skill from the teacher—the referral process and knowledge of community resources. For the most part, however, parents who attend such groups have only the normal range of concerns and general discussion of typical behavior often restores a parent's confidence in his ability to solve his own problems.

Program objectives are listed as follows:

1. The acquisition of knowledge relating to human development and behavior with primary emphasis on the preschool period.
2. The development of an evaluative attitude and of selectivity in consideration of the information presented.
3. The application of such new learnings and understandings as the individual finds appropriate to his use.

Based upon these objectives, there is expectation of:

Receptivity to new ideas.

Increased understanding of human differences and a more objective and accepting attitude toward other persons.

The acquisition of more confidence in self with a resulting reassurance in the role of a parent and as a person.

The determination and acceptance of obtainable goals.

Development of self as a member of the community capable of accepting responsibility and making an effective contribution.

A heightened appreciation of understanding of the preschool child achieved through supervised practice in the use of suggested techniques, record keeping, observation of teacher demonstration, and group participation.

Increased appreciation and enjoyment of children.

We see these things happening in varying degrees. Many mother students state that they have come to this experience confused by the mass of advice given in the literature on parent-child relationships. Many have been viewing their own children with concern that is then lessened by the perspective gained through seeing other children and by their association and sharing with other mothers who have common interests.

Classes provide opportunities for parents to practice successful child supervision methods, to observe their own children with greater understanding and, with the guidance of a trained teacher, to evaluate their experiences. Although these efforts lack definitive research, parents report greater understanding and confidence and increased patience and sensitivity to the meanings of child behavior. They note changes in their own behavior particularly in the use of positive rather than negative reinforcement in response to children's behavior, and strengthened self-image in terms of their mothering abilities and the importance of this role. They sometimes report influence on their behavior years later.

Interest and experimentation with new ideas by fathers is also reported. Some teachers arrange night meetings for fathers and others have conducted Saturday classes for fathers and children. Grandparents may also be involved, some attending with the children of working parents. The sharing of the anecdotal records with the parents, records on which the teacher makes interpretive written comments, are often used to clue in the absent parent. These are read with interest and lead to family discussions and ideas are even sent back for group consideration.

A wide range of possible topics of discussion surrounding the young child is covered in a course outline and constitutes material which can cover a three-year period of study when done on a once a week basis. Course outlines are provided to teachers to indicate the broad range of possible discussion topics but are not used in a sequential fashion. The needs, interests, and sophistication of each group are determining factors in program planning. The teacher does take a responsible educational role in introducing content based on student expectation, apparent areas of strongest interest, and greatest need. At the same time, the teacher is alert to the opportunity to widen the horizons of parents to areas in which they have not seen the importance nor the potential.

This combination parent-child program was started in Los Angeles in 1935, a couple of years after it was initiated in Pasadena, California. Effective parent education must involve seeing, hearing, and doing and the opportunities provided by this program and by parent-participation nursery schools and cooperatives have been called "practice teaching for parenthood." [10] The union of cooperatives and adult education is common in California and from there spread to the states of Washington and Maryland through the work of Katherine Whiteside Taylor.

In the cooperative the major learning opportunity is from participation, whereas the child observation weekly meeting emphasizes discussion and observation and participation is just a part. The cooperative is more likely to have a monthly or bimonthly parent meeting but the principles of good parent discussion are the same in either type of group. Some such programs, however, are more inclined to use lectures and resource persons rather than a study program of the type we are advocating here.

As the parent student moves beyond his interest in the preschool child, other programs of study are available to him. A booklet prepared by the Los Angeles City Schools to acquaint the public with study opportunities states, "Today, with specialization viewed as essential in so many major areas of pursuit, it is only natural that people are interested in learning more about parenthood and family life. Scientific findings point more and more the significance of childhood experiences and the effect of intrafamilial relationships on the developing personality. The role of parent and family life education, therefore, is an important one in providing guidelines for making family life more effective."

Here the objectives of parent education classes are listed as offering parents:

1. Relevant information concerning research and current ideas in the field of child development, family life education.
2. Suggested techniques for gaining objectivity in their person-to-person relationships.
3. A supportive atmosphere in which they are encouraged to reappraise their individual situations.
4. A broadened viewpoint to facilitate their role for functioning in family life.

The classes are "custom-fit" to meet the special needs and interests of the participants. Long-term classes include broad coverage of all aspects of today's scene which affect family life, such as: the merging roles of men and women; changes in sexual mores; the mass media; civil rights issues; the definition of responsibility, and so on. The impact of these cultural conditions are then evaluated in terms of family life, with emphasis placed on the study of children's reactions.

Classes are established for the more detailed discussion of children in specific age groups or for focusing on one aspect of human relationships such as common behavior problems, discipline and guidance, mental health, the role of women, home–school cooperation, as well as the unique problems of the retarded child.

DISCUSSION GROUPS

Discussion group classes may meet for a two- to two-and-a-half-hour period once a week for an entire school year, for one semester, or for a series of six to twelve meetings. We have serious reservations about the value of the short-term class of six to ten meetings. This, however, is what planning groups often want in the belief that parents will not wish to make a commitment for a longer period of time. Consequently attempts are made to leave the series open-ended and frequently groups do request that study go on once the group members discover the experience meaningful to them.

Classes are conducted in such a way as to encourage the participation of students. The teacher opens each meeting with a presentation for background material relevant to general interest that she and the class members discuss and evaluate. Advance planning with a parent committee (these groups are usually PTA sponsored) has led to some tentative decisions about the areas of interest. Trained in the skills of group dynamics as well as subject matter, the teacher keeps the discussion on a meaningful level. He is watchful that each individual has an opportunity for self-expression, controlling the situation to prevent anyone from monopolizing the discussion. The teacher uses all of the skills described in the chapter on group process. At the end of the meeting there is a summary of what has been covered and an announcement of the topic for the next week, either decided previously, or by the group at this time.

In addition to the discussion method, the following techniques may be offered to the class:

> use of audio-visual materials
> book reviews
> role playing
> guest speakers
> panel discussion
> workshops
> field trips
> children's classroom observations

FOR PARENTS OF ELEMENTARY-SCHOOL-AGE CHILDREN

Discussions centering around children of this age are about the stages of individual development in relation to the family, home life, school, and neighborhood. The most popular discussion topics concern person-to-person communication and rapport, competition, discipline, sex education, responsibility, and friendships. Parents are concerned also with their children's education; therefore, special classes are offered on how the child learns and the nature of the school curriculum, including such things as new math for parents. Most recently parents were offered a city-wide opportunity to study how children learn to read, the approaches of the school, and how they as parents enhance the learning process. As programs are developed around the current concerns and immediate interests of parents, we see them become engaged in parental role assessment and grow in their own awareness of the many more possibilities for educational experiences specific to their parental tasks.

CLASSES FOR PARENTS OF ADOLESCENTS

Influenced by the attention which is now being focused on the so-called teenage subculture parents and their adolescent children find themselves frequently in conflict. Traditionally, this is expected as children change physically and emotionally after puberty, yet today's parents are baffled by the prevailing climate of opinion in which the peer group influence and customs appear to undermine parental strength. In an effort to cope with their children's struggle for independence as well as the infringement of middle age upon themselves, parents find maintaining rapport with their adolescents a major problem. Classes in which these controversial issues are studied objectively enable them to come to terms with the relinquishment of their adolescent children to approaching adulthood. Whenever possible these classes are held in the evening in order to include fathers, and at times, the teenagers themselves.

SPECIAL CLASSES

There are several areas which require concentrated study in order to adequately explore special needs and teachers who have been trained in these subject areas are available. They are:

1. Leadership training
2. Modern marriage and the family
3. Preparation for parenthood
4. The one-parent family
5. The role of women in today's world
6. The retarded child

7. The physically handicapped child
8. The gifted child
9. Understanding the underachiever
10. Sex and family life education: birth to adolescence
11. Sexuality and the adolescent
12. Sharing responsibility for the teaching of values

Even though continuing efforts are made to interpret the value of small group discussion with about twenty to twenty-five registrants, meeting over an extended period of time, some sponsoring groups (and some administrators) are still desirous of the large lecture series with a known speaker. If there are to be a number of speakers, specialists in the particular aspect of the subject, the role of the parent education teacher is to introduce the program, act as discussion leader, and present a summary at the conclusion of all meetings. While still questioning the effectiveness of this type of educational program in contrast to the discussion group, we realize that many persons prefer this type of learning and do find facts usable. Hopefully the lecture series will whet the appetite of the participants to seek more intensive learning situations with more involvement over a necessarily longer period of time.

Although study groups and lectures are usually initiated at the request of sponsoring groups, most often the PTA, there is an increasing number of school-initiated programs. Recognition is being given to the importance of developing methods of reaching parents who heretofore have not been involved. Several such educational programs have been given in the specialized areas of narcotics education for parents at the time of the children's instruction in junior high school. Classes for parents of children on probation, understanding the adolescent in poverty areas, and even telephone teaching for parents of the shut-in handicapped are new. The latter involves telephones placed in the home for instruction of the child, and group discussion is achieved for the parents of these children on a hook-up making this possible.

CHANGING EMPHASES AND APPROACHES

Today's program, as well as the one we project, contains similarities and differences when compared to the one launched in the late 1920s and early 1930s. From a 1933 issue of the California

Congress of Parents and Teachers magazine we learn that mothers meeting together in the study circles talked about children but the talk was impersonal and centered around the child in general rather than any one child in particular.

The content is described as some phase of growth and development which served as a basis for discussion, such as obedience or individual differences. The participants are said to have received assurance and relief from the commonality of concerns. New knowledge and varying viewpoints and methods provided food for thought and led to increased skill in child guidance. More observant mothers were believed to lead to sympathetic understanding as a basis for mutual respect between parent and child. Class members and leader alike contributed knowledge, experience, and objective thinking.

Dr. Laws saw the goals (and most programs have adhered fairly closely to these goals) of observation and suspension of judgment, understanding of children's play and other activities, self-understanding and knowledge about development as leading to the application of the scientific method and problem-solving. More effective guidance and management of behavior, a responsive parent who provides security through love and understanding appear to be the product of study hoped for. Gartzman [11] stressed observation of child behavior and methods of guidance as leading to understanding of developmental patterns, individual differences, and resulting in improved parent guidance.

From the 1961 issue of the state booklet on parent education, we find that the subject matter and practical hypotheses for parent education are drawn from the social and natural sciences. "This (knowledge) parents use as they work toward their goals of emotional security and happiness for themselves and their children. As parents learn to accept their children and enjoy them as they are, they find themselves able to progress comfortably in their relationships with their children." [12] Again, the assumption is that with knowledge parent-child relationships are enhanced.

Certain things are constant. Knowledge from the behavioral sciences has been a consistent part of the program. However, that knowledge has changed, become more extensive, has presented evidence in contradiction to some formerly held beliefs. An example of this is the previously held concept that intelligence is fixed and determinable by the genes in contrast to the idea that it is modifiable and the IQ is probably only a measurement of the moment, at best.[13] The belief that intellectual development depends on experience, on the child's transactions with the world, did not prevail in the past. Much teaching of parents about children was, and still is, based on the concept of "ages and stages," of sequential development as a law. Some knowledge still holds; much has been added; some theory has been disproved and there are new concepts and beliefs.

Certain assumptions appear inherent in the early literature of the movement. There appears to have been a strong commitment to the idea that sympathetic observation, understanding of the nature of children, understanding of self, and knowledge would lead to parental confidence, acceptance, and enjoyment of children, constructive guidance, and a nurturing atmosphere. For many people this has, no doubt, been true. Participants in groups attest to this fact. With the move away from the parent as a nurturer of his child's unfolding, predetermined development, and toward the parent as a vital mediator between the child and his growth-enabling environment, there is a whole new dimension in the parental role.

Another historical commitment of the California program has been to the problem-solving process with personal decision-making as a goal. This remains constant because it is practical and is what happens in any event over a period of time. Advice-giving just doesn't work most of the time and is rarely taken even when asked for.

As to processes, discussion was (and is) held as the best approach to true parent learning and understanding. What has been added from experience is greater knowledge of how the process works, a greater use of focus to facilitate learning, and a wide range of techniques. Impetus has been given to the analysis of the discussion method by leaders who feel the need for improving their own skills and practice. Those in the field of teacher education have found it necessary to analyze the process in order to more effectively transmit this knowledge to the ever-growing numbers of parent educators demanded by an expanding field.

Observation remains an important learning tool. There has been an increasing emphasis on teaching parents how to observe and a refinement of skills in teacher use of the parent records as a tool for discussion. As we learn more about the meaning of behavior, parents are taught more about what they are seeing as they observe. A focus on learning enables a more objective view of behavior.

Goals have become more precise. In 1934 it was thought that the parent gained interest, appreciation, habits, and skills from psychological research findings and from his fellow parents. In 1968 parents still gain information, although different information, and they evaluate and apply this as they see fit. More attention is given to the process, the teacher's role is carefully considered, as are the varying needs of individuals and groups, their developmental stage, the stage of the world in which they are operating, and the increased knowledge about how adults learn.

The most important emerging change we see at this time is a clear-cut conception of the parent role as that of a teacher of his child. As he sees himself in this light, something positive may happen to his perhaps rather battered self-image as a parent. Here, as in all other aspects of life, role confusion is serious and deleterious to effective functioning. If I as a parent am to teach my child to learn, to value, and to relate to others, can I be taught effective methods of teaching? Does the society in which I live value my role, believe I can be educated for this function, provide an educational experience which will contribute to my effective functioning?

Increasing knowledge of the interrelatedness of the social, emotional, physical, and intellectual process has implications for new approaches and emphases in parent education. The parental role takes on new significance if we see development modifiable in both rate and sequence and its potentials created through transactions with the environment. The parent—the family—is and creates the major portion of the growing child's environment. When child development is viewed as an orderly unfolding, facilitated and enhanced by love and acceptance, by patience and understanding, the role is primarily one of nurturance rather than teaching and facilitating the search for meaning. When the parent role is a teaching role, there must be goals and knowledge about how to reach those goals. There must be an awareness of the process of learning.

While many parents have concerned themselves as teachers of their children in respect to appropriate behavior, attitudes, and values, their methods have been talking to the child, directing, imposing. Some have an awareness of their teaching by precept, but all too often they have taught without understanding what they were teaching, why, and certainly with little understanding of how. As educators, do they know the limitations of teaching by telling to do? To tell a child to speak politely to his grandmother, and rewarding that behavior with pleased response, is a limited concept of the teaching-learning task. This is not to say that the parent does not give this kind of instruction and reward this behavior, but that he might be helped to see the vast array of teaching in which he can and does engage. The implicit teaching opportunities in daily interactions between parent and child need to be seen by parents and skills in affecting them are a teachable content in parent education.

We are not unaware of the concern of many that through such self-consciousness parents will lose warmth and spontaneity, but believe that an enhanced concept of their role will add pleasure and enrich the relationship between parent and child. We know and must communicate that every life situation does not have to be grimly pursued to wring all possible meaning from it. Instead we would wish to communicate the excitement of helping a child grow in understanding and consequent responsibility for his decisions.

A thoughtful and understanding approach to life is increasingly important in today's world. The individual must make decisions, he must know why he has made them, he must constantly choose between alternatives. He cannot amass the entire body of knowledge; old traditions may not be useful guidelines nor appropriate to situations not yet conceived of, therefore, practice in decision making and the search for meaning are essentials for living. When the parent perceives this as an appropriate role, meeting an increasingly important need, his next question then is how.

CONCERNS OF MIDDLE CLASS PARENTS

The response to the programs we have described here has been primarily that of the middle class, although in the last few years pioneering and successful attempts have been made to reach the disadvantaged poor. As the interest in parent education grows and it is seen as a factor in breaking the cycle of poverty, as social scientists speak of the hidden curriculum of the middle class home as a strength that is lacking in the poor home, some might be inclined to suggest that parent education is needed only by the poor.

However it is part of the middle class life style to see education as an approach to enhancing their role function. Many have used it, although as has been pointed out, by no means the majority. From the parents who use communication sources, we project the general concerns of middle class parents. Judging from parents' reports, they reflect many concerns in common with those who deliberately seek out resources.

Many persons believe that in addition to the strengths provided in the middle class home in preparing the child for school and learning, there is an unhealthy emphasis on grades and too rapid push toward premature accomplishment. The grades and the fact of reading before school become the symbols of future success for the child as well as status giving acts to the parent. Parents want their children to be happy, they say, and they equate that happiness with successful achievement in school now, to getting into the right college later, and winding up with the good job. They want their child to be content, but they want him to achieve. They want him to be thoughtful and considerate, but they also want him to be competitive enough to do better than others. Reading before school entry and high grades for the school child become the proof that they are on the right track.

What methods do they use to spur a child on? Do they know that criticism, punishment, comparisons are not powerful motivators? Do they know that there is a drive toward competence and positive ways in which to nurture that drive? Do they see the role of learning in their children's development? Many persons do but many more do not. Methods need to be seen in relation to goals. Methods of the moment may not lend themselves to the accomplishment of future goals.

We have seen that, in terms of today's complex world and the never greater need to order massive knowledge effectively, love and a stimulating environment are not enough if the child is to relate what he is seeing and doing to a growing awareness of how the world works and his place in it. From birth the child strives to order his experience so that he can use it. But he needs help. To provide concrete experiences alone fails to take full advantage of his intellectual potential. Often without clarification, he may form incorrect conclusions that block accurate perceptions of reality. Children need adult guidance in sorting information so that their experiences are educative rather than miseducative. New methods of emphasis and guidance must be developed for teachers and parents in order to enable this process to occur; to enable adults to play a vital role as a learning resource—listening, explaining, interpreting, answering, and asking questions. These are specific skills that parents can be taught in parent education.

Again, this focus is not to deny the role of the affective factors, love and nurture, essential to the growth process. Attention must be paid to the role of the self-image and the emotional interaction between parent and child. The key point is that the encouragement of intellectual development is integral to, rather than destructive of, healthy social-emotional growth when the time and the pace is right. Thus the role of the parent in the development of the competence of the child is seen as basic to the development of motivation and the desire to succeed. These in turn have a direct effect on the social and emotional qualities of the parent-child relationship.

We believe that there is knowledge that can be taught in parent education; that it may be a much less threatening starting point for the parent than the area of emotional relationships. Parent educators need to experiment with techniques designed to use this knowledge as content, as there are few intervention programs in spite of the repeated references in the literature to the vital importance of the parent role.

The parent needs to conceive of himself as a teacher. He will be attracted to education for this purpose. He can be taught how the child learns and the skills for his role as a teacher.

SUMMARY

California has a long history of parent education as an integral part of the school system, but in spite of the advantageous circumstances it has not reached the numbers of persons that its founders anticipated. Until recently it has had primarily a middle class clientele that in turn has influenced goals, content, and method. It has been based on the belief that information provided in a problem-solving setting is conducive to enhancement of parent role competence.

The Los Angeles City Schools program is extensive and its growth has continued since its inception in 1926. Teachers are trained paid professionals and the stimulus for establishment of classes comes in a large part from the Parent Teacher Associations. This follows the state pattern of a cooperative relationship between the State Department of Education and the California Congress of Parents and Teachers.

Goals, content, and method have shown changes but many of the original purposes and procedures are still usable and sound. Perhaps the lack of clarity as to what parents can anticipate gaining from such study has limited the number of users. The communication of a message to the affect that parents are teachers of their children and can learn competencies for this role might attract more persons as well as interest more administrators in the program potentials.

REFERENCES

1. Gertrude Laws, *Objectives and Suggested Procedures for Parent Education in California,* No. 13. Sacramento: State of California Department of Education Bulletin, July 1, 1934, p. iii.
2. *Ibid.,* pp. v–vii.
3. Herbert Stolz, "Characteristics of the California Program," *California Parent Teacher,* Vol. 10, No. 1 (September 1933).
4. Gertrude Laws, *Public Schools and Parent Education,* No. 22. Sacramento: State of California Department of Education Bulletin, November 15, 1935.
5. *Ibid.,* p. 6.
6. *Ibid.,* p. 3.
7. Gertrude Laws, *Parent Education Manual,* California Congress of Parents and Teachers, 1946.
8. Norejane Johnston Hendrickson, *A Brief History of Parent Education in the United States.* Columbus, Ohio: Center for Adult Education, Ohio State University, 1963. P. 63.
9. Burton R. Clark, *Adult Education in Transition.* Berkeley, Calif.: University of California Press, 1958. P. 149.
10. Katherine Whiteside Taylor, *Parents and Children Learn Together.* New York: Columbia University Teachers College, 1967. P. 231.

11. Pauline Gartzman, *A Study in Parent Education*. Pasadena, Calif.: Pasadena City Schools, 1935.
12. Milton Babitz, *Parent Education—Curriculum, Methods and Materials*. Sacramento, Calif.: Bulletin of the California State Department of Education, Vol. XXX, May 1961. P. 1.
13. Walter B. Waetjen (Ed.), *Learning and Mental Health in the School*. Washington, D.C.: Association for Supervision and Curriculum Development, N.E.A., 1966. P. 51.

6

Parent Education
in Low-Income Communities

EXPLORING ASSUMPTIONS

In order to explore the validity of programs aimed at enhancing parental competence for parents living in poverty or near-poverty, it seems important to consider several questions: (1) What is the reality of poverty or near-poverty for family life? (2) Is there a culture of poverty? (3) Is there a place for parent education in low income areas? (4) If so, what are the problems in program development? (5) What role can education play in the total picture? and (6) What are the basic assumptions of a learning-valuing focus in programs aimed at increasing parental competence of poor parents?

THE REALITY OF POVERTY AND NEAR-POVERTY
FOR FAMILY LIFE

About one half of all American families do *not* live in the middle-class manner projected so tantalizingly through the mass media. Roughly one fourth live badly according to minimum standards of food, housing, work, opportunities, and the material things associated with these.[1] They have little money, virtually no savings, no economic security. They cannot buy in large amounts and thus receive less for their money. Employment, if at all available, is scattered, irregular, and often without satisfaction. There is extensive borrowing, constant indebtedness, use of second-hand clothing and furniture, overcrowded and inadequate housing, and lack of privacy. The poor have a higher death rate, lower life expectancy, lower levels of mental and physical health and nutrition.[2] Lack of a sense of power is reflected in a lack of participation in labor unions or organizations that strive together for better conditions. Lack of access to the benefits of the system leads to a focus on immediate satisfaction, with its accompanying violence, sexuality, alcoholism, and less concern for delaying today's gratification in favor of some future goal.

Another fourth of the nation's families, while they are usually able to sustain steady employment, need to use most of their energies to keep themselves from slipping into poverty. The insecurity of their job situation in the face of increasing automation creates a high level of anxiety. The lack of autonomy or choice about the type of work they do leads to frustration and dissatisfaction.[3]

While there is great variety in lower class family life—from the multiproblem, chaotic disorganization of the jobless hardcore poor to the traditional, highly structured, religiously based family whose adults are employed—these families share the pressures of economic insecurity, poor living conditions, low social esteem, discrimination, poor education, significant differences in style of life, values, aspirations, and perception of self. Contrary to the middle class family whose economic security allows it to maintain itself and provide its children with essential skills for entry into society, the lower class family often cannot educate its children, cure their ills, provide them with jobs, or effectively control their behavior.[4]

Lower class cultures contain themes reflecting these needs. There seems to be an aversion to planning, to thinking about the future except with anxiety and fear, a pervasive suspicion and distrust of the larger world which is seen as threatening not only because one has so little control over what happens to the individual, but because there seems to be so little reward for effort. Thus, self-reliance is less a virtue and dependence on outsiders accepted as a necessity and even as desirable.[5]

The low income family often fails to carry out its socialization function because it does not enable the levels of perceptual, linguistic, and cognitive development achieved by most middle class children. The conditions responsible for this lack of development lie within the nature of the environment, the view of the world to which these children are exposed, the components of experience available.

Basic growth factors, essential to any development, may well be missing. Lois Murphy spells them out in this way: (1) an active, sustained, emotionally supporting mother-child relationship can rarely evolve if a mother is exhausted, depressed, apathetic, resentful, or, as in many upper-lower homes, is placed in a submissive role with little or no emotional sustenance from her mate; (2) an interesting, patterned, adequately rich sensory-motor environment that can provide intrinsic satisfactions for looking, listening, manipulating, exploring cannot exist in a meager, empty, dismal, colorless environment or where the parent does not perceive his mediating role in his child's experience; (3) the kind of variety and change adapted to the tolerance of the child and sufficient to keep his interest in newness and his curiosity alive is not forthcoming in a life that is narrow, monotonous, and seldom changing and where the meaning of learning to the child is not perceived; (4) a flexible, yet reliable, time and space structure which will permit both internalization of structure by the child and opportunities to act on, alter, and create structures, as a result of planning and organizing activities, is impossible in a world where there is no routine or pattern of life, or where there is an excessively rigid, adult-centered pattern; (5) active stimulation and encouragement by the environment is not part of the pattern in homes where children are typically squelched, repressed, discouraged from talking and exploring, as well as not talked to, read to, provided new experiences that stimulate their development; (6) the presence of rewarding, satisfying objects of identification, the model of the "good" adult who is interested in the child and thus stimulates internalization of socially active, constructive patterns of behavior is not possible where the father is not present, or is unable to fulfill his cultural role, or where the mother's own needs and pressures are so overwhelming that a wholesome assumption of the parenting task can never evolve.[6]

The chances are far greater, then, that the experiences essential to learning how to learn from one's experience are not available to many low income children. They are often raised in adult-centered households in which there is considerable pressure on them to grow up as fast as possible and to make their own way in the world. Discipline tends to be physical rather than psychological, with the result that there is parental control over outer behavior, but little over the inner life of their children. Rules are taught mechanically, without reason or justification, to be obeyed or violated as the situation permits. Care of children is custodial, and the emphasis on external behavior rather than internal intention.[7]

The life experiences of the very poor militate against the democratic child-rearing life style that is conducive to the growth of values, skills, attitudes and behaviors essential to full participation in a complex society. The development of basic trust in people, the capacity to respond to and generate response from others, to communicate expressively, to see oneself as a whole, worthy person, to feel in tune with the standards of the mainstream culture and to develop effective ways of governing one's behavior in relation to others are all dependent upon a stable parent-child relationship.[8]

The democratic approach, found to be conducive to the child's mental health, means an approach that takes into account the rights and responsibilities of all members of the family—including parents. It also means an approach that allows for discussion and debate but eventuates in rules to which various members of the family are expected to adhere. It cherishes a disciplined, rather than an archaic, individualism. Parents perceive themselves as senior members of the family, with final decision-making power after the evidence is in and after extenuating circumstances have been considered. Parents have equal powers in decision-making, with children allowed increasing self-directive and family-directive rights as they grow older and show their readiness by their own behavior.

It is clear that such an approach requires considerable capacity for self-control, goal commitment, verbal activity, observation powers and comprehension of abstractions on the part of parents. It would seem to require a large margin of self- and financial security and a relatively benign environment. It also requires a sure sense of personal identity on the part of parents, a wealth of "constructive" psychological defenses, and an optimistic rather than depressed life style. In other words, a stable working-class or middle-class society and parental life experience would seem to be more conducive to a democratic child-rearing style than would the life experiences and environment of the very poor.[9]

Without adequate mental, emotional, and physical nourishment, there is a failure of activation, shown in passivity and inertness. There is a failure to invest or find interest in the environment and to develop expectancy and eagerness. There is a failure to develop meaningful perception of stimuli, and thus a failure to develop responsiveness. There is a failure to develop active perception and the drive to reach out to new experience and to learn. There is a failure to develop the integrative processes, the steps in sensory-motor progress that lead to basic concepts about the environment, and a failure to develop the organizing, planning, creating processes that are essential to learning. Thus, there is a failure in the overall capacity for learning.[10]

The lower class family, living under conditions that preclude a large margin of self- and financial security and that can in few ways be seen as "benign," is thus severely limited in carrying out most of its socially required functions. In large families with modest or inadequate resources, maintenance is also modest or inadequate —certainly from the vantage point of the larger society or of ideal social standards. In terms of the family's socializing role, and usually in the upper lower class, children at best are made into good workers—traditional, conservative, anti-intellectual, materialistic and conventional.[11] This value system is in increasing conflict with that system which seems most conducive for dealing with prevailing social conditions and issues; i.e., the valuing of self-realization, social commitment, rational thinking, the finding of new solutions, and the capacity to live with difference and uncertainty.

Kohn [12] sees these differences in values as resulting from differences in the conditions of life of the various social classes. Middle class parental values center on self-direction. Such values evolve from life conditions that require a greater degree of self-direction in occupational conditions. Dealing with the working class, rather than the jobless poor, Kohn finds working class parents' values center on conformity to external proscriptions that proceed from the nature of working-class occupations, ones that require the following of explicit rules set down by someone in authority. In terms of training techniques, middle class parents are more likely to be permissive and developmental in outlook, feeling more obligated to be supportive of their children than are working-class parents who, in their greater sense of obligation to impose constraints, act in a restrictive or traditional manner. In many middle-class families, both parental roles are minimally differentiated and tend to be supportive, in consideration of the child's internal dynamics. This approach grows out of the reality of middle class status placement, which takes access into society for granted. When access is not problematic and realistic goals can be assumed, then parents begin preparing children from the beginning, incorporating into their daily interaction the teaching of skills essential for future-oriented achievement. But working class parents, whose security depends upon their capacity to function as a depersonalized cog in closely supervised occupations, tend to be far more status-oriented and train their children to conform to those behaviors that will enable them to function according to prescription, discouraging those behaviors that would endanger the minimal security they perceive as achievable.

The degree of freedom and sense of self that parents receive from their own life situation is directly reflected in the kind of teaching role they assume in the lives of their children. For the poor and very poor, a sense of alienation, lack of faith in the future, basic distrust of society's institutions, constant insecurity about meeting basic needs all affect the content of parenting. When there are no alternatives, parents are little inclined to encourage their children to consider alternatives, to select, to develop criteria for choice, and to learn the basic elements of decision-making. If the environment is unresponsive, there is little motivation to act and to develop techniques for dealing with the options it might offer at some future time.[13]

Hess [14] has found severe deficiencies in the lower class mother's capacity to interpret the meaning of the child's experience so that he can understand it and develop the cognitive skills for effective and continued learning. Bernstein's research [15] points to the impact of a restricted language code which does not contain the concepts and tools for explaining the world and defining the potential for effective interaction with it.

Bernstein's theory and Hess's observations of the inability of lower-class mothers to teach combine to suggest a more fundamental reason for the deficiencies of lower-class children in school-relevant learning. When a cultural group possesses a distinctive body of knowledge and beliefs which the older generation feels obliged to pass on in some organized fashion to the younger generation, it is reasonable to suppose that the group will develop the language and teaching skills that are needed for such a purpose. Among disorganized and dispossessed minority groups, however, the culture appears to center around attitudes, interests, a style of life, and a scattering of unorganized beliefs and superstitions so unformalized that they may be transmitted without explanation, argument, or detailed exposition. Deliberate teaching is not a normal or necessary part of the adult role in such cultural groups, and neither the skills nor the language peculiar to teaching are developed and maintained. By contrast, in middle-class American society, nearly every adult can and does teach. It is a normal part of the adult role performed almost without awareness, particularly in the adult's relations with children.[16]

While we have seen that, in one sense, the family, over time, has relinquished the function of education to the schools, in another sense we are now seeing that the good family is good precisely because it provides so much of the young child's education, in the guiding of his whole capacity to maximize the opportunities his environment provides, including school. Thus, family life that includes little social interaction, little verbal communication, and little instruction appears to have a causal relation to language and other cognitive deficits of children. The nature of family interaction is seen as a cognitive system in which decision-making, information processing, perceptual differentiation, conceptualization, and problem-solving are significant factors in the child's development of the capacity to "make it" in the larger society.[17]

Looking at the impact of inadequate socialization on the child entering school, we see that when family interaction does not nurture learning skills, children enter school unable to learn. They often do not understand the language the teacher uses; they do not have the words to think or talk about what they know. They do not understand ideas. They cannot see or hear differences and likenesses between objects, sounds, experiences. They are not familiar with school-related tools. They do not understand order. They do not trust the teacher or the school, or see learning as a source of satisfaction. They function passively, focusing on "getting by" and staying out of trouble. It is not that they do not handle many aspects of their immediate experience skillfully. It is rather that they have not developed the capacity for divining the meaning of their experience or the ability to relate that meaning to their daily lives. They do not see themselves as unique or worthwhile, nor do they see the world as capable of being mastered. And so they fail.

IS THERE A CULTURE OF POVERTY?

The prevalent debate about the existence of a self-perpetuating culture of poverty has real implications for program development. The definition of common behavior patterns as a culture implies an inherent valuing process—that it is a way of life in which people find real value and to which they choose to adhere. Working from this premise, programs aiming to change attitudes and behavior can validly be accused of gross imposition.

In many respects, the behaviors of the bulk of families living in or on the edge of poverty form a kind of culture, particularly as they are reflected in the nature of socialization of children. The fact that these behaviors are found in poverty areas across many different cultures, however, leads to the conclusion that these common behaviors represent a system of social and psychological responses to basic human problems and needs.[18]

Many of the basic problems which confront low-income people are essentially the same—such problems as securing the elemental necessities of life, of maintaining a system of social relations which offers at least minimal security, of preserving a sense of self-esteem in the face of a disapproving society, and of finding some meaning to their lives and some plausible explanation for their situation. Given common problems, it is understandable that many of the poor arrive at the same solutions, especially if we consider the limitations that poverty itself imposes in making alternatives available, and the broader cultural heritage which the poor in America share with each other and the rest of society.[19]

It is perhaps more valid to view observable behavior systems as a subculture, recognizing that they exist within a dominant culture which, in this country, is that of the middle class white population. This means that the value system of the dominant culture also pervades the subculture, so that its members are responding to more than one value system.[20] "We seem to forget that the poor—like the prosperous—may cherish and believe in a system of values that they feel they cannot always afford to act on in daily life." [21]

If we find some of America's traditional virtues and values in their purest form to be strong and recurrent even among the most deprived, then it is possibly more fruitful to think of different types of lower class families reacting in various ways to the facts of their position and to relative isolation rather than to the imperatives of a lower class culture. It is important that we not confuse basic life chances and actual behavior with basic cultural values and preferences.[22]

If we view child-rearing practices that militate against a child's developing a capacity for learning as pragmatic solutions to difficult life problems, how do we assess the validity of an intervention program?

IS THERE A PLACE FOR PARENT EDUCATION IN LOW INCOME AREAS?

Without vast reorganization within the school system (which would be reflective of other major social changes) *and* without intensive efforts to make poor parents more fully aware of their teaching role, the number of people ill-equipped to function in the society clearly will increase in direct proportion to the increase in urbanization and technical advance. Exploring all avenues for remediation is an urgent task. Effective parent education programs may be an important such avenue.

We know that parents are the prime teachers of their children and that the content and direction of their teaching is largely determined by socioeconomic-cultural factors. We know that the degree to which the parent perceives his teaching role largely determines his effectiveness in that role. Research has provided us with little information about the impact of parent education programs that focus on parental teaching skills. This is partially because our understanding of the pervasive impact of the parental mediating role is new; partially because of the variety in approach and methodology that makes replication difficult, and partially because of the "ethical" questions raised by the stance of intervention.

From research findings and personal experience we have established that within low income families education is solidly valued and that there is an intense desire that children do well in school. Part of this is undoubtedly based on the realization, often vague, that the complexity of society demands the achievement of a certain level of competence in order to find a place in it. School achievement has come to be accepted as a necessary prerequisite for the good life. Perhaps this view is one characteristic disadvantaged mothers share, in addition to limited financial resources.[23] "Thus, the educational goals of lower-class parents are similar to those of middle-class parents. The differences emerge in knowledge of techniques for reaching the desired end-state." [24] If education is generally seen as valuable by the poor, and poor parents are not hostile to programs aimed at bettering their children's chances in school,[25] what should the thrust of parent education programs be?

WHAT ARE THE PROBLEMS IN PROGRAM DEVELOPMENT?

Programs with an overt or covert focus on changing total behavior systems or on telling parents what they "should do" imply disapproval. Rejection of such programs by the poor perhaps shows a healthy resistance to middle class agencies that demand behavior unrealistic for the situations that people live in. But parents are aware that their children pay too great a price for academic failure, and they may well respond to programs that provide them with skills to do something they deeply desire to do, without doing it in a critical context. The approach that there is new knowledge about how children learn and how parents teach that will help children "make it" in school may unhook us not only from our middle class lens for viewing lower class solutions, but from the implications of inadequacy that plague so many programs aimed at involving parents in the education of their children.

The home and the school are two very different systems; different in structure, expectations, requirements, behavior demanded of children, rewards offered, etc. The child can function in both systems if the systems respect and trust each other.[26] If the knowledge and strengths of the parent are the basic premise of the approach, if the parent is helped to see how much he already knows that can be translated to his children, if he is given concrete skills and is reinforced in his own learning, then his self-concept as a teaching person in the life of his children can be one area in an otherwise difficult life where a deepened sense of competence is possible.

One of the greatest dangers in program development and teacher training lies in the trap of assuming that behavior, values, and attitudes, particularly as they relate to child-rearing, are common to all families living in or close to the conditions of economic deprivation.

> The lower class is not all of one piece. It includes families living in the midst of poverty; others, in precarious respectability; newcomers eager to escape immigrant ghettoes, and old-line Yankees who have seen better days. There are the tender and the tough, the rough and the respectable, natives and foreigners, immigrants, migrant workers, nomads and rebels, the happy-go-lucky and the malcontents.[27]

Expecting a certain life style simply because a family resides in a poverty area, then, prevents a teacher from viewing each parent in terms of his own strengths. Individual assessment of each parent's personal strengths and patterns of family interaction might enhance the usefulness of the program to each participant. The degree to which parents assume a role in establishing some structure for child-care has to be evaluated against the circumstances of the individual situation, the range of alternatives available, and the bases for choice within the context of people's lives. In many low income homes, there is a viable structure, and while it may contain little intellectual stimulation for the child, it does seem to make both parent and child available to enrichment programs.[28] While the conditions of poverty preclude many dimensions of the parental teaching role, as it can be ideally manifested in advantaged homes, it may well be possible to help a harassed mother to see, for instance, that when she screams at her child to "shut up," he will do better in school if she tells him why, because children need to understand the idea of cause and effect. This would seem to have more relevance than telling a beleaguered, pressured human being she has no right to scream.

Perhaps the vast range of conflicting data about the value systems and child-rearing practices of lower-lower, upper-lower, working class families is only important in its effect on where we start, what methods we use to make knowledge available, the language we use to get concepts across. It should have little or nothing to do with the goals we set. Our perspective is a continuum, beginning with parental skill in mediating the learning process and expanding into consideration of decision-making processes in parent-child relationships. This goal is the same whatever the subculture. The starting point, method, speed of presentation may differ according to the learning style of the individual and/or the group. For instance, the question of illegitimate children has little bearing on goals, except insofar as the situation affects the parent's attitude toward self and child. This attitude may well be improved through an increased sense of competence as a parent. The parent educator accepts different behaviors, i.e., harsh discipline, just as she has accepted the more subtle but equally influential manipulative behavior of many middle class mothers, and focuses on those areas of essential parental teaching that the parent can handle.

WHAT ROLE CAN EDUCATION PLAY IN THE TOTAL PROBLEM?

The role of education can only be vital if it is an integral part of a massive national program to eliminate poverty. We raise this point only because, for meaningful programs, it needs to be verbalized to parents. The drastic changes that must be made on a large scale in housing, employment, income distribution, medical care, et al. before full participation in society is possible for the poor must be recognized by and admitted to the parent. This program must be carefully defined as an effort to enable people to make fuller use of necessary changes. Parental concerns regarding existing inequities will be reflected in group discussions and their impact must be seen in order to be dealt with.

We do recognize that parents, or any significant adult, must be involved in the learning process of children in order for appropriate development to occur. Teaching parental skills in building educational competence for children is one area in which parents have both the motivation and the potential for action. There is an ever-growing possibility that this area can be somewhat free of value-imposition, power conflicts, and other knotty questions upon which our society is stumbling at the moment.

Haggstrom points out that the poor are usually caught up and carried along in someone else's reality, with little power to affect the educational programs or policies of any aspect of society's superstructure. Many education programs, as well as programs of other major institutions, do attempt to control the poor, because to focus with integrity and honesty on self-realization potentials as we do with middle class adults would only engender what many see as disastrous confrontation of the present power structure. The price that the minority of persons from low income areas who do become educated must pay in order to enter "someone else's world and adopt someone else's life patterns" is the adaptation of behavior and styles of relationship that are foreign and unattractive to those to whom the education is being extended.[29]

But if total change of behavior is not an implicit requirement of a parent education program, but rather the offering of specific tools by which to improve self-determination and problem-solving skills, then perhaps in some ways power becomes more possible and the essential negotiation between values can take place.

Education through institutions controlled by the affluent society saps motivation [30] and programs tend to be alien, inappropriate, and irrelevant. But perhaps programs that become an accepted part of community service, staffed by parent educators trained in depth to be in tune with the individual and community needs of the area, structured to provide concrete systems for increasing parental competence and to use the immediate experience of the group to widen the range of alternatives, can grow to be appropriate and excitingly relevant to the immediate concerns of poor parents.

It is possible for parent educators to develop real skill in interaction and enable this kind of relevance. The message to low income groups need not be "This will solve all your problems," or "I have come to change your ways," or "The only way you are acceptable to me is if you bring up your children in the middle class pattern." It can readily be "We know something new about how parents teach their children," and the group approach offers ways of becoming a comfortable place to learn together. We need to be clear at every point that parent education does not offer solutions to the vast range of problems that impinge on the poor. It only offers the possibility of giving people some tools by which their children might be more effective within a thus far inadequate school system, and might achieve sufficiently to begin negotiating with middle class institutions in terms the middle class more readily understands.

Just as the reassessment of professional tasks is underway in order that new careers for the poor can be seen as a meaningful innovation, so reassessing the teaching role of parents—heightening parental competence—can be seen as one approach to one part of the problem. We do know that the poor are powerless to function, to make demands on the power structure, without accruing sufficient functional skills to articulate their needs so that the establishment will hear and take heed. Perhaps this is one way in which this process can be stimulated. As a measure of the maturity of our society, we must make an all-out effort to assure that heredity is the only factor that keeps people from realizing their potential. Increasing the competence of parents in their effectiveness as the prime teachers of their children may be one way.

WHAT ARE THE BASIC ASSUMPTIONS OF A LEARNING-VALUING FOCUS FOR POOR PARENTS?

In developing a viable approach to parent education programs in low income areas, we would then function on a set of assumptions:

1. We assume that at this point in our society, mastery of the vast common base of knowledge is essential to any degree of successful participation in society, and that this mastery demands the capacity to cope with the experience of school. (We recognize the urgent needs for schools to make this essential learning more possible for the experientially disadvantaged, but bad schools do not negate the need for education.)

2. We assume that there is more awareness of the kinds of experiences children need to be able to actively manage the knowledge they must accrue.

3. We know that the middle class parent, who can more realistically set goals for his child, plays a constant teaching role in his child's life, steadily helping him make sense out of his experience.

4. We know that parents whose lives are severely restricted by poverty do see education as a path to a better life for their children, but lack the competence to play a mediating-teaching role with their children.

5. We are aware that there is a broad range of values, attitudes, behaviors, and skills within the category of "low income" parents and that this group has many differential strengths.

6. We are aware that most parents want to be competent parents, that apathy and hostility are often defenses against feeling inadequate.

7. We are aware that most parents know many things that would help their child find meaning in his experience, and we assume they would be receptive to approaches that would help them see that these understandings need to be translated to their child in the ways that young children understand.

8. We assume that if it is the parent's job to send to the schools children who are ready for and motivated to learn, and if being a parent doesn't automatically bring the knowledge and skills to do this job, then agency-based programs must help parents see themselves as their child's most important teacher and must provide some tools for effecting this teaching task.

If you can show me how I can cling to that which is real to me, while teaching me a way into the larger society, then I will not only drop my defenses and my hostility, but I will sing your praises and I will help you to make the desert bear fruit.[30]

IMPLICATIONS FOR CONTENT: A DEMONSTRATION PROGRAM

Since the onset of Head Start and compensatory programs at the elementary and secondary levels,* there has been an upsurge of recognition of the urgent need to involve low income parents in the learning process of their children. Efforts are made to involve parents in school management, as aides in the classroom and in educational programs aimed at enlisting parents in sustaining the learnings their children gain in school. There has been a persistent search for a frame of reference that will provide the kind of entry into parents' awareness that is not intrusive, that builds on rather than negates the parents' integrity and present knowledge. We present here the initial phase of a project that explored the applicability of a learning-valuing focus to programs for Head Start parents.

With a focus of changing parents' conceptualization of themselves as teaching people in the lives of their children, an overall program for the involvement of parents in the Hawaii Head Start summer program was developed in 1967. The program included

* See section on Low-Income Parent Education Methods in Selected Bibliography.

orientation of Head Start teachers for effective involvement of parents, both in the classroom and in parent discussion groups. Teacher experience in dealing with parents, in both of the selected emphasis areas, and opportunities for effective training, were minimal. To mitigate this problem, a series of six television programs* were produced. These programs were shown on the educational television network throughout the state once a week during the six-week Head Start program. The State Department of Education authorized the use of Head Start classrooms for child care and provided parents with a meeting room equipped with a television. Teachers used the 15-minute films as the basis for their weekly meeting with their parent groups. A manual for parent participation was developed, which included the television scripts and suggestions for effective use of parents' time. The films were previewed by the teachers in the preprogram teacher training sessions and discussion techniques explored. Both the scripts from the television programs and suggestions for guiding discussion are included here to illustrate the use of a learning-valuing focus for education of low income parents.

HELPING HEAD START: SCRIPT I

This summer your child is in the Head Start program. It will really be a great time for him. We would like to make it a special time for parents too.

Head Start has really hit the headlines for the last few summers. Everyone talks about it. When we finally learned that there are many kinds of experience that help a child get ready for school, Head Start seemed to be one important answer to every child's getting a good education. And we've been working very hard on building the best kind of children's program we can.

But there is something else the schools had to learn, and that very important fact is that the child's first teacher is you, the parent, and this whole program simply will not work if teachers and parents don't learn how to talk together, listen to each other, learn from each other, and work together all the way.

---

* These films were developed by Jean Fargo while Asst. Professor of Home Economics, University of Hawaii, with the total cooperation of The Hawaii State Department of Education, Hawaii Office of Economic Opportunities and the Hawaii Educational Television network.

So this series of programs is a way of sharing with parents how important they are, and why we think so. You know, most parents don't realize how much teaching they do, how many things they know that children need to learn. And they don't know that this teaching and this learning can go on in an everyday way, without any big changes. Really all it takes is looking at what you already know in a new way—looking at what you know and realizing that children aren't born knowing all that you know and they need help to learn how to make sense out of the world around them.

Before we started on this series, I asked a group of Head Start parents what they would really like to know from a program like this, and they asked some very good questions, like: What's Head Start all about? Why do children need a Head Start to make it in school: What goes on in the Head Start classroom? Why does the teacher plan her program the way she does? Does she really care about our children? Why is there so much fuss about language and talking? What do you mean there are things parents already know that help children get ready for school? What things? How can we help?

Pretty good questions. And what's more, we're going to try to answer them all! But first, here are four very big, really important facts that we are convinced are true:

> *You Are Important to Your Child*
> *You Know Many Things You Can Teach Him*
> *You Can Talk about All These Things with Him*
> *This Means He Will Do Better in School*

Now, let's start at the beginning and talk about what Head Start is all about. When you and I were four years old, I don't remember anyone saying *we* needed a head start. In fact, a very wise and special grandfather asked me "Why are we pushing the children? All they need is love and time."

That's true. Children do need love and certainly they need time to grow in their own way and at their own pace. But life is harder today. We can't get a decent job anymore if we don't have an education. We can't even manage our everyday lives if we don't know what to do about application forms, public transportation, installment payments, and thousands of other things.

That four-year-old son of yours grows up and his first job may be, say, a gas station attendant. Look at what he will need to know for a job we think needs little special training. He will need to know how to read; write; do arithmetic; understand how a car works; and listen to, understand, and deal with people. Plus he will need to be healthy, to like himself and other people, know how to live on a regular schedule, and be dependable. If any of these skills are hard for him, he'll have a hard time holding down this job.

And that little daughter of yours. When she grows up and starts out as, say, a nurse's aide, look at what she'll have to know, and know well: how to read; write; do arithmetic; understand and deal with people under stress; how to study and learn new things. Plus she will need to be healthy, to like herself and other people, to know how to live on a schedule, and be dependable. If she gets stuck on any of these things, they'll find someone else who can do the job, and she'll miss that chance to have a fuller life.

So, yes, children need love and time. But things have changed, and maybe we need to take a look at how we use that time, when children are very young. We know now that children need to know many things before they get to school, so they'll understand what's going on there. We know now that if we start early—not pushing, but helping them make sense out of the world around them, opening their eyes to the fun of knowing things, parents and preschool teachers can work together to help children do better in school.

So children need a head start because times have changed since we were young. There's more to learn to get along; we have to start teaching it even in kindergarten, so that children have to be readier to learn than they used to be.

How do we begin? We start with health. When a child doesn't feel well, he doesn't learn well. A good physical check-up tells parents lots of things they can't find out themselves. We parents are not trained to tell whether our children's eyes are working right. But if they can't see the blackboard, or the print in the book is blurry, it's hard to learn to read. Eye problems are often easily corrected, but only if we know the problem is there.

We parents aren't trained to test a child's hearing, but he won't understand what's going on in class if he doesn't hear well. Ear problems are often easily corrected, but only if we know the problem is there.

All children have the right to be protected from diseases, so we check to make sure they have all their vaccinations. And we make sure that we know why they have runny nose, ears, and eyes so this can be controlled. Teeth in bad shape make it hard to eat and that brings many other problems. All these things mean that some of our children really don't feel very well much of the time, and that means they don't feel like doing their learning job any more than we feel like doing our job when we're sick. So a good physical check-up and a plan for treatment is step number one in getting a head start.

The next step should be taking a look at the other problems families have. The fact that life is harder today really shows up in the number of daily problems families live with, not just you and I, but millions of families in every neighborhood all over the country. So this summer, there will be more people working in Head Start, just talking with families, listening to their problems, and helping them find the best way to do something about them. I don't know about you, but I have a hard time thinking about my children when my own problems are staring me in the face.

And last but not least, there is the children's program. You know, when parents first watch a program for four-year-olds, you usually hear them say "But they're just playing, they're not learning anything. What's so Head Start about that?" But parents quickly come to understand that we're not trying to teach them how to read, write, and add. We now know that there are many things a child has to understand before that more formal learning makes any sense to them at all. Children need to learn *how* to learn, and that's what Head Start is all about.

Parents will have a chance to watch a four-year-old who comes to school feeling confused, not very safe in this strange and different place, not really understanding what he should do here, and then begin to explore the fun of learning about colors and creating his very own pictures, maybe for the first time; beginning to get the control of his arm and hand muscles that he will need later for writing; learning that teachers are nice and that they care very much how he is feeling and learning; learning that things come in many different shapes and forms by having a chance to get in and work with things, because that's how young children learn; learning this with new friends and finding that working together can really be fun; playing happily and developing healthy bodies and using up all that energy in good kinds of ways; eating good hot meals that busy mothers don't always have time to fix; finding out that those strange looking foods people say are so good for you really don't taste so bad after all; getting a regular rest so that they have enough energy for everything else.

When parents have a chance to share this learning and find ways to help it grow, ways the whole family enjoys, then parents really understand that together we are sending to kindergarten a bright and more ready child. Then next summer when you hear new Head Start parents say "But they're just playing. They're not learning anything," you can smile wisely, give the teacher a wink, and give those parents the good word.

Head Start is for you too. When you put a morning in working with the teacher, helping serve juice and many other things, it doesn't take long to learn the ropes. And the teacher can use all the help she can get. Bikes need fixing, equipment needs painting, going on trips needs extra hands, stories need reading, games need playing, and the teacher needs to know many things about your child that only you can tell her.

In other words, Head Start needs parents. Let me repeat that the most important thing we have learned in the last few years of Head Start is that this whole program simply will not work without you. That's how important you are.

Next week, we will go into the classroom and show you just what's going on there, how it helps a child get ready for kindergarten, and how you're already helping all this happen at home. I know you'll enjoy talking these things over with your teacher and your neighbors. You all have a lot to give to each other.

Thanks so much for watching, and see you next week.

SUGGESTIONS FOR DISCUSSION
FOLLOWING FIRST PROGRAM

1. This is a good time to have a resource person available, not for speaking, but for answering questions about the medical component, how it works, what the role of the social work aide will be, and so on.
2. Stress the fact that the need for parents is very real. Daily volunteering

is the contribution in kind of the community and if it is not fulfilled, the cost of additional personnel will need to come out of another part of the children's program.

3. Try to have an active parent from last year's program there to describe the kinds of things parents did in the classroom assisting the teacher and how she/he felt about the experience; a veteran father to outline the kinds of things fathers can do that mean a great deal to the total program.

4. Have the simple rules you have worked out for parents supervising specific areas printed on big cards, so that you can graphically illustrate how easy it is to learn the ropes. Stress the fact that parents will get a chance to just watch for a morning to get a feel for how the program goes, that no one is expected to grab onto the job all at once. Don't worry about language. THE IMPORTANT THING IS THAT THE PARENT IS THERE. We want parents to know what's going on in the classroom, and in order to really do a job with very young children, WE NEED THEIR HELP.

5. You might consider breaking the group into three smaller groups, with a specific task for each, so that parents will feel immediately involved because they are doing and giving something:

   a. One group of parents who would like to learn some of the simple ways of working in the classroom. Don't try to cover the whole program. Select two or three aspects, i.e., supervising easel area, block area, sitting at lunch tables; have simple rules spelled out; teacher and veteran mother (or aide) role-play some typical situations. Do this in the most relaxed, humorous, ungrim manner you can manage!

   b. Perhaps a group of fathers, with a veteran father if possible (but not essential), giving them a list of the equipment repair or building needs for them to consider together; instruments they play, skills they have that can be shared with children.

   c. For parents who are not ready to make this kind of commitment, a group around a table working on preparation of materials for the children's program, or considering a list of materials they might be able to provide from home.

6. A parent may raise a question about how her child will react to her being in the classroom. Assure her that many children respond by clinging. She can feel free to move through the morning with her child and you will help her gradually move into the program, once her child feels safe and comfortable in school.

7. End meeting with much warmth for parents' concern and positive feelings about the summer experience.

HELPING HEAD START: SCRIPT II

Hello, we're very glad you're watching tonight. It's good to be able to talk to so many parents. Nice things happen when parents and teachers talk together.

Remember last time we talked about why parents and teachers need to give our children a head start. Teachers work in their teacher way at school; that's their job. Parents help in their parent way at home, and we're learning that *that* help is part of the job of being a parent.

We talked about the fact that these days, if our children grow up with a good education, they can hold good jobs to build their lives around. And when we parents look ahead for what is in store for our children, we now know we have to think about that when they are very young. There is so much more to learn than there used to be. And Head Start, with parents' help, is a place where children can learn about the world they live in, so that when they get to kindergarten they won't feel lost or confused or out of things. They'll know what's going on; their eyes will be open to the world, and they will know how to learn.

Today we would like to show you something about what is going on in the Head Start classroom, and how it will help your child make more sense out of what he will find in kindergarten.

In kindergarten, children need to know how to tell one color from another, because we talk about so many things in terms of what color they are. That's one important way of seeing that one thing is different from another. Here, in their four-year-old way of learning, through seeing and feeling and doing over and over, children are learning what the colors are, so that when they get into kindergarten they will understand when the teacher says, "Color this box red and the other box blue." If they know their colors well, they won't get stuck. They can do their job. And all children, just like adults, need lots of practice before they really know something well.

And in kindergarten, children need to know that things come in many different shapes and sizes, because we describe so many things by their shape and their size. Here in Head Start, in his four-year-old way, your child is learning about shapes and sizes, really getting in and working with them, so that when he gets to kindergarten and, for instance, starts learning the alphabet, he can remember the shape of an A, B, or C because they're like a triangle, rectangle, and circle and that helps him remember the difference and hold it in his mind. And if he really understands what "big" and "small" mean, he can see the difference between big and small letters. All these things seem simple, but not when we remember that when children are born, they don't know any of these things.

You know, most of our children spend their first five years without much routine. But when they get to kindergarten, bang! they're expected to be able to sit still, follow a routine, really listen. That's hard to do if you've never had much practice. So here, in Head Start, they are beginning to learn this hard job, so that when they get to kindergarten, they can really know how to pay attention, understand the need for order, and sit still long enough to learn.

Another thing children must know to be ready for learning is that some things are the same and some things are different. Understanding this helps us make sense out of new information. What part of this new thing is the same as something else I know about, what part of it is new? In Head Start children are working on learning not just to look, but to really *see* the things around them, so that when they get to kindergarten and start to learn about letters, they can see, for example, that the "o" and the "c" are the same shape, but there is a small difference that helps them remember which is which.

In kindergarten, children need to know about themselves, and to feel good about themselves, because when you feel good about yourself, you feel more like learning.

So in Head Start, he works on this, too, learning about himself, how he looks, how he feels, thinks, acts, so that when he gets to kindergarten and the teacher says, "Tell me about you," he breaks into a big, warm smile and tells her all about who he is.

And in kindergarten, children need to have a lot of words and be able to use them, because that's the main way the teacher can tell what children understand and what they are learning. Here, in Head Start, they are learning about the words for things and practicing using them, so that when they get to kindergarten, they have some of the tools they need for asking questions, explaining things, and for thinking. Language is really the key that opens the door to learning.

Head Start then is a time when this bright and shiny four- (and five-) year-old of yours is really being taught four basic ideas in many different ways. He is being taught that:

> *He is important*
> *He can do many things*
> *He can talk about all those things*
> *And so, school will be a safe and happy place*

But six weeks is a very short time to learn so much and five hours a day is not very long. And that's why parents are so important. Remember we talked about how parents don't realize how much teaching they do, and how many everyday things they do that help a young child learn what he needs to know. I don't mean the sitting-down teacher-kind of teaching. I mean just all day long in what we say and do. Let's look at those Head Start shots again and I'll show you what I mean.

Remember here children are working on being able to tell one color from another, because it is an important way we talk about things. Think about all the times you tell one thing from another by its color. At home you are helping your child learn color everytime you tell him to bring his red shirt, or put the blue plate on the table, or ask your child to tell you the colors in the paintings that come home from school.

Here they're learning about different shapes and sizes by working with them, matching them, seeing them side by side. At home, you've been helping them learn this every time you say, "How about cutting all the square things out of an old magazine, or putting the different size cans away on the shelf, or how about looking at sister's old school workbook?"

The teacher starts with big pictures and short fun stories until children are ready to listen to longer stories and are more interested in hearing the beginning, the middle, and the end. At home you've been helping your children like to listen every time you sit down and talk with them about what they're doing, or ask them to tell you what that TV cartoon was all about, to see if they really hear the story and not just a lot of meaningless noise.

At school, the teacher is talking about same and different, and then letting them see, touch, taste, smell the difference, because that's how young children learn and remember. The apple and tomato are both alike in some ways. They are both red and they are round and we can eat them. But they are very different in the way they look inside, feel, taste, and smell. And children need to be able to really see when things are different, and have the words to tell you not just the name, but all the many other things there are to say about it. At home you are helping them learn this every-time you let them taste, feel, smell, see, and hear many different things *and* you *talk* about them together.

Now here at school, the teacher helps each child find out about himself and the things that make him the same as other people and the things that are special just about him. At home, you've been helping him learn this everytime you give him a job he can do that makes him feel big, give him a small place to keep his own things, listen to what he has to say.

And here, he's learning the words for things and how to talk about what he knows and ask questions about what he doesn't know. At home, you've been helping him learn words every time you talk to him, really stop a minute to pay attention, ask him questions about what he knows so that it helps him think about things. I really think that the questions parents *ask* their children help them learn how to think much more than the questions we *answer*—which is comforting because sometimes children's questions are very hard to answer.

You see, home and school are very different from each other —and they should be. At school, it's the teacher's job to teach all day. It's a job that keeps her very busy. At home, we have a million other things to do, and if your home is anything like mine, it's noisy, full of people, and so much to do that you don't always feel like answering a thousand questions or even asking them. But the little time we do have, we can use to really build in our way on the same things the teacher is building in her way. That means we are really working together, helping our children learn the facts about the world that we parents already know and that our children need to be told about, so that school and learning will be fun for everyone—parent, child, and teacher.

Today we talked about some of the things children need to

know so that they will be ready for the kind of learning that comes in kindergarten. They need to know colors, and they need time and practice learning all of them. They need to know how to describe things, to see sameness and difference and have words for talking about shape, size, texture, number, and many other qualities. To learn, children have to know how to listen and enjoy it, and that takes practice. To learn, children need to feel good about themselves, so they will want to speak up and ask questions; so they'll really undesrtand. Teachers work on these things in their way; but parents have many ways of teaching too.

Now, are you beginning to take a new look at those four big facts we talked about? They really are very big and very important:

> *You Are Important to Your Child*
> *You Know Many Things You Can Teach Him*
> *You Can Talk About All These Things with Him*
> *When You Do This, He Will Do Better in School*

Next week, we will talk about this whole big question of language, and how we can work together on this. You know, the fact that you watch this program and come to these meetings means a great deal to your child. Thanks for coming, and see you next week.

SUGGESTIONS FOR DISCUSSION
FOLLOWING SECOND PROGRAM

1. Good time to point out (covered in Program Six) that these are all ideas that take a long time to really grasp; that we are not expecting all the children to come out at the end of a short six weeks with all these skills mastered. This is just the "start" part of Head Start. We are much more concerned with real understanding than we are with speed.
2. Kinds of questions that might get some discussion rolling:
   What are the things you liked about this film?
   Did it tell you anything new?
   What are some other ways parents teach?
3. If you're feeling ambitious, you might think about having a potluck supper at 6:30 P.M., a brief demonstration of some activities with the children at 7:00 P.M. (perhaps two tables of activities and one group demonstrating work with language) and then sending the children off

to their supervised time in their own room, while parents watch and discuss TV program.

4. Good time to have selected materials around to talk about the kinds of learning going on as the children work with them. Talk about the kinds of learning that happen when children play with blocks, work puzzles, cut and paste, etc. If you have a children's painting collection from other classes, show how the preschooler progresses from the scrubbing stage through beginning form to representational pictures; what it means to the child, how this development takes time, and the meaning to him of having a place for display for his work at home, even when it looks like nothing to adults.

5. If questions come up about the nature of kindergarten that you cannot answer, ask group if they would like to have a kindergarten teacher come to one of the meetings to discuss this with them. Then make sure you work this through ahead of time with the kindergarten teacher so that you are together on what you are saying.

6. If you feel it is working, break again into smaller groups to continue the kind of planning that might have started at the first meeting, and to encourage other parents to take a look at some of the ways they can work within the program.

HELPING HEAD START: SCRIPT III

Hello. We're off again for a look at another part of Head Start. By now you really know that it's a double parent-teacher job. You've seen some of what goes on in the classroom; you've watched your child in this new part of his life. And you know that because there is so much to learn today, parents and teachers can do many things that help a child be ready to learn, even before kindergarten —so that when your child gets to kindergarten, it won't be a strange and different place. He won't feel lost and confused. Nobody likes to feel like that. Kindergarten will be much like his Head Start classroom—more children and less adults. But he will know how to handle the things that happen there. He will be ready.

Today let's talk about talking. School is a very wordy place. Why? Because language is the main way we have to teach. Children need to know how to use words in order to think and to learn, and language learning is the hardest part of school for many children.

Now lots of times we don't need words to let people know lots of things. Our children don't need words to tell us they're happy or sad or angry or all tied up about something. In fact, babies do very well letting us know something is wrong with just a good, loud cry. But children do need words to ask questions, to explain things, to help them think about things, and to let people know what they know. That's what school is all about. The teacher cannot know what a child understands and what else he needs to know unless he has the words to tell her about it.

You can listen to your TV from the kitchen or the porch and know pretty well what's going on without seeing the picture, right? Like when you hear a gunshot, coming from the TV set, you pretty well know somebody has had it. But when you're watching TV and the sound goes off (teacher mouths words soundlessly) . . . what I said was, you have a hard time making sense out of it. You need the words to tell you exactly what's going on. All over the country, in more places than people realize, the language we use with our families, in our homes, with our friends, is different than the language we use in school. This doesn't mean that one language is better than the other. It only means that our children need two languages. He uses one language with his family and friends and gets along just fine. He learns to use another language because that's the language we use for teaching.

Remember we talked about the things your child will need to know when he grows up and starts out on an average kind of job? Reading, writing, arithmetic, understanding how things work, knowing how to get the information we need—all these things are taught in what we call standard English. But the school *wants* children to hold onto their home language, because it's a very important part of family life, and family life is very important. To his home language, we add other words and other ways of using words so that school will be easier—and that's also very important.

Take a look at this picture. The teacher wants to know what a child sees and understands about a picture, because so much of what we learn in school is about things we have never seen and places we have never been. We learn about them through pictures and words. A child without many words to use may say, "The boy looks at the water." He may see other things but not have the words to talk about them. The teacher would like him to be able to tell her about all the things he sees, all the white things, things that live in the water, things that go on the water, that fly above the water, what the smoke from the steamer tells him about the direction of the wind—so many things to see and say.

Head Start teachers are working on giving children some more ways of using words: some to talk about the many things they already know but didn't have words to attach to them; some they need for new things they learn so that they can think about and remember them.

How does the teacher teach about language? Well, the first thing she wants children to know about language is that everything has a name. If something just flashes through your mind without a name to tag on it, you can't think about it or remember it very well.

So the teacher spends much time being sure that the children know the names of things around them, the children around them, the things they see and do, so that things begin to fit together. And she goes over the whole sentence with them—"This is a carton of milk; This is a plate." A child may very well know "carton of milk" or "plate," and how he pronounces it isn't too important. Putting that statement in a whole sentence *is* important. When he knows how words go together to make sense, he understands what he hears.

Then, the teacher wants the child to know that when there is more than one thing, we talk about it with different words. So that when the teacher says, "Show me two pears," he really understands that the "s" sound on the end of the word means that he is to think about more than one. "Is this a pear? No, these are pears." This seems simple, but it is really a hard idea to grab onto. It takes practice before children really understand and know how to change words and find the one that tells just what he wants it to.

Another part of language the teacher is working on is helping children really see that there are many things to know about one simple thing. We saw last week that the apple and tomato are the same in many ways and different in others. We can say about both of them that they are red and round, and they are things we eat; but one is hard and one is soft, one is crunchy and the other mushy. Now look at this block and this ice cube. They are both square, with the same number of sides and corners. The sides are smooth, they are hard. But this one is cold, slippery, and it melts.

And this one is made of wood, doesn't melt, and has many colors. Many things need to be said about these two objects in order to tell the whole story about them.

Another tool for thinking that children need is the ability to talk about where things are and how to compare them to other things. Each word that tells us where something is is different, and means something different. If the block is here, the child needs to say that it is *on* the book; if here, *next to* the book; if here, *behind* the book; if here, *under* the book.

And number position and size: children need to be able to tell us that something is first, or second, or last; and that something is small, bigger, biggest. All these kinds of rules help children understand how one thing compares to another and how it all fits together.

Now, another way we learn to think about and talk about what we know is being able to put things in groups. There are so many different things in the world that we remember them better if we can figure out what group they belong to—like keeping people straight by figuring out what family they belong to. The teacher is giving children names for these things—an airplane, a truck, a boat—but the children are also learning the word "vehicle" because all things that take us places are vehicles. So when a child sees something he's never seen before, and sees that it takes people somewhere, he knows that it is a vehicle of some kind, and in his mind, he remembers it with all the other things he knows are vehicles. He then has a way of storing that new information.

It's the same way with other groups, like food, or furniture, or animals, or tools. He discovers the rule for that group—if we can eat it, it is food—and it helps him fit new information into what he already knows so he doesn't lose it. All of these items are food, but if he were asked to make a group of all the long things, he would pick out the cucumber; all the round things, he would pick the orange, and so forth. And so he learns to put things in different order, depending on what the problem is.

These are some of the rules about language and thinking that the kindergarten would like children to already understand when they come to school. That's why we work on them in Head Start. Let's look at them again:

Everything has a name.

When there is more than one, we use different words.

There are many things to know about one object, and it takes many words
to talk about all these things.

`Many things have opposites, and knowing that helps us figure them out—
what they are and what they aren't.

We need special words to tell about the shape, size, number, color, texture,
and position of things.

Things belong in groups and knowing that helps us remember them.

So we've been looking at what the teacher does to help children learn how to think and how to talk about what they're thinking. This is the teacher's job and in her job, she finds many ways to
give the children fun things to do so that they will have something
to talk about together, and she gives them words to help them do
that.

We parents don't need to teach in this way. First of all, we
don't have all this lovely equipment, or special time. But the next
two times together, we'll show you some more of the things we're
learning about how parents can help this learning grow in lots of
easy, when-we-have-time ways. Next time we will take some of the
trips your children will be taking, so that you can see what they'll
be learning and can then really help them talk about their experiences. After that, we will go into the home of a delightful Head
Start family and see just how many ways there are that parents are
teachers too.

So until next time, keep remembering:

> *You are important to your child*
> *You know many things you can teach him*
> *You can talk about all these things with him*
> *All this means he will do better in school*

Thanks so much for watching, and see you next week.

SUGGESTIONS FOR DISCUSSION
FOLLOWING THIRD PROGRAM

1. Good time for teacher to talk about her own positive feelings about
this approach to language:

—that we are much more concerned about children understanding the rules and ideas about language than with pronunciation;

—that you are delighted with this kind of chance to let parents know how we are working with language in the Head Start program;

—that you are also comfortable with the approach that children need to hold onto their home language, too, and parents should in no way be concerned about their own language in working in the classroom—it's the talking together that we care about.

2. If you have time, print the six basic ideas about language on a large card so that parents can refer to it to form their questions. It's impossible for anyone to remember a series like this from just viewing or hearing once.

3. Talk about how the children are responding to the language sessions. Relate any humorous anecdotes you might have noted.

4. If you feel you can handle it, demonstrate with the children some of the ways in which you are working on language. Even if the children don't respond, or the whole thing falls apart, you're teaching a great deal about the time learning takes, your ability to completely accept their children, your feelings about "mistakes" in responses, and your stress on "really working and thinking hard," if you can handle this kind of situation with humor, ending with "We'll work on this together tomorrow" kind of feeling.

5. If you have your parent committee working on planning trips, have them report on plans, previous trips, what the children learned, etc. By all means show or have parents show any slides or movies you have taken, stressing the importance of parent help, the kinds of things parents do to make these excursions real learning experiences—and indicate this is the content of next week's program.

6. See if some of the parents who have been working in the program will share their experiences with the other parents.

7. If ending with working groups has been effective, ask parents to share what their group has been working on. In a group that is essentially training for classroom participation, keep moving into other curriculum areas spelling out role of volunteer parent and discussing experiences.

HELPING HEAD START: SCRIPT IV

Today, we're going on some special trips, some of the trips our children will be taking in the next week or so. Going places and seeing new things is a big part of the program in Head Start, and we'd like to show you why.

We're taking these trips in a small group today, for two reasons. You can get a much better idea of what each different experience means to each individual child when there isn't a crowd. And it helps us see why we try to have as many adults as we can in the Head Start program. It shows us that when parents and other people in the community volunteer to help out in Head Start, each adult can take four or five children and really be there to answer questions, to point out what a child might not be seeing, to make the trip come alive for the child, and to make it even more alive by helping the children talk, draw, sing, dance, play about what they see when they get back to school.

Today we're off to the fire station, the farm, and the library. The children went on different days, of course, so the experiences didn't get all jumbled together. These are three places within easy reach, three places that hold lots of learning for children.

And here we come, eyes wide open with excitement, feeling all jiggly inside, up to the fire station, where that nice fire captain is waiting just for us. This is the beginning of understanding that there are many people in the community we live in whose job it is just to help us when we need it. And young children learn that big idea best when they can really see, shake hands with, climb up on the trucks of real live community helpers like these.

There's no better way to help a child learn to listen than to tell him something he's really interested in—told to him by someone who really knows. And how many times in a lifetime do you get to know what it feels like to be a big, brave fireman and ride where the heroes ride. Playing, pretending that you're someone else in some other place is an important thing to learn how to do. Children have to do that to learn history, geography, to learn about other people in other lands in other times. They will never be there; they have to be able to imagine what it is like.

The children wanted to know how they put out fires that were higher than the truck. Before we went on this trip, the teacher read them stories and talked about the kinds of things we might see, so that when we got there and saw the real things, we could understand it all better and know what questions we wanted to ask. And when we get back to school, we'll spend lots of time talking and remembering and reading some more and wondering and digesting what we're living through right now. But it's good to learn how to talk to people.

Firemen (in Hawaii) help people who are having trouble swimming and need to be rescued and this is the boat they use. Climb in and see how it feels and how it works and imagine that you are speeding to the rescue, bells clanging, waves slapping the boat. "Why do you need two big motors, Mr. Chief?" "Because it's very important that we get there as fast as we can, so if one motor doesn't work, we have another to take its place," says the nice captain who knows how to talk in children's language. Is there any place but Hawaii where fire engines come equipped with bright red surfboards? The children see that these surfboards are different from the ones their big brothers have. We talk about how they are different. They are longer and heavier and they have handles. "How come?" "What do *you* think?" asks the fireman. "Maybe because they have to carry two," says one thinking child. "Right," says the captain. "If these are used to rescue people, there has to be room for two people on them. If they are bigger than a regular board, they need handles so that they can be carried as fast as possible." Everything has a reason, and if you know how to ask questions, you can find out what that reason is. We learned lots about what firemen do. Next time we hear the siren wailing through the town, we'll have a much better idea of what is happening and remember this trip. "Thanks, Mr. Fireman, 'bye."

And another trip day, out to the farm: will the farmer be as nice as the fireman? "He's smiling," says Debbie, as we walk toward the cows, and this means this will be a nice trip too. He tells us lots of things about those big cows. "They don't look that big in our books, teacher." "Have you ever been this close to a cow before?" "Gee no, teacher." We saw that they are black and white and big and they look kind of sad and they have a deep, low moo and they will be ready to give milk when they have reproduced and they look very shiny and healthy and well-cared for.

This happens to be a demonstration farm where they work on what is the best feed for farm animals, and that means we get to see chickens. We have seen chickens before, of course, but never in numbers like these. The eggs feel warm, not like when they come out of the refrigerator. Loren asks if there is a baby chick in there and the farmer tells us that if we keep the egg in a good, heated place and for a long time, the baby chick will hatch. It seems like the clucking and bobbing heads and warm fresh eggs and flying feathers go on for miles.

And up to see the pigs with just a few children—it's a good time for teachers to listen, for children to talk and ask questions. What a great place to talk about big and little, because baby pigs are very little when they are one week old and big pigs are just huge when they are grown. We take a look at different kinds of families in the world. We talk about the difference between being a human baby and an animal baby. We have a chance to pet a baby pig, who is not really very happy about being taken away from his mother and brothers and sisters, and we talk about how animals sometimes have the same feelings people do—they get scared when something new and strange comes into the picture. And the children really practice their language: this pig is big, these pigs are fat—and a new one—these pigs are not nice to smell. "Thanks very much, Mr. Farmer. This trip gives us lots of things to remember and talk about when we go back to school and then home to tell our families."

And one day, a quiet, easy trip to the nearby library where, in the cool rooms, the librarian welcomes us, because she thinks it's a good idea for children to know and love books. And the voice we use here is the same quiet, inside voice we learn to use at school (unless we are out on the playground), so it's good to practice. This librarian likes to read stories to children. She enjoys it as much as they do. She picked a good story, with action and rhythm in the way it reads, and pictures that really show the meaning of words we hear. We sit still and listen because we really want to hear how it ends, not just because someone told us to. That's real listening. Just watch how they listen. Are they ever this quiet at home?

And books aren't just for being read to you. Books are things you can explore on your own. Trying to think about what the story is telling by looking hard at the pictures is fun. Watch Debby. She's really reading that picture. Finding favorite books and plopping down in any old comfortable position—books are to enjoy in your own way. And there's more to see in the library. Look, up and down the rows, there are all kinds of books—"Wow, maybe when we get bigger, we can read some of those on the top shelf, the kind with little pictures and lots of print." Books about everything—

things we know and things we'll never learn about any other way.

And it's no fun coming to the library if you can't check out some books to take home. Besides we feel pretty important when the librarian very seriously checks out the books we chose. Maybe she thinks we're important too. Maybe she thinks we know how to take good care of books and keep them in a safe place when we're not reading them, so we can bring them back for other children to share. So it's time to say goodbye and thanks for the great story. We checked out the one you read us, so we can read it again.

And so back to school we go, chattering all the way because we have so much to talk about; we did so much together. How does the teacher use these trips to help children learn? Well, in the first place, she takes trips because she knows young children learn best by really doing things and being there, and then talking about their real experiences. For days children will be saying that their paintings are fire trucks and chickens and baby pigs; at the clay table they'll make fresh, warm eggs and round, fat cows; they'll be building rescue boats and farms and chicken coops; their books about fire engines and farms will mean so much more. And in many ways they'll learn, the way fours and fives learn, about themselves and the world around them, playing out what they see and hear and feel.

But parents are good trip-takers too. And a walk about the block or a trip to the grocery store has as much learning in it as a trip we took today. Maybe this is something you can talk about tonight.

Next week, we're going into the home of a Head Start family and show you just how much teaching you already do! Until then, thanks so much for watching, and see you next week.

SUGGESTIONS FOR DISCUSSION
FOLLOWING FOURTH PROGRAM

1. If possible, take a trip the day before this program, involving as many parents as possible, so that these parents can share the experience with other parents.
2. If you haven't done so previously, talk about the trips you have taken using any visual aids, examples of children's work that was stimulated by the trip, the kind of learnings, etc.; how you prepared for the trip, what the children saw, the role of mothers, what you/children did with the experience back in the classroom.

3. Ask parents to think and talk about the kinds of learnings that are possible if we take another look at everyday experiences, i.e.:
    a. Taking a walk (What can you see, hear, feel; what kinds of questions can parents ask about shape, size, sound, color, light, shadow, etc.?)
    b. A trip to the grocery store
    c. The park
    d. The beach
    e. Parents' other suggestions
4. If parents would like to think about a last day or last week get together, what kind of planning and who would like to be involved?
5. Remember to constantly encourage questions about any aspect of the program and if you feel you can't answer them fully, ask for and make suggestions about who might come and do this more completely.
6. If your parent group is not too aware of the total range of community facilities that are available for enriching family life, bring in some of this kind of information—brochures from the various facilities, big chart that starts with home and branches out showing all the different resources that serve the family. Social worker, or social-work aide, or Community Action Program person can help with this.
7. If continuing to end with work groups, have a group that's working on preparing materials that parents have contributed, so that they can really see how these things are used in the children's program.

HELPING HEAD START: SCRIPT V

We've spent four programs giving you a picture of what Head Start is all about, what goes on in that classroom that helps your four-year-old get ready to understand what he will be learning in kindergarten and the primary grades. Now let's really get into what goes on at home and how children learn and how parents teach in a thousand different ways.

First of all, children learn as much from what we parents do as from what we say. The fact that you make the effort to get your child off to school on these warm summer mornings and to watch these programs teaches your child that you care about him.

What else are you teaching all day long? What is your child learning and how does he feel about it? When you say "time to get up, then we'll have breakfast," your child is getting his first lessons about time, that some things come before others, some things come after. When things often come in the same order, it helps a child remember that order, and helps him handle the routines of school. And when you say, "It's time to brush your teeth," he knows you think taking care of his teeth is important, even if he doesn't like it. When you say, "Do you want to wear your red shirt or your blue shirt?" he feels good that you think he's big enough to make up his own mind, and he is learning to know the names of the colors and tell them apart. When you say, "Put four plates on the table. We need two more cups," he feels good that you need his help even if he makes mistakes, and he's getting practice understanding what the words four and two really mean, that they're more than just words that we count—one, two, three, four, five.

When you have time to let him put things away, he often has to match shapes and sizes and he gets practice seeing differences and how same things go together. He also gets acquainted with the idea of smaller, larger, big, too big that he needs. There are a million things to learn in the kitchen. Once in a while when everyone isn't under your feet and you have a minute, it's a great place to help children learn lots of things that parents know, but children don't.

Just talking about things helps children notice them. Remember we said that the questions we ask children are really more helpful sometimes than the questions we answer; questions about what he is doing and seeing that help him learn to think, figure out how things work, how they fit together, how knowing one thing helps you understand something else.

Children are supposed to be the question-askers of the world. Let's turn the tables on them. What kinds of questions can we ask about everyday things that help children think about them better?

"What happens to the egg when we crack the shell? Does it look different? How? What happens when we cook it? Tell me about the pudding powder. Does it look dry or wet? Does it look like the pudding we had for dinner? What is happening to the dry powder when I add milk? Do you remember what happens when we put the soft pudding into the refrigerator?

When we cut open a papaya and a tomato, do they look the same? Tell me about them. You're really learning to see things!

Look, what's the same about corn and a banana. Right, they're both yellow and long. Right, they both have a peeling. Then how do you know one is an ear of corn? One is smooth and one is bumpy; one is hard and one is soft; they feel different, taste different, smell different. Very good!"

Those books you brought home from the library. If you have a minute or your older children have a minute, sit down and listen and talk and ask questions. Children love to know a story by heart. They don't need to hear every word to get the story and tell it back to you. The important thing is that children learn that books are things that tell us about so much that we may never see ourselves and also let us see everyday things in a new way. Children begin to get the big idea that those funny squiggles on the page stand for something even if we can't read them yet. And when they enjoy poring over books, they can do it quietly when parents need a chance to rest, which we all do!

Back yards that have dirt are great for children. With some old cans and pots and dirt and water, much learning goes on about how things are measured and molded—what happens to water when it's poured into dirt, will the dirt in this big can all go into this small can, will the mud pie hold together if I add too much water? This can be the beginning for a four-year-old's understanding of the problems of measurement—weight and pints and quarts and pounds —that he will get later in school.

And television—TV takes a lot of pressure off of parents, and that's good. But just in passing by, we can ask, "Is that music loud or soft, fast or slow? What does it make you feel like doing: marching, twirling, crawling, or just listening? Which is the biggest bear? Why is he hitting that tiger? Is that man happy or sad? At dinnertime, will you tell me what happened in that story?"

Is there any way, in the middle of all your daily chores, that learning can happen? When you're busy hanging up clothes, can you ask your child for two or three clothespins? That's learning. When you're standing over a hot ironing board, can your child help you put things away, because he needs to know that everything has a place? When you're trying to keep that car running, can your child learn that tools have names and practice finding the right one? When you're making those constant repairs, can your child help for a minute, because learning how to hit a nail with a hammer helps him get his eyes and hands working together and he needs that practice behind him when he has to learn to write. Besides, he feels pretty special about being able to be like his daddy. That's how he learns about what being a man is all about.

And parents are pretty talented. They can hold a fussy baby and help a child get good experience at the same time. About that baby—the more we know about how children learn, the earlier we start to bring the world to him, so he can begin to sort it out. At the end of the day when you've really had it, a box full of things help a child find quiet things to do: a pair of rounded scissors from the dime store, because learning to cut helps him get control of the hand muscles he will need in school to hold pencils and make the lines go the way they should. Old magazines are great for suggesting that they cut out round things, square things, things that are red, pictures with one thing in them, pictures with two things in them. "Make a scrapbook; tell me about it."

Of course, all this talking and doing isn't jammed into one exhausting day, just whenever we can work it in. But everything we've been talking about is part of the new knowledge we have about just how important parents are in getting their children ready for school. It means we all can take a new, fresh look at what goes on every day in our house, what our children are learning all the time, and how they feel about being a person who knows lots of things, and how to do lots of things. And we know that children need thousands of different kinds of experiences and lots of chance to practice their new understandings before they are ready to put all of it to use in the orderly way that school begins to teach them. We've really seen that it just doesn't matter how many or how few things we have around the house; what matters is what we can learn from what we have.

What else does a child need to know when he walks through that kindergarten door? He needs to know that the world is a safe place, that people can generally be trusted, that big people are there to give him love and information and the rules for living; and tell him it's okay when he makes mistakes. That's part of learning.

And those rules—all children need to be told what they can't do, so we can live together without losing our minds completely. But now we know that's not enough. Children also need to be told what they *can* do, so they'll have enough information to make a choice when they hit a problem. You can't stand on the teeter-totter, because it's too dangerous. But you *can* sit on it; that's what it's for. You *can't* get off when your friend is up high because he'll get hurt and we care about him. But you *can* get off when you're both ready.

And that takes us to another rule about life that children need to know—that everything has a reason. Sometimes we feel like doing a job by ourselves; sometimes we have time to let our children help us. Sometimes it's all we can do to get dinner on the table and we don't want to be bothered; sometimes we have time to have a few curious characters around. Sometimes are just for big people because that's the most important thing at the time, like getting off to work. We are learning that even when we are really furious with our children, and want them to be quiet and leave us alone (and we all do), if we tell them that it's because we're tired, or worried, or want to be alone, it helps them understand why things are happening. Then they're more able to predict what will happen—that eventually we'll feel more like smiling and listening. Then they'll learn to have that little inside voice that asks the question, "What will happen if I do this?" *before* they do it. They'll be able to think things through inside themselves, consider alternatives and consequences, and then make a decision. That's probably the most important thing anybody has to learn how to do in this life.

Children need to feel that school will be a safe place for them to be themselves. They learn a lot from the way we say things. If we caution our child to "be good" when we send him off to school, maybe he will think his job is just to sit still, make no noise, be scared that he will get into trouble. But when we tell him to "enjoy school" or "have a good day," he'll get the idea that his job there is to learn things, and he does that best by getting involved, asking questions, feeling free to answer even if he isn't sure he's right, be himself and feel that that's a pretty good thing to be.

So we've learned in the last few years that when a child is really aware of what is happening around him, he begins to feel he belongs in the world in which he lives, that the things he does are important and the things he feels are important, and that he makes a difference to people.

And we've learned in the past few years just how much parents do about seeing that all this happens. Helping parents take a new look at all this growing makes *them* feel they can really do a job. That's why we repeat this message, because it's a new way of looking at things, and big people need practice with ideas as much as little ones.

So, once again

> *You are important to your child*
> *You know many things you can teach him*
> *You can talk about all these things with him*
> *When you do this, he will do better in school*

Thanks again for watching. Next week will be our last time together, and we'll try to pull together all the things we've been saying and you've been discussing with your teacher and your friends.

HELPING HEAD START: SCRIPT VI

For those of you who have followed this series all the way through, congratulations! It has been a full, busy, and happy six weeks.

Way back at the beginnning, we began by saying that Head Start was a good idea because there is so much more to know these days, just to get along in the world, and this means we need to think about how we use our time with children in their very early years. How parents and teachers use this time seems to make a real difference in how our children are able to handle the kind of learning they get in school.

Remember six weeks ago—way back there—we watched a Head Start child who first felt confused, not very safe in this new strange place, not knowing what to do. Then we saw him beginning to explore the fun of beginning to learn about colors and making something all his own, to start to build control of arm and hand muscles for later when it's time to learn to write;

beginning to build that important feeling that teachers are nice and care about you and what you're feeling and what you're learning;

beginning to learn that everything has a name, and that we use different words when there is more than one thing;

starting to see that there are many things to know about any one thing—its color, shape, size, number, texture, its opposite, and that it takes lots of words to talk about all those things;

getting a new idea that things come in groups, and that if we know the rule about that group, we can look around and find lots of things that belong in it, and remember them;

playing happily and developing a healthy body and using up all that child kind of energy in ways that are easier for them and big people to handle;

eating good hot meals that busy mothers don't always have time to fix;

finding out that different-looking foods don't taste as funny as they look;

getting regular rest so that we have enough energy for everything else;

And we saw all the many everyday ways that parents help this learning grow, ways that the whole family enjoys. You know that all this is very new knowledge, this idea that parents do many small things as they live with their children, day by day, that help the child make sense out of the world around him, help him understand what's going on, help him put things together so that he can feel and see his own learning, feel good about it, and think about himself as a learning person.

We have new knowledge about how much goes into getting ready for the more orderly, more formal kind of learning that begins in kindergarten and builds up in the first, second, and third grades to give children their basic tools of learning: the tools of reading, writing, figuring, and the ability to talk about it all. We've just begun to ask ourselves what things a child needs to understand —about himself and the world around him—before he can be at all ready to learn to read and write.

We did know that good health, good food, the chance for active outdoor play and plenty of rest were important. We did know that a child needs to feel that the world is a pretty safe place and that he is a special, worthwhile person just because he is alive. But we sure are taking a harder look at what else he needs help with as he looks at the world around him, to help him see that it's not just a confusing mass of motion that doesn't make any sense, but that there are ideas that help us put things in order so that they can be thought about and talked about and learned about.

And so we are just learning that every time parents take a minute to listen, or to explain how something works or why something happens, every time parents stop to ask a question, it means that a child is seeing something new. He is understanding something he didn't see before, finding out, putting things together, and at the same time he feels so very good inside about someone thinking he is important enough to listen to. He is learning that big people are there to give him love and time and information and some rules for him to use when he comes up against a problem. Then he gets the feeling that school will be fun, a place to work and play and learn, because his parents—those so important big people in his life—think school is a good idea and they're with him.

All these things that very young children need to learn may seem very simple, but they are really very big ideas. And big ideas take a long, long time, and lots and lots of practice with little pieces of them, over and over, before they really take hold.

That's why it's so important to see that Head Start is just a six-week beginning in working with ideas that take years to really understand. So please remember, it's just a beginning. Don't worry if your child is not rattling off colors or pointing out shapes at the drop of a hat. Just remember how long it takes us big people to learn something new!

And don't worry if your kindergarten teacher continues to work in this kind of way on these kinds of learnings. She is picking up where Head Start leaves off. She will know what your child needs much better now that we've had a six-week chance to get to know each special child, and because you now know how important it is to a teacher to be given the chance to share what you know about your child. She needs to learn what you know. Then she will understand when he is ready to move on to the next step in learning. How fast he goes doesn't matter. What is important is that he masters each step along the way. It is much easier to climb up a ladder when you can step firmly on each rung along the way. It is very hard to climb up a ladder when the rungs are missing or so loose they don't hold you up when you need them. How fast he climbs it is not important—how solid the rungs are makes the difference.

I think we saw something else very important. Children can learn two ways of doing things, the ways that work for them at home *and* the ways that make learning easier at school, just as children can learn two languages, the one that works just fine at home, and the standard English we use for teaching and learning in school.

You know, sometimes parents are really put on the spot. Sometimes we find it hard to smile sweetly when our children come home from school and tell us we're not saying things right, or we're not doing things the way the teacher says things are done in school. But we do have a choice about what we do when we feel put on the spot. We *can* tell our children to run along and mind their own business, but deep inside we know this doesn't help them walk that important bridge between our ways and the school way. Our children will be part of that way much more than we ever were. So maybe we can tell our four- and five-year-old that we're glad he's learning school language. We want him to know them both, and they're both important. We parents have to feel good about our own ways, and be glad our children are learning to handle school ways at the same time. It's a hard job, but it's worth it if it helps our kids bring the two ways together and make them work for them.

There are other ways that home and school are sometimes different. At home, children fight a lot. That's the way they often work things out with their brothers and sisters and the neighbor children. But at school, if they are fighting all the time, there's no time left for learning, so in school they learn to use words to solve problems.

Homes are noisy places, so our children often learn to tune out the noise because it is too much to keep in one head. But in school, you know how important being able to listen is; so in school, they learn how to tune in.

At home, big people have lots of other things on their mind besides children, so children don't always turn to adults to explain things. But in school they need to see the adult as a person who guides their learning. Now what we've seen this summer is that when the home and the school understand each other better, understand each other's job and each other's problems, these two ways can really come together a lot. Teachers can really try to understand some of the problems parents face and use that understanding to make school more in tune with what children already know. Parents can understand what the school is trying to do and find so many ways to help them do it.

That's the greatest thing about Head Start—it brings everybody together to work on making life better for children and families. People from all over the state—school people, community action people, just people—got together. They think differently about some things, but they forgot that and worked all Spring and Summer to see that the Head Start programs were as good as they could be; that the children had the happiest, growingest time they could; that parents really felt it was their program and would pitch in and make it work. And it's only when parents and schools find ways to work together, not just in Head Start, but in kindergarten in the Fall and all the way through school; not just in school, but in all the community's needs, that we can all do the job we want to do. That job is to raise children into the kind of adults this battered old world needs, tomorrow's adults, able to love and learn and solve their problems in peace and good will. Now you know, and the schools know, what we mean when we say:

> *You are important to your child*
> *You know many things you can teach him*
> *You can talk about all these things with him*
> *This means he will do better in school*

Remember, whether it's Head Start or regular school or something that needs doing in our community, we can make it work if we all use what we already know, and get in there and help. Your Head Start program worked—because of you.

IMPLICATIONS FOR METHOD:
A DEMONSTRATION PROGRAM

There are many programs in process throughout the country that focus on providing parents with specific skills for enabling their children's learning.* While there are programs aimed at more generalized learning goals (child-rearing methods, child growth and development, family relationships our present concern is with the explicit goal of increasing parents' awareness of and competence in their teaching role. Programs differ in method, some dealing on a one-to-one basis with parents, others working with parents in

* See section on Low-Income Parent Education Methods in Selected Bibliography.

groups. Programs differ in personnel, some using teachers, social workers, or psychologists as the enabling agent; others involving paraprofessionals under supervision.

There is one interesting difference in program goals that might be noted in evaluating programs that "teach parents to teach their children." The focus of the learning approach is not so much to "train" parents to "teach" in the formal, sit-down-and-get-to-it sense. It is fare aimed more at providing parents with an understanding of what a child needs to learn and how he learns it, of the learning potential in a wide range of available learning experiences, of how to bring this experience to the child and to mediate between the child and his experience so that it is meaningful to him. In other words, our goal is to enable the parent to see himself as a teacher of his child, as an interpreter of the world around his child, as a provider of experience in a broader sense than the capacity to conduct a specific teaching task. Although it may seem a trivial distinction, there is a qualitative difference between the parental message "This is how to put a puzzle together," and "Let me help you fit this experience into what you already know, so that you can learn from it."

THE LOS ANGELES PARENT-PRESCHOOL CHILD PROGRAM

The Parent-Preschool Child project, a federally funded program administered by the Parent Education section of the Los Angeles Public Schools Adult Education Division, began in 1963 and ran for four years. The project ended because its unique format did not fit the requirements of funding agencies, and exhaustive efforts to secure other funding failed. The impact of institutional rigidity on the task of generating new programs made the success of this program remarkable. In spite of inherent operational difficulties, the program's success reaffirmed its original premises and the experience provides some valuable lessons.

Rationale

The program assumed that a deep sense of alienation from the mainstream of life with resultant feelings of anonymity and worthlessness, and the overwhelming problems of an impoverished existence made it difficult for poor parents to perceive and feel competent in the teaching role that most middle class parents assume. It was believed that parents in disadvantaged areas were interested in their children's school success and would respond to programs offering them skills in enabling this success.

Objectives, generally, were (1) to develop an awareness of the effect of parent attitudes on children's behavior; (2) to increase understanding of parental skills in guiding children; and (3) to increase knowledge of community resources to strengthen family life.

Specific teaching goals for parents were (1) to support and strengthen their many strengths; (2) to nurture a sense of their own worth as individuals, parents, and citizens; (3) to increase their perception of their children's learning process and their skill in enhancing it; and (4) to provide an experiential basis for stronger home-school relations.

Specific goals for the children were (1) to increase the child's range of experience; (2) to increase ability to communicate and use adults as sources of information; (3) to increase ability to conceptualize and to develop perceptual skills; (4) to increase ability to listen in a sustained and involved manner; (5) to increase the child's sense of self-worth; (6) to develop an interest in learning and to exert initiative in the learning process; (7) to establish expectations of reward from learning and task completion; and (8) to begin to handle emotions in positive, constructive ways.

Program Design

This project provided classes for parents and their preschool children in the designated poverty areas of the Los Angeles School Districts. One certificated parent educator was assigned to each class. Classes met one morning a week for three hours, except for three classes for Spanish-speaking families, which were extended to two days a week to more adequately meet language needs. Parent and child attended classes together. Each session provided both a varied program of activities for the children and a parent discussion session. Teachers worked with the children as a demonstration for the parents, and in discussion groups with parents to clarify the needs of children and parents' role in meeting those needs. As parents' knowledge and skill increased, they worked with the children and discussed this experience with their peers and the teacher.

COMMUNITY DEVELOPMENT

For each three-hour-class, the teacher was assigned an additional two hours for working with community agencies. Along with time for recruiting and sustaining class membership, work with community agencies was essential. Careful interpretation of goals, methods, and approach of this project to agency personnel and community leaders often meant the difference between success and failure—the agencies served as a further source of recruitment. In addition, the teacher's intimate knowledge of the agencies that touch the lives of the parent group deepened both her understanding and her effectiveness.

Community organization concepts were foreign to many of the parent educators. In-service training helped teachers see the task and the techniques involved, and all teachers evidenced growth in skill and enthusiasm for this aspect of their job.

RECRUITMENT

Recruitment in middle class communities is handled simply by printed brochures distributed by the adult schools. Classes are well-established and have a long community history; waiting lists are common. Moving into low income areas necessitated different methods. Simple, easy-to-read flyers were distributed by teachers and currently enrolled class members through all available community outlets. Random home visits were tried with little success. Particularly in housing projects, residents seemed negatively predisposed toward any agency personnel. Teachers felt they were invading privacy. Home visits were limited to people who expressed interest or to new residents referred by housing project offices. Posters, often bilingual, were used. News releases in papers favored by the local community and radio publicity proved effective. Teachers discovered the places where mothers and young children congregated and talked casually about the class. They spoke to PTAs, community organizations, and agency staff meetings. Word-of-mouth proved most effective, in particular when class members began to assume responsibility for involving others in the class. As the teacher became known in the community, mothers sought her out. As she attended coordinating council meetings, she developed relationships with key agency personnel and community leaders that led to sustained support and liaison between class and community.

Sustaining Attendance

Regular attendance is vital to any learning process. Parents of young children have limited time. In low income areas, many have large families, no help, many responsibilities, and inadequate means of transportation. Regular and prompt attendance is often not part of the pattern. Illnesses are frequent. There is often intermittent employment, frequent pregnancy, insufficient clothing. Mothers receiving public assistance usually stay home the day the check arrives. Clinic appointments involving long waiting periods conflict with class time. After a break, it often takes special effort to reestablish attendance. Despite these hardships, there was a developing pattern of regular attendance. Several factors seemed to account for this.

Rapport between teacher and student. The initial and continuing relationship between teacher and each mother was vital to attendance. Making each student feel important called for teachers who were friendly and outgoing, who had a sense of humor, and were deeply interested in and respected people. Speaking to each mother individually each day, greeting her upon arrival with warmth, wise use of the physical surroundings to provide a welcoming atmosphere, were obviously important. Teachers scheduled home visits to new students to complete the orientation and increase rapport with mother and child. An experienced mother was often assigned as hostess to a new student for the first few times. Mothers learned that the student who comes the second or third time usually does not drop out and made reception of new members a group concern. Continuous open enrollment was the rule.

Unconditional acceptance. Teachers quickly learned to establish a "come as you are" atmosphere, and to drop previous "professional" behaviors in favor of casual relating on a more equal basis, indicating their common concerns and feelings. Mothers were helped to feel they did not need to accept the teacher's ideas, that they could comfortably disagree and still maintain a good relationship. The teacher's warm and consistent acceptance of the children was particularly important.

Persistent reaching out. Postcards, phone calls, and visits by the teacher and class members helped absentees bridge the gap back to class. Informing mothers of topics up for discussion or special projects for the children helped. Involving class members in planning for coming events, parties, trips, speakers, films, workshops, demonstrations, and sharing sessions sustained attendance and developed group cohesion.

Class credit. For those students without a high school diploma, credit could be obtained with 80 percent attendance. This motivated mothers to begin working toward completion of an interrupted high school education.

Teachers

Twenty-two certificated parent educators were involved in the project, with experience in low income areas varying from none to three years. General monthly in-service sessions dealt with deepening understanding of goals and skills in parent education. Sessions for project teachers specifically focused on understanding the nature of poverty, curriculum planning, federal programs in the district, community resources, referral methods, and sharing experience.

The teaching task required not only the skills of leading group discussions and working with young children, but an understanding of the learning styles of both parents and children in disadvantaged communities. Teachers' experience was often limited. This meant they were often faced with alien child-rearing and behavioral patterns. They often had to absorb considerable initial hostility and to overcome distrust. They felt they were seen as outsiders, or feared as authority figures. In anticipation of variable culture shock, mental health consultation groups (see Chapter 4, pp. 131–34) were available on a voluntary, free basis. Thirteen of the twenty-two teachers participated in these groups, working through these feelings and strengthening their effectiveness with the student group. For most teachers, the experience was rewarding. They grew in knowledge, understanding, and respect for the strengths of the poor. Conviction about the validity of the program led many to delay accepting other assignments until it was certain the program would not be continued.

Teacher Aides

Although an integral part of the funded program, the provision of teacher aides from the community was only partially and sporadically fulfilled. Agencies assigned to supply aides were not always able to do so. Where aides were used in classes, they were invaluable. Their knowledge of the community and relationship to it provided insights for the teacher and increased the ease of the class members. The learnings for both teacher and aide as they worked through their new relationship were extensive. Only three of the twenty-five aides were judged unsatisfactory. In-service training, essential to ongoing development, is a needed component. When funds for aides were unavailable, volunteers from more advantaged communities were substituted. While they served the classes effectively, the presence of a community-based person added an essential dimension to class process.

Advisory Committees

An overall project advisory committee helped determine participant needs, reactions to programs, and directions for growth. Committee composition included two teachers, one representative of a community agency, an elementary school principal, a prekindergarten teacher, fourteen class members, a PTA president from a participating school, and a teacher aide. The committee's concerted efforts to enable the program were cut short by the withdrawal of funding, but this kind of objective evaluation by a group that combines both the serving agency and those served provides a meaningful structure for keeping a program on its course.

Children's Program and Progress

Although the prime goal of the children's program was the provision of concrete demonstrations of methods and materials for parental observation, the experience had some impact on the children. The equipment, nature, and range of experiences and materials was as rich and broad as funding and teacher innovation would allow. All the traditional activities of a good preschool program were furnished with a deliberate focus on activities that would clearly demonstrate to parents the specific learning for children in both the way the children used the experiences and in the way in which the teacher used the learning situation.

As a result of a well-planned and stimulating program, the children showed considerable growth. They developed greater facility with language; their increased self-confidence and desire to reach out to new experiences was evident. Non-English-speaking children learned some English and were able to function in English-speaking groups. Children developed a sense of satisfaction in finishing tasks, asked more questions, learned to enjoy books, and considerably lengthened their attention span in a wide range of activities. They communicated more easily with the teacher, other children, and adults, and mothers reported a higher level of communication at home. They grew less dependent upon parents in many ways, learned to share and take turns, to handle routines, and to find comfort in the life of the group. Increased capacity to deal with concepts, to recognize colors and shapes, to differentiate sounds, to recall, to be aware of relationships between events were observed. The children seemed friendlier and increasingly trustful of adults.

Parents' Program and Progress

Observation of children's program. Parents had an opportunity to see, do, and discuss under the guidance of the teacher, giving them a chance to test out new behaviors in a safe setting. The feeling that parent and child were learning together reinforced parental motivation to continue these new behaviors in the home. Concrete observations of how children learned coupled with clear explanations of the meaning of that learning made sense to mothers unused to dealing with abstract ideas. Once the learning involved in the activity was understood, mothers could find that learning potential readily available in a wide range of experiences at little or no cost. They responded to those activities and interests that they could most comfortably handle on their own, and were supported by the teacher at each step. They began to see meaning in helping children learn to help themselves, in providing a pleasant atmosphere for routine family activities, in the value of rest, in the meaning of order and routine. The teacher tried to be aware of life situations where following through was too difficult, and she tried to support what was possible for the mother. There was relaxation in inhibiting children's involvement with materials, particularly when mothers experimented with those materials first in their own group sessions. There was a diminution of yelling at children and an increase in quiet conversation and the proclivity to listen. Mothers reported increased enjoyment in their relationships with their children, and a wider range of interaction. They read to their children, used the libraries, and involved husbands in reading and listening to their children.

Use of the group experience. Group discussion went beyond the children's program, once the group became comfortable with the teacher and each other. The teacher's role in these programs involved enabling the wide spectrum of parental concerns to become available for group discussion. While in middle class communities, parents easily verbalize their concerns so that the teacher can readily provide the content and structure that fosters maximum individual growth, teachers found this process initially hard for poor parents. They found they needed to more specifically initiate topics and to employ a wider variety of approaches until sufficient trust and mutual respect developed to enable parents to assume increasing responsibility for determining the direction of discussion. Beginning sessions were related to routines of the children's program because parent participation in these routines were necessary for the smooth functioning of the class. A good learning environment required this minimal involvement. Teachers learned that involvement comes slowly for the organizationally inexperienced mother, and sometimes found they could only enrich the children's program as the mothers' understanding of its meaning grew, and thus their motivation to participate.

Teachers also quickly faced the impact of differential socioeconomic and cultural patterns on attitudes and values as they moved into the usual areas of parental concern. In the area of discipline, particularly, teachers sharpened their skills in accepting attitudes counter to their own and found more effective ways of raising alternatives without imposing upon or negating individual integrity. Focusing on the parent's feeling about the discipline she received from her own parents often led the parent to consider whether she wanted her child to feel that way. Discussing children's responses to teacher's approaches, while at the same time recognizing the different pressures on parents, helped mothers see a broader range of alternative behaviors. Participating in the children's program allowed mothers to test these behaviors on other children before they decided to make any changes in the patterns they had established in their own homes.

Parents frequently raised the topic of the effect of their child's friends and neighborhood children on his behavior. This was a source of great anxiety particularly among those living in congested areas and housing projects. Teachers provided opportunity for discussion, sharing concerns, role-playing, approaching other mothers to get a greater neighborhood consensus, experience in relating to other children, and airing feelings aroused when other mothers disciplined or criticized one's own children. Teachers were also quick to indicate their awareness that this did not solve a multifaceted problem, but that both greater security in what they believed right for their own children and increased skills in communicating with others did provide some tools.

How to control television-watching was a question frequently raised by mothers. They viewed the problem in the usual context of a power struggle. Teachers attempted variously to minimize any guilt regarding the use of television as a respite from children, helped them find ways to use what the children watched as a learning experience, and enabled group discussion of other kinds of activities that would move children away from constant TV viewing and still allow mothers some free time.

The mother as a home manager was a comfortable and favored topic, an area where many had real competencies to share. Areas of further interest were easily and unthreateningly expanded through use of outside speakers and resources. Increased skill in home management led to discussion of how to use the resultant increase in free time.

Mothers responded with enthusiasm to a focus on education and more skillful relating to schools. Fear of school personnel, personal experiences of school failure, lack of know-how for approaching teachers all contributed to the negative attitude low income mothers often pass on to their children as they prepare them for school. However, as a school-based program, the project class provided a real springboard for attitude change in this area. Local school personnel came into the classes, the meaning of parent-teacher contact was discussed, parents role-played parent-teacher conferences, and many parents were able to initiate satisfying meetings with teachers of their older children. Parents visited kindergarten classes with their children, discussed these experiences in the group, related their observations to their own learnings, and generally felt more at ease with a previously overwhelming institution. Some parents were moved to join PTAs and take active roles.

Discussion of health needs and services, presented largely by resource persons, varied in its impact, depending on the speaker. Parents were able to discuss their fears and mistrust of preventive measures and health departments and delineate the real difficulties in obtaining adequate service. In some instances, the teacher attempted to relay this to the agency. In other instances, group discussion enabled hesitant mothers to seek immunization. Planned Parenthood representatives were well received, particularly in Negro communities. Religious controversy needs to be understood and clearly verbalized and accepted. Class members struggled with the question of discussing contraception with their teenage daughters. Teachers, as in most other areas, could only present the range of alternatives and encourage individual decision-making. Sex education proved to be an area where the differential backgrounds of teacher and students made the teacher hesitant to deeply explore the question. Books, pamphlets, and reference materials were found somewhat wanting, and teachers expresesd need for more realistic materials.

The question of prejudice arose frequently, specifically and in the course of other discussions. How to help children develop self-pride and hang onto it in the face of discrimination was the subject of solid and concerned discussion, once the teacher was trusted. Experiences were shared, materials explored for their negative and positive attributes. Discussion of the impact of the civil rights and protest movements on feelings about self, ways of relating this impact to children, and their ideas about the future were lively.

Use of community resources, both to meet needs and to enrich family life, was an area of considerable interest and growth. Guiding this use enables parents to feel more part of a community, discover resources for one's own family, be able to help others in a crisis situation, and be better prepared to handle one's own crises.

The development of children's self-confidence proved a particularly meaningful area of discussion when parents' own growth in understanding and skill could be clearly demonstrated. The parent's feelings of satisfaction with his increased competence was directly related to how his children feel when they learn and are rewarded for that learning, both intrinsically and by the outside world. Focusing observations on concrete examples of children's growth in self-esteem makes this a vivid learning experience for parents.

Use of field trips and discovering the learning inherent in them and the ways to interpret the learning to their children proved extremely valuable. These experiences initiated a large increase in family activities and provided much material for sharing within the group.

Mothers did not express much interest in such topics as feeding problems, children's attitudes toward money and material possessions, or the abstract exploration of teaching values to children. Teachers recognized their own problems in these areas, the need to evaluate their relative meaning and, where relevant, the need to find entry into the subject that is meaningful and visible to mothers.

Obviously, topics generating from the mothers themselves were of greatest interest. Good visual aids, workshop sessions with demonstration and student participation, buzz groups, community events, and personal experiences all amplified the impact of discussions. Teacher-prepared materials, describing a typical situation and offering several alternatives for action, stimulated good discussion. Mothers' growing ability to record observations and use them as discussion material developed in many classes. Teacher verbalization of what the group meant to the individual mother and each one's contribution to the group enhanced relationships and class participation. Parents steadily grew in their ability to express themselves, to consider alternatives, to apply problem-solving techniques to situations as they arose. There was a growth in community involvement, as their in-group organizational experience gave them confidence. Some of the mothers participated in community service projects; others returned to school. When classes were discontinued, large numbers protested to the Board of Education, with articulate descriptions of the gains accrued from participation.

Some Learnings about Method

The group.   The value of the group process is doubly meaningful with parents who feel inadequate in meeting the standards of middle class articulateness, who have strong feelings of mistrust in the efficacy of talk, and who are often loathe to express real feelings in the one-to-one relationship with anyone outside their daily world. Talking informally with one's peers is more in tune with what comes naturally. Common concerns and the stimulus of more verbal parents makes words available and feelings expressible. "The give and take of group membership, the sharing of experiences and the spontaneity of feelings provide the parent with a context in which he can be himself. . . ." [31] The strength and encouragement that parents get from each other as they share experiences and support each other's growth is vital to the learning process. The group atmosphere lets the teacher reduce the role distance through greater informality, easy banter, humor. There is greater chance to establish rapport on a nonverbal level in warm, concerned group discussion. There is a more flexible structure than within the one-to-one relationship for down-to-earth, action-oriented, problem-centered discussion, that combines the thinking and feeling of many people with a common interest. In a group, it is possible for the teacher to temporarily ignore a clear lack of motivation on the part of some members of the group and to concentrate on making the learning so relevant to those who are motivated that the spirit is contagious and movement occurs. With or without the base of an observation-participation experience with their children, there is evidence that the satisfactions parents find in the "family" of the group sustain attendance.

One of the most important factors in the meaning of the group experience for low income mothers particularly is the break it provides in the drudgery and monotony of daily life. If it is a warm and welcoming setting, if there is a level of fun and excitement in the process, the group meeting often becomes the one time eagerly looked forward to by mothers, particularly if there are provisions for child care either in an organized program or supervised by volunteers.

Parents need to know what to expect. It is imperative that teachers immediately provide parents with a clear, concrete grasp of why they are there, what will happen, how it will happen and—depending on agency procedure—the understanding that there will be no long-term demands for involvement. A teacher stating at the start, "You know many things you can teach your children so they will do better in school," presenting an example she knows will clearly demonstrate this premise, and reinforcing this successful effort will move much farther than the teacher who gives a polysyllabic lecture. This may seem an obvious point, but the skill with which middle class–based teachers can put ideas into informal language is often sorely wanting, and is a key area for teacher training.

A concrete demonstration of group procedure can then move, with the support of appropriate visual aids, into an exploration of the learning value to children of many experiences, and into the clarification of parental skill in uncovering that learning and making it available to children. This process depends entirely on the teacher's conception of the range of possibilities, on the facilities available for parent observation and participation, and on community resources. The important factor is making clear and known what was diffuse and unknown, so that expectations are in line with what will actually happen and not more or less than parents feel they can or want to handle.

The time element is important. Parents not used to committing themselves for indefinite periods or to regular demands often need to be assured that classes will not go on forever. Teachers can set a minimum number of meetings, leaving the decision to extend the sessions to the parents themselves. Classes established within the structure of school programs, on a semester or year basis, continue to meet, and the satisfactions of having sustained one's own endeavor over a long period of time are many. There are also values in discovering for oneself the joy of learning, and in making the commitment to additional effort on a personal or group basis.

Parents' learning style. There is general agreement that educationally unsophisticated people find some ways of learning more meaningful than others. Generalizations suggest that they are more action-oriented than verbal; extrospective than introspective; oriented toward problem and symptom rather than inner change; relatively unimaginative; more spontaneous than reflective.[32] These conclusions have had resounding and positive implications on the reassessment of teaching techniques for all educative processes, forcing teachers to break down their material into discrete learning steps, place these steps in some sequence, and thus make learning more meaningful to any learner, regardless of previous experience.

The appeal to make learning functional, relate it to immediate concern, show clearly how and why it can be used in daily life is an important guideline.[33] A child needs to know one shape from another. Why? Because it helps him tell one letter from another, for instance. Yes, but that learning comes later, why do we need to worry about it now? Because it takes him thousands of related experiences to learn and we have to start now. Here, start with this book, this cup, that ice cream cone. What are the shapes? Where else can you find them? Everywhere! The kindergarten teacher will ask Johnny to put his finger on the square. But what if he doesn't know what a square is? Children need lots of time, lots of different chances to deal with an idea. Where's he going to get those chances? From you, his best teacher. What shapes did you find just in the kitchen this week? Did you know you had so many? It helps to look through different eyes at the things around us.

Concrete examples, vivid and striking, clearly illustrating only what the teacher is working on, visual and readily available, are essential tools. Teachers need to search for visual aids that do not incorporate too many other concepts until parents have the essential ideas clearly in mind. Some of the teaching techniques developed by Bereiter and Engelmann [34] are invaluable: i.e., children need to learn one color clearly before another is introduced; or it is more feasible to teach the concepts of short and tall specifically before being concerned with the more complex concepts of shorter and taller.

Teachers need to focus on uncluttered ideas, disregarding nuances, relativities, and subtleties until people are ready. Solid understanding allows the teacher to take thoroughly mastered concepts one step further.

The need for action in the learning process is just as important for parents as it is for children. The task is raised; materials searched; ideas jelled; materials made, their uses role-played, their effects discussed. Parents demonstrate how they handle situations with their children. Trips are taken to put people into learning situations, to make new observations, to approach experiences from new viewpoints. The sessions are flexibly programmed to allow for physical movement, such as active games to be used with children or taught to older siblings to use with the young.

The appeal for sequential presentation of material has been made before, not just in the simple-to-complex order of material, but within the nature of the material itself. A simple puzzle can illustrate graphically for parents the need for perceptual-motor skills, how a child has to learn to talk silently to himself, or what kinds of questions from the mother help a child learn to think through the task. But it can also be used for counting, ordinal counting, developing language discriminating shapes, color, size, position. Each teaching tool contains its own potential, often more fully available to understanding if one starts first with the simplest idea involved.

Reinforcement.   There are two dimensions of this teaching tool to consider here: it helps parents learn; and parents can in turn learn to use it meaningfully as they relate to their children.

When teachers reinforce parent behaviors and responses, they often say they feel phony constantly telling mothers "that's really good," until such a response to each small increment of growth comes to be genuinely felt. Once the experience of the group solidifies, the teacher can pick up on this with parents. "How did you feel when Mrs. Jones told you that was well done? Did it make you want to work at it harder?" This feeling, once recognized, can be related to dealing with children, and the concept of reinforcement can be nurtured, explored, tested, evaluated just as other learnings are. "Why do we recognize positive behavior? Because children need to feel good about themselves and to want to try. How do they learn that? By trying and finding it good—over and over and over."

Another aspect of reinforcement is the continual coming back to old ideas and applying them in different ways. We discussed it in terms of learning to broaden one's range of alternatives for viewing the potential learning in any one material or experience. It is also important in terms of holding on to new learning, and making it constantly available to be applied to new situations.

Broadening the focus. There will be few sessions where the opportunity to pick up on a mother's comment about her child and broaden the discussion range beyond enabling specific cognitive learnings will not be there. The teacher needs to gauge the readiness of the group to examine what the child is learning in experiences less concretely related to school. After the group climate is secure, and mothers feel successful in new areas of competence, they are far more able to look at areas around which there is more anxiety, particularly if attention on the subject is sustained. "What is the child learning? What do you want him to learn? We know something about how children learn. When you decide something is important for a child to learn, how do we go about teaching him? What kinds of experiences does he need? How do you feel about that? Play out that idea. Does it work? Does it feel right? We usually have to poke around in these things longer than simpler things like learning numbers. Jot down how often that happens and tell us about it next week."

Sometimes the teacher may need to limit the range of areas raised at any one time. Randomness and disorganization are often part of a parental pattern, and the group is a valid base for getting some grasp of "If we do this first, we can pay more attention to that next." The teacher's skill in drawing the group back to salient points without shutting out anyone's contribution is important. Here is where her ability to confer quickly with individual parents, around the periphery of the group, can allow recognition and support for feelings that don't get dealt with directly in the group.

In general, the teaching task is not too difficult for the teacher who has a zest for her job, likes to relate openly, teach dramatically, and get her students deeply involved in doing. For teachers working in settings where home visits or individual contact is the rule, the principles are essentially the same, though she will need to function without the sustaining, stimulating interaction that the group provides.

The teacher working with parents of older children will need to apply her understanding of age-level learning processes to the finding of those areas where she can dramatically demonstrate the impact of parental teaching, and then move with a learning focus into broader areas of parent-child relationships.

The Broader Goal of Competent Citizenship

A most exciting implication of the Head Start movement and other antipoverty programs that begin with parents' concern for their children is the development of parent groups that take an active, aggressive role in their community. Project Enable [35] is a noteworthy example of the integration of the goal of community participation into the conceptualization of programs for parents. Many groups, beginning with a focus on the preschool program itself, have moved into taking collective action in community concerns, with edifying results. Parent groups have taken effective action on questions of community services, and community organization and structure. Such action has generated from the experience of working together on a common task. The management of a preschool program provides experience in basic organization skills, in interpersonal relations, and in the awareness of the power of collective action and the perception of self as having power to affect the larger community. To see such learning as a valid outgrowth of programs for parental involvement is important for program planners. Parents who use the parent group experience as a learning place for more effective involvement in what happens to them as people are parents who set a clear model for their children's conceptualization of what it means to be an adult.

SUMMARY

There are many questions to consider in the development of parent education programs for families who live in poverty or near-poverty. The conditions of life generate behaviors that enable the poor to cope with their reality, and there is valid concern that educative efforts not be intrusive.

Yet there is also the reality that the poor value education for their children. Many parents in poor communities respond to programs that direct their attention to the gaining of skills to help their children, without demanding, however subtly, the rejection of all that their experience has taught them. People without power, without a voice in society, may find value in programs that make what they already know visible to them and available for increased facility in their parental and community roles. We can help parents to more competently enable their children's development without imposing irrelevant behavioral standards.

An attempt is made to delineate how the learning-valuing focus and the use of the group discussion method can sharpen program direction and maintain harmony with reality problems. An approach that presents alternatives and fosters individual decision-making may nurture adults' facility to make more effective use of what we hope will be a widening range of choice.

REFERENCES

1. Suzanne Keller, *The American Lower Class Family*. New York: New York State Division for Youth, 1966. P. 2.
2. Elizabeth Herzog, *About the Poor: Some Facts and Some Fictions*, Publication No. 451. Washington, D.C.: Children's Bureau, 1967. P. 39.
3. Keller, *Lower Class Family*, p. 2.
4. *Ibid.*, p. 5.
5. *Ibid.*, p. 72.
6. Lois Barclay Murphy, "Child Development, Then and Now," *Childhood Education* (January 1968), p. 305.
7. Keller, *Lower Class Family*, p. 73.
8. Catherine S. Chilman, *Growing Up Poor*, Publication No. 13. Washington, D.C.: U.S. Department of Health, Education and Welfare, Welfare Administration, Division of Research, May 1966.
9. *Ibid.*, pp. 35–36.
10. Murphy, "Child Development," pp. 304–305.
11. Keller, *Lower Class Family*, p. 75.
12. Melvin Kohn, "Social Class and Parental Values," *American Journal of Sociology*, Vol. 64 (January 1959), pp. 337–351.
13. Fred Strodtbeck, "The Hidden Curriculum in the Middle Class Home." In C. W. Hunnicutt (Ed.) *Urban Education and Cultural Deprivation*. Syracuse: Syracuse School of Education, 1964.
14. Robert D. Hess, "Educability and Rehabilitation: The Future of the Welfare Class," *Journal of Marriage and the Family*, Vol. 26 (November 1964), pp. 421–429.
15. Basil Bernstein, "Social Class and Linguistic Development, A Theory

of Social Learning." In A. H. Halsey, Jean Floud, and C. A. Anderson (Eds.), *Education, Economy and Society*. New York: The Free Press of Glencoe, 1961.

16. Carl Bereiter and Sigfried Engelmann, *Teaching Disadvantaged Children in the Preschool*. New York: Prentice-Hall, 1966.

17. Margaret Faust, "What is a Good Program for Economically Deprived Young Children," *California Journal for Instructional Improvement*, Vol. 8, No. 4 (December 1965).

18. Thomas R. Ford, "Value Orientations of a Culture of Poverty: The Southern Appalachian Case," *Working with Low-Income Families*. Washington, D.C.: American Home Economics Association, 1965.

19. *Ibid.*

20. Herzog, *About the Poor*, p. 8.

21. *Ibid.*

22. Hylan Lewis, "Child Rearing Practices Among Low Income Families in the District of Columbia." Unpublished paper presented at the National Conference on Social Welfare, May 16, 1961. Mimeo.

23. Personal correspondence with Mrs. Norma Radin, Research Coordinator, Ypsilanti Public Schools. Ypsilanti, Michigan, January 23, 1967.

24. *Ibid.*

25. Morris Smilansky, "Fighting Deprivation in the Promised Land," *Saturday Review of Literature* (October 15, 1966), p. 87.

26. Keller, *Lower Class Family*, p. 3.

27. Eleanor Pavenstadt, "A Comparison of the Child-rearing Environments of Upper-lower and Very Low-lower Class Families," *American Journal of Orthopsychiatry*, Vol. 35 (January 1965), pp. 89–98.

28. Warren C. Haggstrom, "Poverty and Adult Education," *Adult Education* (Spring 1965), pp. 145–160.

29. *Ibid.*

30. Ralph Ellison (quoted without reference) in Don D. Bushnell, "The Educational Advantages of the Poor," *Audio-Visual Instructor*, Vol. 12, No. 1 (January 1968), pp. 24–27.

31. Vincent Calia, "The Culturally Deprived Client: A Reformulation of the Counselor's Role," *Journal of Counseling Psychology*, Vol. 13 (January 1966).

32. Robert E. Gould, "Dr. Strangeclass: Or How I Stopped Worrying About the Theory and Began Treating the Blue Collar Worker," *American Journal of Orthopsychiatry* (January 1967).

33. Walter G. Daniel, "Some Essential Ingredients in Educational Programs for Socially Disadvantaged." In Jerome Hellmuth (Ed.) *Disadvantaged Child*, Vol. I. Seattle: Special Child Publications, 1967.

34. Bereiter and Engelmann, *Teaching Disadvantaged Children*.

35. "Project Enable," *Social Casework*, Vol. 48, No. 10 (Dec. 1967).

7

Fostering Parental Competence
in Other Settings

Thus far we have considered the learning-valuing focus for parent education in such settings as child observation groups, Head Start programs, and discussion groups with parents of preschool children. Here we consider the efficacy of this approach in (1) other settings that reach preschool children and their families; (2) programs dealing with the concerns of parents with older children; and (3) concerned with preparing young people for parenthood.

OTHER PROGRAMS FOR PARENTS OF PRESCHOOL CHILDREN

Defining "preschool child" in the broadest terms, from conception to kindergarten entry, we find a wide range of settings where parents can be involved in educational programs, or can be approached from an educative stance.

PARENTS OF INFANTS

Both theoretical and applied research verifies the hypothesis that, particularly for the very disadvantaged, to start enriching the stimulation and mediation level of experience at three and one

half or four years may well be too late. Helping parents conceptualize their teaching role is imperative in meaningful remediative
efforts with the poor. Indeed, if advantaged parents could more
clearly perceive the depth of experience they could provide their
children from the beginning, we might yield a generation of children who are more creative, freely exploring, and competent than
our children generally are now.

Classes for expectant parents need not focus only on the
physical management and emotional needs of infants. Projects concerned with the intellectual stimulation of infants are yielding
much pertinent information that can help parents gain skill in
their teaching role from the moment of their child's birth. Well-
baby clinics are ideal for concientiously integrating parent education into the overall approach of clinic staff in every formal and
informal contact with parents. Public health nurses, with broad
access to parents with newborn children, are a rich resource for
this kind of orientation. Pediatricians, by far the largest group of
"parent educators," need to understand more completely the role
of the parent in fostering growth and development. Some forward-
thinking pediatricians have employed social workers as members of
their professional team to deal more skillfully with parents' problems. If the parental teaching role were the take-off point for working with parents in this setting, more long-range movement might
take place.

DAY CARE CENTERS

Day care centers, the most rapidly growing area of facilities,
are being supported on a national level. There are realistic problems in attempting to work in structured and regularly scheduled
ways with working parents. Their time, energy, and availability is
limited, even though they are interested. Flexible and innovative
programming, socially oriented events to offer some relief to stress-
ful home routines, effective use of the quick, informal conference
as children are delivered and retrieved, all provide opportunities
for supporting parents in what they do teach and in broadening
their perception of their involvement in their children's experience
and growth.

DAY CARE HOMES AND PRIVATE NURSERY SCHOOLS

Day care homes and private nursery schools are significant among services meeting the needs of working parents, but little educative service is offered to the parents themselves. Day care mothers do not see themselves as offering a professional service nor do they receive any training in dealing with parents. Public licensing agencies are understaffed and unable to offer close supervision. However, new legislation covering facilities caring for children in federally funded job-training programs now requires these day care mothers and private center personnel to upgrade their standards. Training institutions are providing courses to enrich understanding of children's needs, skills in meeting them, and skills in sustaining sound relationships with parents. Here, too, training and individual growth might be enhanced if the underlying concept of the role of the significant adult were clearly seen in terms of mediation rather than management.

COOPERATIVE NURSERY SCHOOLS

The cooperative nursery school can be an optimal setting for the learning-valuing approach to parent education, because it involves the parent so much more meaningfully in a learning-by-doing experience. Parents in this kind of preschool are not peripheral; special structures do not need to be planned for their involvement. They *are* the school and without them, nothing happens. The cooperative has tremendous value as a laboratory of adult learning, simply because it requires participation, and thus the learning process is at least assured of being launched. The group process inherent in providing a sound educational setting for children provides parents a concrete opportunity to gain knowledge and skills, clarify personal goals and values, and develop facility in group problem-solving through actual experience.

Cooperative nursery schools exist under many structures, each with their unique advantages and disadvantages. When these structures are viewed in terms of the extent to which the potential for adult learning is maximized, they form a continuum from "least" to "most" conducive to growth.

The informal cooperative, formed casually by a group of interested parents who meet in one or several backyards and led by one or more of the mothers, provides an enriched experience for children and promotes the spirit and style of cooperation within a neighborhood. The quality of the children's program and the degree of involvement and directed learning of the parents varies widely, depending solely on the awareness, sophistication, and leadership qualities within the group itself. The focus is generally on the children, rather than on adult education per se.

The formal private cooperative is formed in a structured manner by a group of interested parents who then employ a professionally trained preschool educator, and establish a specifically equipped setting for good early childhood education. It is the responsibility of the parent group to maintain that setting, pay the teacher, determine program components, participate in facilitating the curriculum as assistants to the teacher.

In many areas, representatives of local schools form councils of parent participating preschools. These councils are concerned with common problems of management, deepening parents' grasp of growth and development concepts, curriculum goals, teaching methods, and parent involvement. They often provide, through meetings, newsletters and community programs, a tie for parents to local schools, colleges, universities, and community resources and stimulate the use of these facilities for increasing understanding of family life and parent-child relationships.

While most cooperatives are formed in middle income areas, there have been some outstanding attempts to establish this kind of experience in low income areas. Some cooperatives raise scholarship funds in order to make their populations more heterogeneous; some reach for subsidization by philanthropic groups; some have entered the Head Start framework; others have a relationship with local welfare agencies so that the mother's allotment is raised to cover tuition.

For the nonworking, low income mother with little or no organizational experience, little adult association or relief from harrassing life circumstances, and a low estimate of her parental skills, the cooperative with wise guidance can be a most fertile base for growth.

For the middle class family with little exposure to people unlike themselves, little feel for other cultures and ways of life, and an inhibiting fear of the unknown, the cooperative bringing different kinds of people together to work on a common task provides a most growth-enabling structure. This dimension of learning to find oneself in other people, whatever their differences, and to make those understandings part of daily life, is probably the most urgent learning task of our times.*

The basic structures within these cooperatives vary, according to the wishes and needs of the parent group, the belief system and effectiveness of the professional teacher, and the physical settings in which they function. The status and area of professional decision-making that the teacher maintains varies with the degree of control desired by the parent group, their concept of what good preschool education is, and whether or not there is a professional teachers' organization with both a commitment to professional standards and some degree of negotiating power. The extent of parental involvement in management, and thus the extent of the learning potential for participating parents, depends upon the way in which the teacher defines her role, her leadership capacities in enabling the involvement of adults, her emphasis on parent education, the decisions of the parents as to the level of their participation, and the degree to which the group is led to learn from its own experience.

While most cooperatives provide much significant learning for both children and their parents, some structures seem to have greater potential for use of the learning experience.

Cooperatives as laboratories for adult education. In Seattle, for instance, parent cooperative preschool groups are an integral part of the adult education extension service of the Department of Family Life, Seattle Community College. Parents register for an adult course, Parent Education Child Study Laboratory, and enroll their child in the laboratory group. The teacher, hired by the group, is selected from the department's recommended list.* A Family Life Instructor is assigned to the group to supervise the

---

* An outstanding example of a consciously integrated cooperative is Heights Cooperative Nursery School, Los Angeles, California, where the mix of race, religion, economic level and cultural background forms the base of the children's curriculum and the parents contribute their unique heritage to enrich the total experience for families.

* An Early Childhood Education Degree program for the training of preschool teachers was initiated in the fall of 1967, thus enhancing the department's capacity to provide professionally trained personnel.

children's program and provide leadership for the parents' learning experience.

The college assumes responsibility for providing: (1) a rich and relevant learning environment for both parents and children, and (2) the structure essential for effective group functioning and satisfying personal growth. Parents' perceptions and expectations for the experience vary so greatly that requiring a minimum level of participation is essential to generate involvement, for only through involvement will each parent be able to decide what might be valuable to him in the experience. Thus, there are established criteria for participation, requiring parents to (1) put in assigned time in the laboratory (usually one morning a week); (2) attend monthly group meetings; (3) attend department orientation programs and workshops; and (4) meet the group-determined obligations deemed essential to individual group functioning.

So that groups can be assured of functioning within the standards of the program, exceptions to these minimum criteria are made only with the approval of the instructor. This enables the group, through the instructor, to openly confront the basic premises of the program, to be aware that they are dealing with a question of principle, and to enter into the problem-solving process fully aware of alternatives and their consequences. For example, should the group be so disgruntled with the disruptive behavior of a specific child that they were nearly unanimous in their desire to expel the family, the instructor would focus on helping the group think through what it values. If the group really feels that children need to learn how to cope with different behaviors without having accepted those behaviors for themselves, how do children learn this if their environment is relatively problem-free? Can this group accept only what is the same and comfortable or can it make room for difference? Do we help children tolerate imperfect situations and deal with them maturely when we sidestep rather than confront? This is a family with a problem. Do we have some resources we can mobilize, using the teacher, the curriculum, and sensitive, directed behavior of interested mothers, to see whether this place can be a safe and helping place for this child and his parents? What information do we need, what resources can we call on that will help us think through this problem?

This stance enables the group to face the problem, define it, raise alternatives, fully perceive the consequences, make a decision, live with it, and look at it again in terms of situational changes. This process gives parents real skills for providing a decision-making model for their own children that can be translated to the family setting. It gives them real tools for working in the community where broader choices are made.

Beyond the requirements of basic participation and the department's commitment to democratic decisions, the full range of concerns involved in the ongoing management of parent cooperatives constitute the core of the group process and are the property of the group. The instructor enables this process, insuring that the broadest range of alternatives are available, providing relevant information, and encouraging maximum involvement in decision-making. Each group is unique, and the group composition changes markedly from year to year. Policies and procedures that were facilitating to one group often prove troublesome to the next. The instructor helps the group reevaluate old decisions in terms of present realities so that children's growth, parents' concerns, and teachers' professional skills are constantly in view and goals projected more meaningfully.

There are three arenas in this program structure where program philosophy is at work: (1) in the learning environment of the laboratory; (2) in the learning environment of the parent group process; and (3) in the learning environment of the instructor's relationships with individual parents. This totality is a statement: "Here is a living demonstration of a philosophy and a way of living it out. We will define it for you and make it visible so that you can use these concepts, these values in operation, to sharpen your own beliefs through choosing to adopt, adapt, reject, or ignore what you see here." Through the teacher, the premises underlying the curriculum and the instructor's stance with the parents, the program says: "Here, in this place, we feel a child needs to learn (to trust himself and others) because this is a cornerstone for further growth. These are the learning experiences we provide to nurture this kind of growth, this kind of learning. How do *you* feel about it? How do you want to feel? Is this something you wish to take into your own belief system or would you prefer to leave it here? What do you need to know in order to make your own decision? What is the range of alternatives?

The instructor proceeds from a basic conviction that there is something to be learned in this setting; that parents will learn through involvement in the experience, and that her role is to mediate that experience with the goal of enlightened individual choice. She defines the premises of the program initially and as they are lived out on a daily basis in what both children and parents experience and in the decisions they make about that experience. She defines the learning process as it happens, helping the group spell out its questions and helping them see their own growth as they gain facility in decision-making and problem-solving. The questions she raises for the group to consider depend, of course, on the way in which she perceives what is happening. The questions she doesn't raise depend on her judgement as to the group's readiness and the direction that she feels holds priority at the moment, in terms of the growth of the group. When parents raise questions, either singly or as a group, the instructor's role is not necessarily to answer them but to (1) show the range of possible answers and how they relate to the parents' own feelings, goals, values; (2) provide a gauge for growth so that parents know they have grown not because of what experience the instructor provided, but because of the degree to which they have made their experience meaningful to themselves; (3) to find her success not in what parents decide but in the fact that they are deciding and (4) to involve herself as a participant in the process and grow with it.

One of the most fascinating dimensions of this kind of structure, making this kind of statement, is the evolving and solidifying teacher-instructor relationship. The professionals, each with his own area of concern, work toward the goal of dealing with the core philosophy so that all areas are in tune. The teacher is working toward helping children accept difference, for example, with the same grasp of program values as the instructor, who makes this kind of learning visible to parents. They are able to relate these underlying concepts to the dynamics of development, at both the child and adult level. They are making essentially the same statement, whether through the children's curriculum, response to individual children, parents' program, or a specific board meeting, so that the underlying philosophy is always brought to bear on immediate experience. This harmony is the ideal situation, of course, and comes only from effort. A department that can train both preschool personnel and family life instructors, allowing great space for individual difference within the overall premise of the program, will perhaps be able to develop the most well-integrated, learning-oriented, parent education structure.

PROGRAMS FOR PARENTS OF OLDER CHILDREN

Skillful programming to meet the full range of parental interest involves two general directions: first, programming preventively to improve the quality of family life; and second, programming in response to specific areas of immediate parental need.

PROGRAMS OF GENERAL INTEREST

In programming preventively, classes, discussion series, and informal structures are provided where parents can consider child growth and development, family relations, woman's role, home management, etc. All these topics bear on helping parents sort out their individual value system and perceive their parental role more clearly. Decisions about how to spend time, energy, and money are all value-based decisions; choices about how to arranges one's home environment to meet the unique needs of family members hinge on deciding what is most important. There is a broad range of points of entry into the wealth of content dealing with human relations, self-actualization, and the competent management of life tasks; they are all doors that lead to raising the same basic core of questions and affecting the process of individual choice. Offerings that examine literature, music, and art for the family are exciting arenas for exploration of the parent's role in his child's learning how to learn from his experience; they widen the alternatives for the value search. Even the large number of offerings commonly collected under the aegis of home economics—cooking, sewing, or decorating—all are anchored in value decisons. Content and process could be more meaningfully integrated if the instructor saw his role in fostering individual autonomy in these settings.

PROGRAMS IN RESPONSE TO SPECIFIC CONCERNS

There are four general areas into which specific concerns fall: (1) parents' need for understanding the changes in content and methodology that have taken place in the schools in order to help their children, i.e., new math and reading; (2) parents' long-range concerns about their own conflicts and anxieties and desire for help in exploring their role, i.e., sex education; (3) parents' immediate and urgent concerns, i.e., adolescents and the related questions of drugs, the "new morality," and protest movement; and (4) unique life problems, i.e., the problems of parents with handicapped children.

Parents and the Reading Skills of Children

Along with new math, the emphasis on learning to read and the changes in approach to this task have been of interest to parents. Most parents want their children to learn to read well; they know this skill is a necessary tool for achievement in our society. For a long time parents have been asking teachers "How can I help my child with his reading?" Unfortunately, for an equally long time, the answer has often been, "Leave him alone. Teachers will teach him to read. It is a very complex process and you may do the wrong thing." Fortunately, there is an encouraging awareness emerging among some educators that no matter how skillful and successful they are in teaching reading, they are not the only contributors to the process. Parents do affect their children's ability to read for better or for worse. Parents are a willing and useful resource that can and should be brought to this important task.

Lloyd's [1] attempts to involve parents in the teaching of reading are indicative of this trend. Here the program planned for education and involvement of parents is not just a public relations nicety, nor is it limited to parents of children having reading problems. "The program is designed to use this parental resource at all times for no teacher, no school, can be assured that each child is attaining his maximum growth if the extra growth possible with parent cooperation is neglected." [2] The program states that this assault has not been haphazard or opportunistic. It has not been casually optional, hoping that parents would care enough to become interested. It has been a planned development to define and to implement the parental role in the child's learning to read.

Reviews of research relative to children's reading (Bloom,[3] Della-Piana [4]) point directly to the importance of the parent-provided educational environment. Specific factors thought to affect the child are parents' aspirations for themselves and their children, language models, academic guidance, stimulation to explore the environment, intellectual interests and activities, and work habits encouraged. Correlations were highest (+80) with the tests of word knowledge and reading and lowest with spelling and arithmetic computation.[5] Couple these findings with the interest of parents and the need for programs dealing with how the parent can help his child and it becomes apparent that here is an area where parent education is needed and would be used.

Our experience is that parents want to help their children read and will attend classes to learn sound ways of doing so. In 1968 the Adult Education Division of the Los Angeles City Schools initiated classes for parents entitled "How Parents Can Help Their Children Read." It was expected that there would be a maximum of 100 classes. Instead, 150 were established. Parents took advantage of these parent education offerings in nearly every community in the city. The key to success seemed to lie in the fact that parents felt genuinely involved in their child's potential school achievement. Parents were learning through the classes how they could aid in their child's education. They felt themselves to be a recognized part of the educational team, and they developed learnings and skills that had meaning to themselves as individuals, as well as parents.

Courses were six sessions of two and one-half hour meetings. Content areas included the following:

1. Understanding individual differences and developmental needs of children.
2. Experiences that develop reading ability,
3. Developing a sight vocabulary and word attack skills,
4. Reading at home: reinforcement of vocabulary and comprehension,
5. Using multi-media,
6. Helping the child who is experiencing difficulty.

Content included general topics for discussion, plus application to both the beginning and continuing levels of reading. Typical parent comments were:

1. The program has made me aware of how important it is to guide our children and provide a good environment for learning,
2. Now I understand and accept my children better because of what I learned,
3. I'm sorry the series is over as I think I could learn even more to help my children read better.

Bloom [6] states that what the parents do, rather than their status characteristics, are the important determiners in the home environment. Parent education course content should include some specific ways in which parents can help their children learn to read. We have already discussed the prereading period of growth and parental effect, but conscientious parental assistance should not stop here. Most parents try to reinforce the school's reading program but they need and want more skills for doing so. They also need reassurance that what they are doing is right. This education should not, and need not, be limited to parents of nonreaders or of those having problems. It should be seen as important to any child's maximum development.

We are aware that intense pressure often backfires. Even when the parent is not pressing his child to achieve, the child cannot fail to be exposed to the tension that surrounds education and its relation to the future. Tensions and pressures are present. Shall we say "Don't let the parent in on the processes of learning for he may damage the child?" Or, is it possible that by making him aware of the importance of what he is doing, then giving something constructive to do and the skills with which to do it, helping him understand what excessive pressure does, we can replace the negative forces with positive ones. To say "Don't tell the parent anything," is not an answer to the problem. This fact is apparent as one listens to teachers' reports (and complaints) about excessive pressure on children.

While a great deal of research has been done to discover what kind of parental environment produces learners, efforts to help achieve such environments have been minimal. Existing programs, for the most part, have been general mental health approaches. Studholme reports of her study, "although the meetings were initially presented to the mothers as 'reading-centered' group guidance meetings, the mothers of their own volition quickly turned to more personal, emotionally-centered subjects." [7] Research has looked more at the parents of children who have problems than at specific ways that parents can help children read. Techniques can be taught. The trained parent tends to become more aware of the child's wide variety of needs and of the many ways in which he develops. Values come into view and a more searching look can be taken at whether or not he is teaching his child what he wants to teach him.

Groups should start with how learning to read takes place and what parents can do to encourage this learning, rather than focus on what parents have done wrong. Parents can look at the positive forces affecting learning to read, such as the example they provide, their expectations, the language models they provide, the academic guidance they can give. They can discuss the motivation stimulated by reward versus punishment, the possibilities of approval for success, the relationship of anxiety to failure. The basic need for someone to talk to and someone to listen, someone to read to and to read to them, can be illustrated. Parents can be taught to observe, to find out, to evaluate and in turn, to teach their children such approaches.

Rather than considering television either an unmixed horror or a convenient baby-sitter, parents can be helped to see the learning possibilities inherent in it, to think of questions and responses about programs that create a learning situation and a force for learning to read. Parents can be taught games to play with their children that improve eye-hand coordination, improve spatial relationships, develop figure-ground perception, and the myriad other skills and capacities upon which learning to read is based. They can be shown the relationship between what they do and the child's learning to read.

In discussing the evaluation of various approaches to teaching reading, Chall states, "and since children are also taught at home by their parents, knowing what goes on after school would also be helpful." [8] We would add that what is taught at home can be influenced by educational programs for parents wherein they are helped toward partnership for children's education, given understanding and skills.

Reading is an essential tool. Parents know this and it is a source of great anxiety to them. They do not all know the dynamics of learning, nor how they can affect motivation. For a very long time they have been blamed for failures, but far less often has the educator taken them into his confidence and shared his knowledge with them. They want to know and they can be taught.

PROGRAMS IN RESPONSE TO LONG-RANGE CONCERNS

Parents and Sex Education

One of the areas of deepest conflict for parents is that of providing guidelines for sexual behavior. This question often becomes the total content of many classes, even when there is initial intention to cover a wider span of family life curriculum. Thus, delineating a learning-valuing focus for examining the parental role of sex education has special importance.

Many books are written on how the parent may teach his child about sex, but few study opportunities are offered. The primary interest today is in the schools' assumption of responsibility for teaching biological information and attempting to influence attitudes and behavior of the young. But the schools alone cannot do the job; the parent again is the prime educator.

The parent may be the forgotten learner. Sexual attitudes and the groundwork for marriage are determined within the family. However, there appears to be little confidence in influencing adult attitudes on sexuality and in their ability to educate the young. Adult reticence and avoidance of children's questions are decried, but little attention is given to improving the situation other than taking the task over from the parents. There is too little thought given to helping family members to consider the meaning of sexuality and sexual behavior, and to keep the results of such consideration in view in their interactions.

It is said that parents don't do the job so other social institutions (generally the schools) must take over. The statement is often made that parents have been negatively affected by their personal experiences with their own parents and are, therefore, unable to assume the task of educating the young for healthy sexual attitudes. Yet most teachers who will take over the institutional responsibility have had the the same childhood experiences; most of them are parents. Will they be able to do in the institutional setting what they allegedly cannot do as parents? Will their attitudes and emotions stand in the way of their teaching role? If the teacher can be trained to educate children toward healthy sexual attitudes, why can't parents be trained for the same task? Parents are going to educate their children even by their silence and thus the child will have two teachers, perhaps teaching opposite ideas and beliefs. The question will always be who shall teach sex education, if attitudinal factors acquired from childhood influence all of us. Can teachers who experience a conspiracy of silence in their own childhood be taught to be family life educators? If they can be taught to teach children about sexuality, why can't parents? Among both teachers and parents, probably some can respond to education in this area; others cannot.

Sexuality is a matter of concern to parents from the birth of their children on. It is reasonable to assume that both parents and teachers should be educated for this task. Teaching skills are of vital importance, knowledge is important, attitudes should be understood, personal values need to be considered. Because every parent influences his child, he should have knowledge he can impart. He should have clearly assessed his own values. He should know how to communicate with his child in such a way that the child does not have to take the opposite point of view merely to prove himself a person in his own right. The parental task should be met with confidence in one's ability to cope rather than withdrawal in panic. The process of valuing here is as important as in any other dimension of living.

Because of concern and anxiety, sex education is probably a good area with which to begin parent study, although bringing it up in a later session of an ongoing class when the group members and the leader are more comfortable with one another has its advantages, too. Inevitably, any parent education group is going to be involved in a discussion of sex; it is inextricable from other aspects of living. Our experience has been that while this ongoing approach to the subject has real values, parents can and will enter a group to study sexuality specifically, and directly, and thoroughly. With talk of "new morality" and the sexual revolution, parents perceive a great need for reevaluation. Such a class will attract the dissident and anti-groups that believe the whole matter should be ignored. A skillful leader, however, can usually handle this advocacy and actually use it to advantage in helping people think for themselves. Confrontation should not be avoided because of the articulate minority. They have been controlling education efforts in this direction far too long.

A program for parents can bring them information about sexual development, the current social scene, and what the school instructional program is bringing to their children. It can help parents see their parental role as sex educators.

As parents view how the culture affects their children's sexual attitudes and behavior and as they determine what should be taught by schools and families, working cooperatively with the schools can be furthered. Insofar as there is an informed and supportive parent group, school programs can continue to improve and change to meet the problems of the day.

Free choice is as much if not more important here than in any area of the content of parent education. Any attempted imposition of values is intolerable to the participants. As always, the decisive factors in whether there will be an environment for free choice are imbedded in the parent educator's commitment to self-determination. The educator should take a look at his own attitudes and beliefs before he can attend to this task. He must be commited to refraining from imposing his own beliefs. He must create an environment where all opinions are accepted and where no one attitude is allowed to dominate unless it is without question the prevailing attitude.

A careful study of topics to be discussed is important. The words chosen are important. They should not be so obscure that no one knows what the program is about. Neither should they be so inflammatory that persons enter to defend entrenched attitudes or protest ideas. We would hope the program is planned around positive attitudes toward sexuality, deemphasing pathology. In our experience working with planning groups, a first suggestion has often been to talk about venereal disease, or strangely, the use of narcotics. Although these matters may be considered within the series, it is well to avoid them as topical headings for they may overshadow the potentials for looking at sexuality as an integral part of normal development.

The following are some titles worked out with care before being offered to the community for study possibilities:

Sex and Family Life Education

Guiding the child from birth to adolescence

1. Is the child a sexual being?
2. Feelings and attitudes about family life and sexuality.
3. Community influence on the child.
4. The facts of human reproduction.
5. Is teaching the facts of life enough?
   Whose responsibility?
   When to talk and when to listen.
6. What the schools are teaching.
7. Preparing for tomorrow's sexuality.
8. Developing responsibility.

Sexuality in Adolescence

1. The urgent concerns of youth.
2. Psychic, moral, and physical consequences of sexual behavior.
3. Sexual behavior and social ethics: Is there a new sexual morality?
4. What the schools are teaching.
5. Do you prepare your child for marriage?
6. Responsible interpersonal relationships.

Here is a timely topic and one of real concern to parents. Even when schools are offering excellent programs for children and young people, the involvement of parents should not be confined 'o gaining their consent. The job of educating children cannot be done by schools alone. Organizations such as PTA should be involved in promoting parent education in this area. The involvement of parents should not be limited to approving program responsibility assumed by the school while they sit passively by. The parents' full role should be recognized and their inevitable partnership with the schools prepared for. Parent educators should be trained for this task as well as educators of children. Study opportunities for parents should be broadly available.

PROGRAMS IN RESPONSE TO IMMEDIATE CONCERN

Relationships between Parents and Adolescents

The area most illustrative of the urgency of programming to meet specific parental concerns is that area most vulnerable to the impact of social change—the adolescent and his family. Parents of adolescents are perhaps the most uncomfortable members of the "over thirty" category. Those with young children are concerned and anxious that their children will face problems and pressures that the parents have never experienced, but they hold the vague hope that the world will put itself together before teen age comes. Those with teenage children do not have this breathing space. They are caught up in the turmoil of change and protest along with their children and are deeply disturbed by the radical differences in attitudes, behaviors, values, and goals between the generations. They are disturbed by the prevalence of drugs and the "new morality," threatened by the rejection of their concept of achievement, and distressed by the great national strife within which we live. They find, to their despair, that they no longer speak the same language as their children, and thus are unable to communicate with them. Fear evokes rigid clinging to old values. Rigidity causes selective cognition and blocks the search for common values. Young people are so much more sophisticated in today's ways that parents cannot define their teaching role. Though they may have accepted the need to move from the task of management to the position of consultant, they find that their children do not wish to make use of parental experience.

It is imperative that schools and mental health agencies provide structures within which parents can explore their urgent concerns and share their anxious confusion with other parents, under the guidance of sensitive and trained personnel. Confronting the challenges that the young are forcing adults to face is a painful process. It demands deep soul searching; it means exposing one's sense of failure and frustration. If the parent can engage in this process in the safety of a group, supported by the common feelings of others who share his problem, the search for new solutions becomes more feasible. Those new solutions may well be the reaffirmation of long-held values, arrived at after thoughtful reexamination in the light of change. On the other hand, old values may be redefined as parents encounter new insight into the concerns of youth and find validity in their struggle. This is an essential process. Thousands of adolescents, some as young as twelve years old, have left their homes to live, if only temporarily, in communal settings where they need not face the gritted teeth of parents who cannot "understand." Tens of thousands of other young people stay in the tense and conflicted nest, yearning for the freedom that will come with age.

These are precious years. They have always been turbulent, but they could and should be a time for warmth, for active engagement in the learning process as emerging adults interact with senior family members who are equally involved in their own growth, in an atmosphere of mutual respect for individual integrity. Parents need to learn skills to evoke this kind of growing climate. They must conceptualize their role in providing a model for active management of experience and for the ability to cope with change. If they have not seen the growth of their children as an open-ended, becoming process before, they may be available to changing their perceptions in the face of the discomfort they feel in their present stress.

The learning-valuing focus within a structure that fosters individual decision-making would seem to be the only relevant process. Parents' role with their adolescent child is precisely in the area of helping him to interpret the meaning of his experience, to make that meaning sharpen the youth's capacity to deal more effectively with his life. Thus, parents need to develop skill in asking the kinds of questions that help their child think through his experience with greater clarity and awareness of long-range consequences.

One of the parents' prime functions is helping their child define what he values. They do this most effectively by being clear and confident in their own value system, and thus not threatened by rejection or difference in the way their child chooses to live. While parents of an adolescent have far less control than parents of a preschool child over the kinds of experiences their child may have, they can help him learn from those experiences and decide what he values in the light of that learning.

With a learning-valuing focus, the parent educator has a visible and cogent role in such parent groups. He enables the group to define concerns, provides relevant information, spells out the conflicts in the context of the realities of today's society. He insures that all the alternatives are seen, the consequences of parental decisions fully explored. He confronts emotions, and he unites the alienated with the stream of group concern. He questions until individual choice is a solid, consistent decision. He encourages the trial of new behaviors and helps the group become a launching and reinforcing place for new perceptions. He models the kind of growth-enabling, sorting, and choosing process that is such an essential component of parental competence.

Programs for Parents of Handicapped Children

Programs to meet the special needs of parents whose children are physically, neurologically, or emotionally handicapped begin most effectively at the preschool level (or at the point of diagnosis of the disability) and continue through the time during which special management is necessary. While the substance of child growth and development knowledge is relevant, there are many areas of reassessment necessary to help parents deal with the problems handicapped children pose. Parent educators in these programs need specific understandings as to the nature of the handicap, its impact on growth and development, an awareness of realistic expectations and the capacity to deal with the special problems of guilt, pressures, and physical demands parents face.

The group process is particularly meaningful as parents come to terms with the reality of their task and the force of their feelings about it. Mutual support and sharing of experience, guided by a sensitive educator, can be a prime factor in helping a troubled parent find a balance between the demands of his parenting task and his capacity to meet those demands. The questions "What does my child need to learn?" "What do I want him to learn?" "How can I provide the kinds of experiences and mediation that will enable that learning," all need to be answered within the context of a frank assessment of the effect of the disability, if known, and current knowledge of expectations. The question of appropriate discipline becomes enmeshed in feelings of guilt about the etiology of the disability. Confusion about expectations leads to punitive pressure on the one hand, or overprotection on the other. The special demands of the handicapped child lead to distortion of relationships with normal siblings. Negative or discomforting responses from other people lead to demands for conformity the child may not be able to meet. Thus, the parent educator must have skill in helping parents face the reality of their problem, perhaps before parents are then able to look at what learning is possible and how they can effect it; what they value and how they use these values to deal with their responses to daily events.

PROGRAMS PREPARING YOUNG PEOPLE FOR PARENTHOOD

The ideal point of entry for an educational approach to the parental task is perhaps at the junior high level, where programs involving young people in exploring the nature of the parent role are beginning to take hold. In many secondary schools, child development classes are combined with observation and participation in school-based preschools, either cooperative or public day care centers, where students can gain insight about young children and watch the learning process in action. Here, questions of guidance and essential curriculum are considered, theories of growth and development discussed, and personal reference to one's own family style explored. The concept of a parent as a significant teacher of his child and the skills involved in parental competence provide a realistic framework within which the student can begin to perceive the nature of a role he will eventually assume.

Classes in senior problems, family life, marriage and the family, are becoming more prevalent in high school curricula. The recognition of the role of learning in the active management of one's life; the importance of gaining facility in decision-making, problem-solving, and the selection of values; the clarification and mediation of individual experience are all dimensions of adulthood and parenthood. Presenting the parental role as one involving teaching and the competent enabling of development gives young people a chance to see that this job requires specific, attainable skills and does not just come naturally.

College and university offerings in all areas of human development should provide the opportunity for young adults to view their future parental roles as vocational in concept and should offer the kind of structure, content, and process that engenders clear direction and specific skills.

SUMMARY

In this chapter, we have considered the applicability of the learning-valuing focus for the entire range of programs dealing with parents and future parents in a wide range of settings and agency structures. Stress is placed on programs that help the new parents see their potential for impact on the full development of their children through the nature of their interaction with them. Parents are connected formally or informally with expectant parent class, well-baby clinic, day care homes and centers, private nursery schools, and cooperative preschools. They respond to a broad spectrum of adult education offerings related to improving the quality of family life, from cooking and sewing to the changing role of women, all of which hold great potential for fostering individual autonomy and decision-making in the parental role.

Programs responding to specific interests range from new math for parents to meeting the challenge of adolescence, all of which hinge significantly upon the growing capacity of the parent to gain competence in enabling his child's development, to sort out his values in the light of available information, and to gain skill in putting those values into practice. Programs for parents of handicapped children look at the impact of disability on the overall learning and development of their children and focus on the vital need to place priorities on family goals—a process that demands conscious delineation of values. Programs in schools, churches, and community agencies aimed at preparing young people for parenthood may well be given a more sturdy structure through helping young people see their future parental role in terms of its teaching function.

REFERENCES

1. Helene M. Lloyd, "New York City's Program for Developing the Role of Parents in the Reading Progress," *The Reading Teacher*, Vol. 18, No. 8 (May 1965).

2. *Ibid.*
3. Benjamin S. Bloom, *Stability and Change in Human Characteristics.* New York: Wiley, 1964.
4. Gabriel Della-Pianna, Robert F. Stahmann, and John E. Allen, "Parents and Reading Achievement: A Review of Research," *Elementary English,* Vol. XLV, No. 2 (February 1968).
5. *Ibid.*
6. Bloom, *Stability and Change,* p. 124.
7. Janice M. Studholme, "Group Guidance with Mothers of Retarded Readers," *Reading Teacher* (April 1964).
8. Jeanne S. Chall, *Learning to Read: The Great Debate.* New York: McGraw-Hill, 1967.

8

Development of New Forms
and Solution of Old Problems

The field of parent education provides opportunity for development in a variety of ways. It also has many existing problems that stand in the way of further development. We pose both the possibilities and problems in this final chapter in the hope that others will view them as we do, as challenges and opportunities.

NEW FORMS

SCHOOL BASED PROGRAMS

If it is the responsibility of parents to send to the schools children who are ready and motivated to learn, and to sustain and nurture growth, the schools must offer parents assistance in meeting the demands of the task. If being a parent does not automatically confer the knowledge and skills essential for competent preparation of children for school, then schools must accept responsibility for organizing the pertinent knowledge and making it readily available, in a usable form, and on an ongoing basis. As elementary schools move closer, as they are doing throughout the country, to incorporating preschool programs into the school system itself, planning a format that includes the parent in the process of education is essential. As the child moves ahead in his education, the parent must understand something of the educational process and see the importance of his own teaching role. In addition, he needs a resource for acquiring the skills he must bring to the task.

Looking first at the preschool child and his parent, we propose that the team of the preschool teacher, preparing the child for his school experience, and the parent educator, preparing the parent for his role in sustaining this experience, can be a highly effective one if it is administratively nurtured and built practically. Many preschools have attempted to include parent education within the scope of the teacher's task. Some parent programs have integrated the children's curriculum as part of the parent educator's role. Teachers of children and teachers of adults need different skills and knowledge. When the task is combined the teacher must have both sets of skills. Such a combination can and has been done but it makes for greater demands in terms of background and experience. In some instances it may be more practical to form a team of two separate teachers and to develop their skills in working together effectively. Preschool teachers can work with parents on a one-to-one basis; however, it is the group process that may well offer the most potential for adult growth in that short period when the child is in preschool and at a time when parents are more open to exploring their role. It is the parent educator whose training most adequately equips him for enhancing the learning potential of the group.

Parent education should not stop when the parent sends his child to school, for the parent continues to be an important part of the educative process. Parents need schools for their children and schools need parents as partners in the process of educating children. The parent educator with a working knowledge of school philosophy, goals, and curriculum as well as the parent education skills can be an effective member of the school team. Parents acquire skills for supplementing the formal education of their children and in the process understand the school and solidify the ties between home and school. The parent educator can serve as a liaison between home and school and assist the faculty in its understanding of parent attitudes and problems.

An even more comprehensive approach to involving the family in the educational process is demonstrated in what we have chosen to call the Family Center. If we are committed to viewing the family as vital to the education of children, and thus to seeking the full assistance of the family in the educative process, then such a plan has merit.

THE DEVELOPMENT OF FAMILY CENTERS

The concept of a Family Center as part of the educational institution offers great promise for new approaches to building family strength and contributing to the partnership between home and school. Parents, those significant adults in the lives of children, need a place where they can learn to improve their skills for providing their children with an environment for optimal development. An educational program for adults, related to the school and highly visible within the community, should have strong attraction for parents. Family centers would be of use to all families and of particular value to low income families with their limited resources, their frequent alienation from the school, and their lack of basic skills. In view of the ever present lack of funds, perhaps these centers should be started in disadvantaged areas where the need is greatest.

The Need for Fully Functioning Families

For children to fully use the educational experience of the school, they need a home environment that provides the learning-to-learn experiences, parents who value education, and parents who see themselves as important to the ways in which children learn. Children need parents and teachers who understand each other's goals, who work cooperatively and supportively. In such centers parents could learn more about child behavior, more about child-rearing practices and their effects on learning, more about the importance of their own role. When parents are engaged in education, they get implicit recognition of the value of learning that affects the motivation of children. In addition, such centers could provide educational opportunities for a wide range of personal development, such as the possibilities of community participation, and the acquisition of basic skills for home-related tasks like home management. Such a program, conveniently located, could do much to build home and school partnership.

With an expanding background of knowledge and experience in the use of problem-solving skills, parents become more able to raise children who see themselves as worthwhile, are able to trust adults, approach learning with zest and are able to make meaningful use of formal learning. There must be a dual approach to the goal of increasing parental and familial competence. Provision of information and knowledge concerning all facets of child rearing and family living must go hand-in-hand with the exploration of parental, familial, and cultural values and attitudes that affect adults' ability to understand and act upon the information and knowledge that is theirs. Parents must learn to assess, to evaluate, and perhaps to alter their performances as they affect:

1. The development of a family value structure commensurate with the today's demands,
2. The growth of the individual family member's positive self-control,
3. The relationships of the individual member to formal education, to employment, to the community.

Program Design

The centers should be housed in separate buildings located on elementary school grounds. They should be open day and evening and become community centers in a true sense. In this way they can serve recreational as well as educational needs. Family activities can provide topics for group discussion of the meanings of behavior and the understanding of relationships. Both formal and informal educational approaches can be used.

The areas of study possible in a center are numerous and should include:

Preparation for parenthood.
Infant and parent interaction, the need for stimulation, etc.
Study of the preschool child, his development and learning.
Relationships to the school and the parental role in education.
Understanding, relating to, and guiding the adolescent.
Basic skills, basic education, and language learning.
Development of home management skills.
Relationships to the community: its resources, their use, areas for improvement.
Citizen responsibility and potentials for civic action.
The family as a consumer unit.

Training for homemaker services.
Training for aides and volunteers in schools.
Older family members, problems and opportunities for service.
Teacher understanding of the community and its families.
Family-centered social events, teenage activities.

These might be only a beginning with other areas of concern and interest becoming evident as the center clientele becomes established.

Outreach

In communities which do not function easily in a formalized educational setting, an outreach to parents is essential. Parents must learn what education has to offer. They must be exposed to educational possibilities in an environment where they are at ease, not defensive. Such an environment is the home. Trained aides could be utilized to enter the home to do the selling job for education that experience has shown is necessary with adults in such communities. The aide, an important member of the center staff, could serve as recruiter, interpreter, liaison agent. He could meet over coffee in kitchens with parents who have never before been given reason to believe that the educational institution is available to them on terms that are flexible and not threatening. Through such an approach, it would be possible for parents to feel that education can help them and their children to use the schools to meet their own educational needs and desires.

The Young Child

When faced with educating the disadvantaged child, there are still many problems not being met. No easy answers are yet available. Bear states:

In addition to the learning problems manifested by the disadvantaged, there are social problems and problems of attitude towards education, schools, authority, and adults. This schism in the adult-child relationship cannot be overlooked in planning long-range effects of such programs. Two possible solutions to this problem were suggested: first, the child might be encouraged to seek more information and aid from his teachers, attempting to perpetuate the close relationship initially established between the preschool child and adults who express an interest in him. An equally important step would be to increase the amount and degree of contact between families—especially mothers, who are probably the most significant adult to the preschool child—and social institutions, such as the school, attempting to establish a better foundation in the home environment for generalization of behaviors which intervention programs aim to produce in the child.[1]

The family center should be a program that concentrates on some of these problems. Parents may well hear the message that they are influential in fostering creative intelligence. Intervention programs designed to influence parent-child relationships need to be instituted before birth and maintained continuously. With evidence pointing to the need for earlier intervention, to start with the parent in the prenatal period might offer preventive programs rather than correctional efforts. Instruction of mothers in infant stimulation is the starting point of many experimental programs. The mother is the logical one to instruct. If during those first three years of life, a child needs opportunities for sensory-motor stimulation, perceptual discrimination, verbal interaction with an adult, individual attention, linking of related words and objects, encouragement toward perseverance with tangible and verbal rewards for relatively competent performance,[2] then parents can be taught to contribute to this task. Much lay literature begins with "Parents should . . . , but parents must know why if they are to enlarge on what they are already doing. They must see how the child responds. They need to see someone else do these things, see the use of materials, observe the impact of increased interaction. Then they can make a sounder contribution to what is known about optimal environments for children's development.

The centers should provide a place for constructive experiences for the preschool child. The children's program should be conducted by persons knowledgeable and qualified in the areas of child development and should be offered to groups of children from an early age. Parents would be observing and participating and the school learning for the child would thus be extended into the home. Home influences would be less likely then to be working in opposition to the child's school experiences. The parent's image of himself would be influenced. Hess [3] has said that the meaning of deprivation seems to be the deprivation of meaning in the early cognitive relationships between mother and child. Unless the mother is involved in the process of the child's search for meaning, that child's experience means far less to him. The centers can provide an enriched environment for the very young child with simultaneous education for the mother and thus meet the current concern that intervention at four years of age is not early enough.

With such early involvement of the parent, there should be a real chance of influencing parental attitudes toward schools and education. As parents understand what the school is offering their children, their role can become increasingly supportive. The parent image of a teacher will be influenced by this early experience. The demonstration of how a child responds to and is interested in an interested and responsive adult (the demonstration teacher) cannot but help the parent widen his concept of his own role in the teaching of his child. Values and attitudes that are being taught to the child are being considered by the parent at the same time. The common goal of developing a learning-thinking child is a joint venture and not one where schools have taken over because parents have failed.

The parent's facility becomes increased as he sees his enabling role as the teacher of his child. He sees the importance to the child of assessing his own values and engaging his child in the process of valuing and practicing the decision-making process. These skills are directly related to enhancing the child's use of the educational opportunities. A learning-focused approach to education is completely compatible with this setting.

Related Areas

Parents, in their search for competence, frequently become aware of their educational needs that lie beyond the relationship of home, child, and school, but that basically affect the educational achievement of the child. As an illustration, the self-concept of parents has been proved to have a direct effect upon the child's self-image and his academic school achievements. The ability of the parent to cope successfully with his community, thus increasing his own sense of personal value, has direct bearing upon his child's school accomplishments. An approach to increasing parental self-confidence, when it is coupled with the adult's relationship to the family group, can provide a highly meaningful laboratory experience. A basic education or English as a second language class, combined with subject matter in the many areas of family living, could be a doubly meaningful experience. Homemaking courses can be approached as integral to the child's welfare.

To strengthen the family, the parent needs to look at the larger community, either with a need to obtain specific services or information, or with a need to move into another area of community participation. Knowledge of the community, its services and opportunities to serve, should be part of the curriculum.

Many services within communities are not utilized because of lack of awareness of their existence or their function, and sometimes because of the attitudes of an agency's staff. Parent educators have a vital function in the building of two-way communication between agencies and the community of families they serve. This suggests the possibility of providing training for the staffs of other agencies, both in community awareness and in techniques of adjusting to the cultural expectations of the communities. Such training could also be made available to school personnel.

The training of parents and others interested, for child care positions, might be accomplished as an adjunct to a parent–preschool child program. Aides might be trained for Head Start and other prekindergarten programs. Future aides could be trained for the centers. It has been demonstrated that both women and men can be trained for such jobs and find placement within their communities.

The preparation of parents to serve as volunteers within their children's schools has already been done on a limited basis. Each school with its own specific needs in a specific community could benefit from such volunteer training. Parents need not be the only persons to serve as volunteers, however. The grandparent group in many neighborhoods is a source of potential volunteer power. Volunteer training, when geared to a particular school, provides opportunity for interpretation of school objectives, methods, and problems in a unique and personalized fashion.

Such possibilities for active involvement in learning and its purposes can be readily communicated. With a planned program of outreach and a convenient location, the center should be able to overcome the problems of reaching heretofore reticent families. The existence of such centers would be evidence of institutional recognition of the importance of the parental role, of the function of families, of the place for education in the enrichment of families. The visibility of the center should communicate a message of belief in the importance of parents and the necessity for family involvement.

Anticipated Results

For the parent there can be clearer definition of his role as a prime teacher of his child and increased personal competence. He can come to see himself as important to and capable of affecting the child and the family environment. He can understand and assume an active teaching role, seeing the potentials for teaching and developing skills for the task. He becomes aware of the need to engage in the process of valuing and the teaching of values to his children. The parent understands the goals of the school, prepares his child for the school experience, and actively relates to and assists in the school. The distance between home and school is bridged.

The parent is provided an accessible opportunity to increase his skills in basic education or, if necessary, the learning of English. Provision is made for learning other home related skills. He may learn to be a more effective consumer, to understand and apply the principles of good nutrition, of health care, of safety practices, of home maintenance and beautification. The older family members can come to see a place for themselves in home and community.

The employment of aides should do much to tie the center and the community together as well as to provide employment that might serve as preparation for other jobs. New careers are developed from the training for aides, homemaker services, and child care.

Learning about community resources can lead to more effective use of them, as well as community participation and active responsibility for its functioning. Considerations of modes of attacking community problems can be followed by individual or group action directed toward improvement of the community and its resources. From this should grow a sense of ability to affect one's own life, to be a change agent within the community. Perhaps a stronger sense of community would come from such a central effort wherein people assess their situation and the potential for making an impact on the community, and then find that through planned action they are not as powerless as they had assumed.

Family-centered social activities might lessen the sense of isolation that large city living has created, of loss of supports provided by the old, more stable neighborhoods of the past. One would grow to know one's neighbors, to become identified by common purposes, and to develop a sense of responsibility for others.

Teachers need to understand the people of the communities they work in, the families of the children they teach. The family life educator can help teachers and families understand each other. The family center has the potential to be a central point of understanding of family relationships, for focusing on the skills families need to secure inner strength, and for the effective interaction of home and school.

PARENT EDUCATION AND LITERACY TRAINING

There has been some experimentation in combining family education and literacy training. A limited number of parent education programs have included the teaching of basic skills; a few have used the setting of parent education to teach English as a second language to Spanish-speaking people. The exploration of possible methods to implement this logical combination of goals has just begun, thus the materials considered here are tentative and incomplete. We are convinced, however, that this area holds new and exciting possibilities.

We must give immediate consideration to whether the basic education programs are realistic. The use by UNESCO of literacy education as a starting point for meeting crucial educational needs of emerging nations is strong indication to consider literacy education among program goals. There is a real need for intensive study to determine the feasibility of combining family life content with literacy training.

We have made suggestions for a total adult education effort (i.e., the family center) aimed at optimum development of parents as significant adults in the lives of their children. Along with the obvious gains in self-realization for parents as individuals, involvement in educative programs provides a positive model for children. When parents find value in learning for themselves, they will communicate this value to their child. When parents engage in the learning process themselves, they are telling the child they value education. When parents become more aware of their own learning process, they can be more sensitive to the experiences of their learning child. Thus, basic education is an integral part of the offerings of a family center.

When we look at the problem from the other direction, i.e., bringing family and parent education designed for literacy education, the most obvious step is the inclusion of that content into the curriculum of literacy education. All too often, when the subject of such a combination arises, there is the tendency to think only of an adjacent child care program that will free mothers from the care of their children so they can more freely attend to learning to read and write. We are speaking, however, of a specific curriculum derived from both literacy training and family life education, a combination that should offer "learning while learning." One might object that the content of parent education is appropriate only to mothers. Yet the research in child development is replete with indications of the significant role of the father in the child's development. Even those students who are not parents either will eventually be or hold some prominent place in the lives of children around them.

If we accept the principle that education must be relevant to the interest and experience of the learner, then family life content in literacy materials has broad appeal. The learner finds much that is immediately usable and is motivated to study further. Even when the teaching style does not include discussion of content, there will be incidental learning. This has been done to some extent with particular emphasis on content dealing with health and consumer education and the availability and use of community resources.[4] The interpersonal relationships within the family, and more specifically, the parent's role as teacher of his child, have had less attention.

Are the goals and methods of parent education transferable to the teaching of literacy? The parent educator attempts to provide a structure wherein parents can see the importance and the dimensions of their teaching role; obtain information to broaden the base of their child-rearing decisions; and consciously determine their own directions as they assess the content gained from the teacher, the group, and their own experience. Is this proper content and process for the task of educating for literacy?

Even though learning to read and write are important, teaching for skills alone sells the educative process short. People learn best when self-determination is part of the process. Assisting others to become autonomous problem-solving persons is a goal that should be a part of any educational process. Choosing and valuing are applicable to any learning situation unless the educator views his students as receptacles into which he is pouring information in the hope that they will come out in a new shape of his making. Without offering the opportunity of choice, the end result is solely the acquisition of facts and skills. The parent education method as we have described it—the use of the discussion method with a learning-valuing focus—should be useful in a setting where the primary purpose is to teach a person to read and write. With a relevant content and student involvement in the process, the learned skills can be more meaningfully used.

If we deal with a particular parent-child relationship, the parent is inevitably led to certain considerations. An adult learner may question the statement, "Johnny learns from both his parents and his teachers." If he had thought that only teachers teach, he may wish to explore what it is *he* teaches, how does he teach it. Discussion leads to exploration of daily life for evidence of this process, and to a continuing search for greater understanding. Are there other ways to teach what one wants to teach? How does one decide what he wants his child to learn? Aren't one parent's decisions different from another's?

Discussion is time consuming but it can serve as a motivational force. The student becomes involved and may want to explore other materials that offer other ideas. From discussion can come consideration of thoughts and feelings, a beginning to see oneself as a decision-maker, an increased awareness of the impact of each decision on one's concept of himself as an effective parent. New skills in conducting the kind of internal dialogue the competent parent needs emerge and strengthen self-concept. The teacher does not stop with simple presentation of material but enables involvement through questioning—"Is this valid for you? Does it help you see a reality problem more clearly? Would you act on this new information?" The ability to read is not the sole goal; assessing the meaning of the content to one's own life enriches the skill. The student in literacy programs is a member of a family—often a parent—a wage earner, a member of his community. He must be able to read; he also must have immediate evidence of the value of reading to his life. The skills essential to participating in the democratic process are learned in family interaction. If the democratic process can be made visible and skills provided to guide it as it occurs naturally in daily family life, these skills can be extended from the initial family experience to the larger community.

There is much that is applicable to this question of relevance of material to the learners' experience, in programs for teaching children to read. In the language experience approach, for instance, some students may dictate material to the teacher that arises directly from some immediate family concern. The vocabulary used to describe the personal experience is then built upon; later, all the students write of their own experiences. This material serves as a basis for discussion. It has been found that materials relevant to one group, subculture, or community are not necessarily meaningful to another. Thus, content derived from the lives of the students themselves is a direct expression of interests and concerns; relevance is clear.

Many educators believe words that are emotionally laden for the learner are learned more quickly and retained more accurately over time than neutral words. Student-created materials are expressed in the words of the learner and thus have more emotional significance to him. Perhaps there is a guiding principle in the fact that graffiti is sometimes the product of the nonwriter and is often read by the nonreader.

Skills alone do not make an educated man. Skills outside the context of experience are less likely to be used. To teach for the acquiring of skills without a reality base for and practice in their meaningful use is to limit the learning potential in the educative process. Thus the goals and methods of the parent education process are transferable to the task of literacy education.

FAMILY PLANNING AND PARENT EDUCATION

The goals, methods, and content of parent education are of use in family planning programs. The stimulation of rational choice and the emphasis on the decision-making process are compatible with the goals of family planning. Some efforts to urge voluntary birth control threaten some individuals and may provoke resistance.

Respect for individual choice and faith in the ability of individuals to make their own choices wisely and to act upon them, are essential to any effort to achieve broad acceptance of population control efforts.

The need for population control is well recognized. Predictions of demographers and other social scientists regarding the dire effects of sustained population growth underscore the need for immediate action. This problem is less urgent for our country, but only quantitatively so. We need to act and although programs are being increased in number and effectiveness, we are not making full use of available know-how. Services do not meet the demand. Funding of additional programs is not being legislated at an adequate rate. All possible approaches must be explored.

Family size and spacing of births is a complex matter affected by social, psychological, and economic factors. As Chilman indicates, "family planning programs and policy personnel need to differentiate their own impersonal perceptions, goals and motivation from those more personal ones of those they seek to serve." [5] A parent education program might add another arena for reconciling the family planning goals of the society as a whole and those of the individual. The society has a stake in the quality of family life; that quality can often be related to family size. But the decision to limit a family is a personal one. The method of working with families should be one that respects the personal quality of those decisions rather than one that attempts to manipulate those decisions "for the good of society." While the end results of family planning for society and for the family are compatible, reasons for deciding on smaller families are different among different families. That difference must be respected and that respect communicated. Thus the process of valuing as it can evolve within a parent education setting may hold potential for programs focused on family planning.

Even though the demand for birth control services currently exceeds the supply, it is still vital to educate for awareness of such resources as there are and individual decisions regarding their use. Some parent education programs in low income communities provide experience in this area, indicating that there are many women who were vaguely aware of resources for birth control but who did not, until the question became the property of their parent group, have a full picture of what was available or of the range of questions underlying any related decisions. Parents should have greater access not only to relevant information but to structures within which they can assess what the information means to them.

OLD PROBLEMS

LACK OF PUBLIC UNDERSTANDING

Most people cannot tell you what parent education is. This is not surprising in view of the struggle within the field itself for consensus. Until we can come forth with a succinct definition and delineation of what can be gained from involvement in parent education, we reach only a limited few. Parents are concerned about their child-rearing practices. They wish to increase their competence. They reach out in many ways for direction.

We are beset with two opposing ideas of the purpose of parent education. On the one hand is the spectre of domination; on the other, the crusade for consensus. Few parents really want to be told what to do; few educators with any understanding of human behavior wish to spout directives. To some, the concept of education for parents is seen as social engineering, an anathema in a democratic society. To others, the term education implies domination and exact prescription. To the adult, the idea of being robbed of his right to make his own decisions, particularly in this area so close to his emotions, is totally unacceptable.

The crusaders for consensus are more likely to be prescribing for other people. There is a way to do something; all of those other people ought to do it that way. Parent education, then, is thought of as good for one's neighbors and less adequate relatives. Rather than manipulation, it is open imposition. Parent education should be neither. Programs should have goals that are clearly communicated. When those goals are the learning of processes rather than specific facts, they are more difficult to communicate. Ways must be found to get this message across.

The pendulum swings in this field as in others. We have moved from the stance of specific advice-giving to its opposite. But people want and expect information in an educational setting; and there *is* information about the dimensions of the parental teaching role. Information need not be uncontestable to be useful; debate stimulates clarity and enhances individual involvement in the decision process. The parent educator who operates from a sound base of information he believes is profoundly useful to parents brings a high level of commitment to programs and enriches the content level of students' concerns.

The people who decide where the educational dollar goes must also receive the message of parent education loudly and clearly. Budgets of schools and social agencies are chronically limited. Administrators with no awareness of the need for services to parents will make no commitment to their development. These leaders are clearly aware of the need for language programs for the foreign-born or job training programs for the untrained or jobless. Education to improve the quality with which each new generation is prepared for society is less obvious both in need and impact that is statistically measurable. Preventive programs are less justifiable. Yet parent education *is* basic education and may well make a qualitative difference in the way children are led to use the materials the society offers for growth and contribution; it may well be preventive of conditions that require expensive remediation. Showing the validity of parent education efforts is part of the work community planners must achieve.

Parent education is not just intervention at point of crisis, although it can and does serve this purpose. These parents with immediate, hurting concerns are totally responsive. But parental competence can be developed before problems become serious and distort the pattern of family life or change the direction of potential growth.

Interpretation of goals is not the only outreach problem; specifying method is also difficult. Parents want to know what is going to happen, how a discussion group can make a difference. They want to know what the process will be and what elements of control will be left to them.

Programs need to state clearly that change means choice, choosing from a realm of possible choices. Parents need to know that the parent educator presents possibilities for better understanding and for action, encourages the making of choices that are most real for individuals. All parents have faced confusion and indecision about questions involving their children. Learning to deal more effectively with confusion and indecisiveness is a goal parents would want to achieve. They need to know they can become involved in a process that can effect this learning. New ways are needed to interpret new approaches.

THE NEED FOR TRAINED TEACHERS

The lack of trained personnel is a continuing problem. Many programs fail under inexperienced, untrained leadership. When program goals are not clear to the leaders, they cannot be achieved by the group. Knowledge is not enough; philosophy and consistent methodology are needed to make it usable. A teacher may recognize the futility of passing out advice, but not have the skill for enabling personal choice. A teacher without adequate training may have little insight into his own motivation and thus use the group to meet his own needs. Colleges and universities and more specifically, departments of adult education, could logically undertake the development of training programs that help teachers see themselves as integral components of expanding continuing education programs. There are many established departments that could develop their offerings to provide a major sequence for the training of parent education personnel.

RESPONSIBILITY FOR PROGRAMMING IN PARENT EDUCATION

National level policy is essential to encourage and support programs for family development and increasing parental competence. There must be public recognition and acknowledgement of society's need for strong families. Far too often national level recommendations for family life education are based on pronouncements of family failure. Parenthood is seen as a matter of instinct and somehow that instinct has failed. Any parent worth his salt should have no problem with his parent task. Therefore, programs are needed only for the inadequate. This message is not readily welcomed by large groups of parents. However, with a policy that clearly supports education for family life as an integral offering of developmentally based adult education programs geared to enhancing competence in key life roles, the aura of remediation will gradually vanish.

Strangely enough, we do not place the cast of failure on any other dimension of society's responsibility for passing on vital knowledge from one generation to the next. In the field of child development and family relations, however, the researchers and professionals research and study, yet provide little or no opportunity for parents to consider, sort, and integrate pertinent information. The family absorbs much of the blame for most of our social problems—mental illness, delinquency, dropping out, alcoholism, suicide, illegitimacy, etc. It must adapt to the demands of a highly mechanized economic system. When that society blames the family for many of its social ills yet accepts no responsibility for providing adequate skills, it is simply scapegoating.

Some efforts are made. In some areas, parent education programs are provided within public school adult education programs, but these are few. In other communities, programs are mounted by private agencies. In other countries—France, Belgium, and Switzerland—for example, private agency programs have partial government subsidies. In Yugoslavia, they are apparently part of an extensive government-supported adult education program.[6] Some programs evolve from concerns of universities and colleges; others exist temporarily under short-term grants. It should be obvious that a solid financial base is essential to program continuity; this kind of base is most available through governmental support.

Professional organizations related to the field must turn their attention to the concerns of parent education. Vigorous leadership can and should be assumed by interdisciplinary groups, e.g., the National Council for Family Relations. Adult education professional groups, such as the National Association for Public School Adult Education, the Adult Education Association of the U.S.A., and others can play an effective role in interpreting and promoting programs. Organizations in the field of early childhood education are particularly cognizant of the need to reach parents. The Association for Childhood Education International, the National Association for the Education of Young Children, organization of parent participation preschools, other education associations such as the National Education Association, have a vested interest in fostering programs. Mental health associations are closely allied. Active, aggressive leadership in all these areas could move the field of parent education from its present marginal status to a position of significant impact.

Lay associations have played a powerful role in what has been achieved thus far. Without the consistent, enlightened leadership of the National Congress of Parents and Teachers, parent education would not have moved beyond an occasional experimental group. Without the effort of the California Congress of Parents and Teachers, California's outstanding program would have remained minimal. The concept of the professional parent educator has evolved directly from this organization's ability to conceptualize such an educative function.

The Child Study Association of America has promoted program development and refined practice. Their publications have contributed in a major sense to the growth of the field. Recently innovations in program design and setting have contributed new insights and directions for expansion.

The International Federation for Parent Education, with its headquarters in Paris, France, serves as a consulting agency to UNESCO and stimulates programs on an international level. The International Conference brought home the realization that wherever the recognition of need, there are common questions and concerns, common unresolved issues. The Federation's goal of bringing together people with these common concerns to share insights, pool knowledge, and work toward new solutions hold great potential for program growth.

There is an urgent need for a national organization soundly based on government support, as is the National Institute for Mental Health. Such an organization could more effectively define philosophy, coordinate goals, effect training programs, develop guidelines for leadership, and consider the range of settings within which parent education could function. As recognition of need becomes ever more clear to increasing numbers of concerned professionals and community leaders, a clearing house is vital to rapid growth.

THE NEED FOR RESEARCH

We are in accord with Brim's assessment [7] that evaluation remains the most difficult problem in the field. Some aspects of this question were explored in Chapter 3. The issues Brim raises in evaluation are placed here as a way of assessing the objectives of a learning-valuing focus.

As stated in Chapter 1, there is an urgent need for parent education programs to have the following attributes:

1. A teachable content that is adaptable within many different agency formats.
2. Content meaningful across a broad range of class, cultural and subgroup factors.
3. Parent educators who *are* educators, providing the range of alternatives and the process essential to individual decision-making.
4. Flexibility in focus depending upon where people are, but sturdiness in framework and process to enable learning.
5. Visibility as programs aimed at extending present capacities rather than remediating present inadequacies or failure.

The implications for research in programs meeting these criteria are obvious. Many evaluation problems derive from differences in goals, philosophy, methodology, and quality of personnel from one program to another. The differences are often so great that findings from one study are frequently not relevant to another. Findings from a variety of studies do not readily allow for generalization. The relative effectiveness of a program with a clearly specified philosophy applied to a wide range of settings could be more reliably measured if there were consistency in the aforestated variables from one setting to another, or if these elements were systematically varied. That is, if structured, agency-based group-oriented programs were sustained with a common core of goals, philosophy, method, and level of personnel, measurement instruments could be more accurately developed. There is a pronounced need to assess one approach against data derived from other approaches.

The aim of parent education programs has been to improve the mental and physical well-being of children by altering parents' behavior through education. These changes should be reflected in the child's adjustment and behavior.[8] Valid instruments have been hard to come by. In measuring parental attitude change, the Parent Attitude Research Instrument has been the focus of greatest effort.[9] This scale measures attitudes of parents toward selected socialization tasks and toward their role in the process. While it does reflect attitudes, a problem evolves in determining whether parents' responses are influenced by social desirability, what they think they "should" feel. A problem also arises in the attempt to link changes in parental attitudes with actual changes in behavior on the part of both parents and their children. Unfortunately, there is still little empirical evidence to support any of the links in this assumed chain of events.[10]

The problems encountered in valid measurement of behavior in a setting natural enough to insure the observation of truly representative functioning are many. They are perhaps partially overcome through the intensive, naturalistic, living-in methodology developed by Oscar Lewis.[11]

Rather than the global, nonquantifiable aim of improving the mental and physical well-being of children by altering the parents' behavior through education, a more specific thrust seems appropriate. The goals of such an approach would be to increase parents' awareness of and competence in their teaching role; to increase the skill with which parents use the substance of daily life to nurture their children's competence in dealing with their experience and in finding meaning in that experience; to sharpen the parent's capacity to define his own values and use them to make his daily child-rearing decisions consistent with long-range goals. To be measurable, these attributes must be translated into descriptions of specified, observable actions—behaviors that clearly indicate the presence of skills or the extent of learning that has become operant.

The ultimate criteria of effectiveness of program, then, would not only be found in the increased competence of the child in his physical, social, and intellectual interaction with his environment— his general capacity to learn from his experience. The criteria would also encompass the measurement of observable behavioral changes on the part of the parent. Increased awareness of his teaching-mediating role, a greater facility for perceiving the learning potential in daily life situations, evidence of problem-solving skills, perception of the value base of his decisions, provide a more viable set of measurable factors than previously possible.

Once observable behaviors are articulated, there are several avenues for the development of research instruments. Perhaps the most intriguing is the use of videotape recording of parent-child interaction. Although not all biases can be eliminated from the selection process, this new tool has great potential for use in parent education programs. It provides an opportunity for parents to observe and reobserve their own behavior and that of their children, a chance to see response systems in operation. It provides an objective view of the dynamics of the interaction process and has been found to generate a high level of commitment to change, a factor essential to any growth. The use of videotaping and micro-teaching has taken hold in many educational programs throughout the country. The potential for reliability in evaluation is enhanced. Videotape recordings of parent-child interaction prior to and following a focused group experience can be used to develop an objective evaluation instrument. Videotaping also allows for objective team assessment: the parent, the parent educator, the group members, other professional personnel can all participate in assessing the change or lack of change in the nature of the parent-child interaction system, and a basis for intervention can evolve from discrepancies in what is perceived. Incidents can be played and replayed. Evaluation need no longer rely on subjective anecdotal recording or recall. Replay allows for evaluation of one dimension of the dynamics at a time with a high level of objectivity. Once groups are comfortable in a working relationship, videotaping can be used to record the group process and individual movement within a group, for a variety of purposes. Such a tool would be most effective in studies of group process, socialization, parent education personnel training, group self-measurement, and would also furnish material for interpretive films so sorely needed in this field.

There are interesting possibilities for developemnt of measurement instruments that would reflect parental problem-solving skills prior to and after involvement with program content. Questions posing representative parent-child interaction incidents, reflecting typical daily child-rearing decisions, "What would you do if . . . and why?" may produce measurable differences in parents' perceptions of the dimensions of the interactive process. Attitude measurement scales which focus more specifically on determining the parents' concept of himself as a teacher of his child may yield growth in conceptualization of the nature of his task. The issues to investigate are fascinating and varied. Much more scientifically based effort is needed.

The most obvious concern is not merely the lack of a core philosophy that would enable integration of purpose and procedure so that one could more lucidly determine what to measure. We are equally blocked in valid observation and evaluation efforts by the lack of instruments specifically designed to measure what current programs attempt to effect. Once a workable framework and methodology have been generated, the next step is the careful delineation of measurable observable behaviors and the designing of valid instruments by which to measure them.

CONCLUDING STATEMENT

Parent education evolved as a field because parents knew they needed information and sought it from the social and behavioral sciences. They found, however, that none of these disciplines had the language or method to relate to parental concerns. Initial attempts, while fragmented and pedantic, have clarified the issues. The cumulative experiences have been synthesized into a unique entity—parent education.

Now we view parent education as a field, as a means by which information, understanding, and experience can facilitate the interaction between parents and children. It is not a global panacea for the problems of our complex and turbulent society. It does imply that available knowledge can be organized and attuned to clarifying the role of those who prepare each new generation.

REFERENCES

1. Robert D. Hess and Roberta Bear, *Early Education*. Chicago: Aldine, 1968. P. 230.
2. *Ibid.*, p. 8.
3. *Ibid.*, p. 103.
4. *Curriculum Guide and Resource Units for Personal and Family Development in Adult Basic Education* (Prepared by the National University Extension Association, Washington, D.C. for the U.S. Office of Education, Division of Adult Education).
5. Catherine Chilman, "Fertility and Poverty in the United States: Some Implications for Family-Planning Programs, Evaluation and Research," *Journal of Marriage and the Family*, Vol. 30, No. 2 (May 1968), p. 222.

6. Information obtained at annual meeting of The International Federation for Parent Education, Leeds, England, April, 1969.

7. Orville G. Brim, Jr., *Education for Child Rearing*. New York: The Free Press, 1965.

8. *Ibid.*, p. 269.

9. See E. S. Shaefer and R. Q. Bell, "Development of a Parent Attitude Research Instrument," *Child Development,* Vol. 29 (1958), pp. 339–361; M. Zuckerman, B. B. Riback, E. Monashkin, and J. A. Norton, "Normative Data and Factor Analysis on the Parent Attitude Research Instrument," *Journal of Consulting Psychology,* Vol. 22 (1958), pp. 165–171; and Wesley C. Becker and Ronald S. Krug, "The Parent Attitude Research Instrument: A Research Review," *Child Development,* Vol. 36 (1965), pp. 329–365.

10. Fortune V. Mannino, Julia Kisielewski, Exall L. Kimbro, Jr., and Barbara Morgenstern, "Relationships between Parental Attitudes and Behavior," *The Parent Coordinator* (October 1968), p. 237.

11. Oscar Lewis, *The Children of Sanchez*. New York: Random House, 1961.

Bibliography

919 - 784 - 9105

The following references are by no means an effort at total coverage. They represent key readings that provide entry into the broad range of concerns that have implications for the field of parent education from which the reader can proceed.

CONTEMPORARY SOCIETY AND THE FAMILY

Readings that provide a grasp of the impact of social and technological change on the role and function of the American family:

Bardis, Panos D., *The Family in Changing Civilizations,* New York: Associated Educational Services Corporation, Simon and Schuster, 1967.

Bell, Norman W. (Ed.), *A Modern Introduction to the Family* (rev. ed.), New York: Free Press, 1968.

Borke, Helene, "A Family Over Three Generations: The Transmission of Interacting and Relating Patterns," *Journal of Marriage and the Family,* (November 1967), pp. 638–648.

Braceland, Francis J., "Emotional Problems of Contemporary Life," in Robert D. Strom and E. Paul Torrance (Eds.), *Mental Health and Achievement,* New York: Wiley, 1965.

Brenton, Mryon, *The American Male,* New York: Coward-McCann, 1966.

Bronfenbrenner, Urie, "The Split-Level American Family," *Saturday Review of Literature* (October 7, 1967), pp. 60–66.

Burgess, E. W., "The Family in Changing Society," in P. K. Hatt and A. J. Reiss, (Eds.), *Cities and Society,* New York: Free Press of Glencoe, 1957.

Cavan, Ruth S., "Subcultural Variations and Mobility," in H. T. Christense (Ed.) *Handbook of Marriage and the Family,* Chicago: Rand McNally, 1964, pp. 535–581.

Chilman, Catherine S., "Families in Development at Mid-Stage in the Family Life Cycle," *The Family Coordinator,* (October 1968), pp. 297–311.

Duhl, Leonard J. and Antonia H. Chayes, "Individual, Family and Community," *Journal of Home Economics,* 56 (October 1964), pp. 579–585.

Edwards, John N. "The Future of the Family Revisited," *Journal of Marriage and the Family,* (August 1967), pp. 505–511.

Ellis, Barbara Gray, "The Family Perspective and Family Interaction," *Child Welfare,* 46 (February 1967), pp. 83–88.

Etzioni, Amitai, "Basic Human Needs, Alienation and Inauthenticity," *American Sociological Review, 33,* 6 (December 1968), pp. 870–885.

Farber, Bernard, *Family: Organization and Interaction,* San Francisco: Chandler, 1964.

Friedan, Betty, *The Feminine Mystique,* New York: Norton, 1963.

Geiger, Kent H. (Ed.), *Comparative Perspectives on Marriage and the Family,* Boston: Little, Brown, 1968.

Goode, William, "Changes in Family Patterns," in John N. Edwards (Ed.) *The Family and Change,* New York: Alfred A. Knopf, 1969, pp. 19–32.

Goode, William, *World, Family and Revolution Patterns,* New York: Free Press, 1963.

Handel, George, *The Psychosocial Interior of the Family,* Chicago: Aldine, 1967.

Hartman, Ann, "Anomie and Social Casework," *Social Casework,* 50:3 (March 1969), pp. 131–137.

Heiss, J., *Family Roles and Interaction: An Anthology.* Chicago: Rand McNally, 1968.

Hess, Robert D. and Gerald Handel, *Family Worlds,* Chicago: The University of Chicago Press, 1959.

Hill, Reuben, "The American Family of the Future," *Journal of Marriage and the Family,* 26 (February 1964), pp. 20–28.

Hill, Reuben, "Challenges and Resources for Family Development," in *Family Mobility in our Dynamic Society,* Ames, Iowa: Iowa State University Press, 1965.

Hill, Reuben, and R. H. Rodgers, "The Developmental Approach," in H. T. Christensen (Ed.), *The Handbook of Marriage and the Family,* Chicago: Rand McNally, 1964, pp. 171–211.

Hollingshead, August B., "Class Difference in Family Stability," in Richard Cloward and Herman D. Stein (Eds.), *Social Perspectives on Behavior*, Glencoe, Ill.: The Free Press, 1963.

Kephart, William M., *The Family, Society and the Individual* (2nd ed.). Boston: Houghton Mifflin, 1966.

Leslie, Gerald R. and Kathrun P. Johnsen, "Changed Perceptions of the Maternal Role," *American Sociological Review*, 28:6 (December 1963), pp. 919–928.

Lifton, Robert J. (Ed.), *The Woman in America*, Boston: Houghton Mifflin, 1965.

Mannes, Marya, "Is the Old Family Circle Dead?" *Family Circle* (August 1968), pp. 37–38.

Martindale, Don, "Timidity, Conformity and the Search for Personal Identity," *Annals of American Academy of Social and Political Science* (July 1968).

McKinley, Donald G., *Social Class and Family Life*, New York: Free Press, 1964.

McNassor, Donald, *This Frantic Pace in Education*. Address to the Long Beach City Schools Counselors Association and Psychological Services Administration Staff, Long Beach, California, October 3, 1966. Mimeo.

Mead, Margaret, "The Life Cycle and Its Variations: The Division of Role," *Daedalus* (Summer 1967), pp. 871–876.

Meier, Dorothy L. and W. Bell, "Anomie and the Achievement of Life Goals," *American Sociological Review*, 24:2, 1959, pp. 189–202.

Merton, Robert K., and Robert A. Nisbet (Eds.), *Contemporary Social Problems*, New York: Harcourt, Brace & World, 1966.

Miller, Daniel and Guy Swanson, *The Changing American Parent*, New York: Wiley, 1958.

Mirande, Alfred M., "The Isolated Nuclear Family Hypothesis: A Reanalysis," in John N. Edwards (Ed.), *The Family and Change*. New York: Alfred A. Knopf, 1969, pp. 153–163.

Montagu, Ashley, *The Humanization of Man*, New York: World Publishers, 1962.

Olim, Ellis G., "The Self-Actualizing Person in the Fully Functioning Family: A Humanistic Viewpoint," *The Family Coordinator*, (July 1968), pp. 141–148.

Pollak, Otto, "The Outlook for the American Family," *Journal of Marriage and the Family* (August 1967), pp. 305–392.

Parsons, Talcott, and Robert F. Bales, *Family, Socialization and Interaction Process*. New York: Free Press, 1965.

Riesman, David, "Some Questions About the Study of American Character in the Twentieth Century," *Annals of the American Academy of Political and Social Science,* (March 1967), pp. 36–47.

Riley, Matilda W., "Socialization for the Middle and Later Years," in D. A. Goslin, and D. C. Glass (Eds.), *Handbook of Socialization Theory and Research,* New York: Rand McNally, 1968.

Rodman, Hyman, "The Changing American Family," in Hyman Rodman (Ed.), *Marriage, Family and Society: A Reader,* New York: Random House, 1965, pp. 249–258.

Rodman, Hyman, and Talcott Parsons, "View of the Changing American Family," *Merrill-Palmer Quarterly,* 11:3 (July 1965), pp. 209–228.

Rosenstock, Florence, and Bernard Kutner, "Alienation and Family Crisis," *The Sociological Quarterly* (Summer 1967), pp. 297–404.

Sirjamaki, John, *The American Family in the Twentieth Century.* Cambridge, Mass.: Harvard University Press, 1953.

Smith, Ruth H., Donna Downer, and Mildred T. Lynch, "The Man in the House," *The Family Coordinator,* (April 1969), pp. 107–111.

Smith, William M., Jr., "The Family Roles of Modern Man," *Illinois Teacher of Home Economics,* (Fall 1966–67).

Sofer, Elaine Graham, "Inner-Direction, Other-Direction and Autonomy," in S. M. Lipset, and Leo Lowenthal (Eds.), *Culture and Social Character.* Glencoe, Ill.: Free Press, 1961, pp. 316–348.

Strodtbeck, Fred L., "The Family in Action," *Child Study,* 34 (1958), pp. 14–18.

Sussman, Marvin B., "The Isolated Nuclear Family: Fact or Fiction?" *Social Problems,* Vol. 6 (Spring 1959), pp. 333–349.

Talmon, Garber J., "Social Change and Family Structure," *International Social Science Journal,* Vol. 14 (1962), pp. 468–488.

Useem, Ruth, "Changing Cultural Concepts in Woman's Lives," in H. Peters and J. Hansen (Eds.), *Vocational Guidance and Career Development.* New York: MacMillan, 1966.

Vincent, Clark, "Family Spongia: The Adaptive Function," *Journal of Marriage and Family,* Vol. 28, (February 1966), pp. 29–36.

Yinger, J. Milton, "The Changing Family in a Changing Society," *Social Casework,* 40 (October 1959), pp. 419–428.

THE SOCIALIZATION PROCESS

The nature of child-rearing patterns, parent-child interaction systems, as they reflect the socialization process; factors of class, culture as they affect the parenting act:

Alexander, T., "Child and Society: Excerpts from Biocultural Approach to Psychological Development," *School and Society,* 97 (April 1969), pp. 241–247.

Baldwin, Alfred, J. Kalhorn, and F. H. Breese, *The Appraisal of Parent Behavior,* Psychological Monographs, Vol. 63:4, No. 299, 1948.

Bandura, A. and R. H. Walters, *Social Learning and Personality Development.* New York: Holt, Rinehart & Winston, 1963.

Baumrind, Diana, "Parental Control and Parental Love," *Children,* 12, 1965, pp. 230–234.

Baumrind, Diana, "Effects of Authoritative Parental Control on Child Behavior," *Child Development,* 37:4 (December 1966), pp. 887–907.

Baumrind, Diana, "Child Care Practices Anteceding Three Patterns of Preschool Behavior," *Genetic Psychological Monographs,* 1967, 75, pp. 43–88.

Baumrind, Diana, and A. E. Black, "Socialization Practices Associated with Dimensions of Competence in Preschool Boys and Girls," *Child Development,* 38, 1967, pp. 291–327.

Becker, Wesley C., "Consequences of Different Kinds of Parental Discipline, in M. L. Hoffman, and Lowis W. Hoffman (Eds.), *Review of Child Development Research,* Vol. I, New York: Russell Sage Foundation, 1966, pp. 169–208.

Benedict, Ruth, "Continuities and Discontinuities in Cultural Conditioning," *Psychiatry,* 1938, 1, pp. 161–167.

Block, Jack, "Personality Characteristics Associated with Fathers' Attitudes Toward Child Rearing," *Child Development* 26, 1955, pp. 41–48.

Boehm, Leonore, and Martin L. Nass, "Social Class Differences in Conscience Development," *Child Development,* 33:3 (September 1962), pp. 565–574.

Boehm, Leonore, "The Development of Conscience: A Comparison of Children of Different Mental and Socioeconomic Levels," *Child Development,* 33:3 (September 1962), pp. 575–590.

Boek, Walter E., Marvin Sussman, and Alfred Yankauer, "Social Class and Child Care Practices," *Marriage and Family Living,* 20 (November 1958), pp. 326–333.

Bowman, Paul, "Family Role in the Mental Health of Children," in E. Paul Torrance and Robert D. Strom (Eds.), *Mental Health and Achievement.* New York: Wiley, 1965.

Brim, O. G., Jr., "Personality Development As Role Learning," in I. Iscoe and H. Stevenson (Eds.), *Personality Development in Children.* Austin: University of Texas Press, 1960, pp. 127–159.

Brody, G. F., "Relationship Between Maternal Attitudes and Behavior," *Journal of Personality and Social Psychology,* 2 (1965), pp. 317–323.

Bronfenbrenner, Urie, "Socialization and Social Class Through Time and Space," in T. Newcomb, and R. Hartley (Eds.), *Readings in Social Psychology*. New York: Holt, Rinehart and Winston, 1958.

Bronfenbrenner, Urie, "The Changing American Child—A Speculative Analysis," *Merrill-Palmer Quarterly*, 7:2 (1961), pp. 73–84.

Bronfenbrenner, Urie, "Soviet Methods of Character Education: Some Implications for Research," *American Psychologist*, 1962, 17, No. 8 550564.

Caldwell, Bettye M., "The Effects of Infant Care," in M. L. Hoffman and Lois W. Hoffman (Eds.), *Review of Child Development Research*, Vol. I. New York: Russell Sage Foundation, 1964, pp. 9–87.

Church, Joseph and Joseph Stone, *Childhood and Adolescence* (2nd ed.), New York: Random House, 1968.

Clausen, John A., "Family Structure, Specialization and Personality," in M. L. Hoffman and Lois W. Hoffman (Eds.), *Review of Child Development Research*, Vol. II, New York: Russell Sage Foundation, 1966, pp. 1–54.

Clausen, John A. (Ed.), *Socialization and Society*. Boston: Little, Brown, 1968.

Devereus, E. C., Urie Bronfenbrenner, and G. J. Suci, "Patterns of Parent Behavior in America and West Germany: Across-National Comparison," *International Social Science Journal*, 14 (1962), pp. 49–506.

Dyer, E. D., "Parenthood as Crisis: A Re-Study," *Marriage and Family Living*, 25 (1963), pp. 196–201.

Elkin, F., *The Child and Society: The Process of Socialization*. New York: Random House, 1960.

Erikson, Erik, "Identity and the Life Cycle," *Psychological Issues*, 1:1 (1959).

Erikson, Erik, *Childhood and Society*. New York: Norton, 1963.

Erikson, Erik, *Identity: Youth and Crisis*. New York: Norton, 1968.

Foote, Nelson, and Leonard Cottrell, *Identity and Interpersonal Competence: A New Direction in Family Research*. Chicago: University of Chicago Press, 1955.

Gordon, I. J., "Beginnings of the Self: The Problem of the Nurturing Environment," *Phi Delta Kappa*, 50 (March 1969), pp. 375–378.

Goslin, David (Ed.), *Handbook of Socialization Research and Theory*. New York: Rand McNally, 1969.

Havighurst, R. J., "How the Moral Life is Formed," *Religious Education* (November–December 1962), pp. 432–439.

Hoffman, M. L., "Child-Rearing Practices and Moral Development: Generalizations from Empirical Research," *Child Development*, 34:2 (June 1963), pp. 295–318.

Hoffman, M. L., "Parent Discipline and the Child's Consideration of Others," *Child Development,* 34:3 (September 1963), pp. 573–588.

Hoffman, M. L., "Personality, Family Structure and Social Class as Antecedents of Parental Power Assertion," *Child Development,* 34:4 (1963), pp. 869–884.

Inkeles, Alex, "Social Structure and the Socialization of Competence," *Harvard Educational Review,* 36:3 (Summer 1966), pp. 265–283.

Inkeles, Alex, "Social Structure and Child Socialization," in John A. Calusen (Ed.), *Socialization and Society.* Boston: Little, Brown, 1968, pp. 73–130.

Kantor, Mildred, J. C. Glidwell, I. Mensh, H. R. Demke, and M. L. Gildes, "Socioeconomic Level and Maternal Attitudes Toward Parent-Child Relationships," *Human Organization,* 16 (Winter 1958), pp. 44–48.

Kohlberg, L., "Development of Moral Character and Moral Ideology," in M. L. Hoffman and Lois W. Hoffman (Eds.), *Review of Child Development Research,* Vol. I. New York: Russell Sage Foundation, 1964, pp. 383–431.

Kohn, Melvin, "Social Class and Parent-Child Relationships," *American Journal of Sociology,* 68:4 (1963) pp. 471–480.

Korner, Annaliese, "Mother-Child Interaction: One or Two-Way Street," *Social Work,* 10:3 (July 1965).

Littmen, Richard A., Robert C. A. Moore, John Pierce-Jones, "Social Class Differences in Child Rearing: A Third Community for Comparison with Chicago and Newton," *American Sociological Review,* 22 (1957), pp. 694–704.

Malinowski, Bronislaw, "Parenthood—The Basis of Social Structure," in Marvin B. Sussman (Ed.), *Sourcebook in Marriage and the Family* (2nd ed.), Boston: Houghton Mifflin, 1963, pp. 40–47.

Maccoby, Eleanor E., "Early Learning and Personality: Summary and Commentary," in Robert D. Hess and Robert Meyer Bear (Eds.), *Early Education.* Chicago: Aldine, 1968, pp. 191–202.

Maslow, A. H., "A Theory of Human Motivation," in Don E. Manachek (Ed.), *The Self in Growth, Teaching and Learning.* Englewood Cliffs, N.J.: Prentice-Hall, 1965, pp. 246–268.

Mead, Margaret, and Elena Calas, "Child-Training Ideals in a Post-Revolutionary Context: Soviet Russia," in M. Mead and M. Wolfenstein (Eds.), *Childhood in Contemporary Cultures.* Chicago: University of Chicago Press, 1955, pp. 179–203.

Medinnus, Gene R., *Readings in the Psychology of Parent-Child Relationships.* New York: Wiley, 1967.

McNeil, Elton B., *Human Socialization.* Belmont, Calif.: Brooks Cole, 1969.

Meerloo, Joost A. M., "The Psychological Role of the Father," *Child and Family* (Spring 1968), pp. 102–116.

Nichos, R. C., "A Factor Analysis of Parental Attitudes of Fathers," *Child Development,* 33 (1962), pp. 791–802.

Parke, R. D., "Some Effects of Punishment on Children's Behavior," *Young Children,* 24 (March 1969), pp. 225–234.

Parsons, T., "Family Structure and the Socialization of the Child," in I. Parents and R. F. Bales (Eds.), *Family Socialization and Interaction Process.* Glencoe, Ill.: The Free Press, 1955, pp. 35–131.

Perlin, Leonard, Marian Yarrow, and Harry A. Scarr, "Unintended Effects of Parental Aspirations: The Case of Children's Cheating," *The American Journal of Sociology,* 73:1 (July 1967), pp. 73–83.

Pease, Demaris, "Family Forces Influence Child Behavior," in Joe L. Frost and Glenn R. Hawkes (Eds.), *The Disadvantaged Child: Issues and Innovations.* Boston: Houghton Mifflin, 1966, pp. 382–388.

Pederson, Frank A. and Kenneth S. Robsen, "Father Participation in Infancy," *American Journal of Orthopsychiatry,* 39:3 (April 1969), pp. 466–472.

Schaefer, E. S., "A Circumplex Model for Maternal Behavior," *Journal of Abnormal and Social Psychology,* 59 (1959), pp. 226–235.

Schaefer, E. S. and Nancy Bayley, "Maternal Behavior, Child Behavior and their Intercorrelations from Infancy thru Adolescence," *Monograph Society for Research in Child Development,* 28:3 (1963, whole No. 87).

Sears, R. R., Eleanor Maccoby, and H. Levin, *Patterns of Child Rearing.* Evanston, Ill.: Row, Peterson, 1957.

Sewell, William H., "Some Recent Developments in Socialization Theory and Research," *The Annals of the American Academy of Political and Social Science,* 349 (1963), pp. 163–181.

Sewell, William H. and A. O. Haller, "Factors in the Relationship between Social Status and the Personality Adjustment of the Child," *American Sociological Review,* 24 (August 1959), pp. 511–521.

Silverberg, William V., *Childhood Experience and Personal Destiny.* New York: Springer, 1964.

Smith, M. B., "Competence and Mental Health: Problems in Conceptualizing Human Effectiveness," in S. B. Sells (Ed.), *The Definition and Measurement of Mental Health: A Symposium* (in press).

Stendler, Celia B., "Sixty Years of Child Training Practices," *Journal of Pediatrics,* 36 (1950), pp. 122–136.

Stolz, Lois Meek, *Influences on Parent Behavior.* Stanford, Calif.: Stanford University Press, 1967.

Taconis, Liba, "The Role of the Contemporary Father in Rearing Young Children," *Educational Research,* 11:2 (February 1969), pp. 83–94.

White, Martha Sturn, "Social Class, Child Rearing Practices and Child Behavior," *American Sociology Review,* 22 (December 1957), pp. 704–711.

Whiting, J. W. M., "Socialization Process and Personality," in F. D. L. K. Hsu (Ed.), *Psychological Anthropology: Approaches to Culture and Personality,* Homewood, Ill.: Dorsey Press, 1961, pp. 355–380.

Winch, Robert F., *Identification and Its Familial Determinants.* Indianapolis: Bobbs-Merrill, 1962.

Zunich, M., "Relationship Between Maternal Behavior and Attitudes Toward Children," *Journal of Genetic Psychology,* 1962, pp. 155–165.

LEARNING PROCESS

Readings on the nature of the learning process, development of cognitive skills, motivation; the role of parent interaction, the effect of child-rearing practices on intellectual development:

Almy, Millie, "Spontaneous Play: An Avenue for Intellectual Development," *Young Children.* May, 1967, pp. 265–276.

Almy, Millie (Ed.), *Early Childhood Play: Selected Readings Related to Cognition and Motivation.* New York: Selected Academic Readings, 1968.

Almy, Millie, Edward Chittenden, and Paula Miller. *Young Children's Thinking.* New York: Teachers College Press, 1966.

Ausubel, David, "Stages of Intellectual Development and Their Implications for Early Childhood Education," in Peter B. Neubauer (Ed.), *Concepts of Development in Early Childhood Education.* Springfield, Ill.: Charles C Thomas, 1965.

Bereiter, Carl and Siegfried Engelmann, *Teaching Disadvantaged Children in the Preschool.* Englewood Cliffs, N.J.: Prentice-Hall, 1966.

Bernstein, Basil, "Social Class and Linguistic Development: A Theory of Social Learning," in A. H. Halsey, Jean Flound, and C. A. Anderson (Eds.), *Education, Economy and Society.* Glencoe, Ill.: Free Press, 1961.

Bing, E. "Effect of Child-Rearing Practices on Development of Differential Cognitive Abilities," *Child Development* 34 (1963), pp. 631–648.

Bloom, Benjamin S., *Stability and Change in Human Characteristics.* New York: Wiley, 1964.

Bruner, Jerome, "The Will to Learn," *Commentary* (February 1966), pp. 41–46.

Bruner, Jerome (Ed.), *Learning About Learning, A Conference Report,* Washington, D. C.: U. S. Government Printing Office, 1966.

Bruner, Jerome, "The Growth of the Mind," in J. F. Rosenblith and W. Allensmith (Eds.), *The Causes of Behavior.* Boston: Allyn and Bacon, 1966.

Caldwell, Bettye M., "What is the Optimum Learning Environment for the Young Child," *American Journal of Orthopsychiatry* (January 1967), pp. 8–21.

Caldwell, B. V. and L. Hersher, "Mother-Infant Interaction During the First Year of Life," *Merrill-Palmer Quarterly,* 10 (1964), pp. 119–128.

Cohen, Elizabeth G., "Parental Factors in Educational Mobility," *Sociology of Education,* 38 (Fall 1965), pp. 404–425.

Crowne, D. P. and others, "Some Developmental Antecedents of Level of Aspiration," *Journal of Personality,* 37 (March 1969), pp. 73–92.

DeBoer, Dorothy L., "Annotated Bibliography on Early Child Learning," *Education,* 89:1 (September–October 1968), pp. 40–42.

Dittman, Laura, *Early Child Care.* New York: Atherton Press, 1969.

Dixon, Norman R., "The Home as Educative Agent," *Educational Leadership* (April 1968), pp. 632–636.

Freeberg, Norman E. and Donald T. Payne, "Parental Influence on Cognitive Development in Early Childhood," *Child Development* (March 1967).

Fort, J. G. and others, "Cultural Background and Learning in Young Children," *Phi Delta Kappan,* 50 (March 1969), pp. 286–388.

Fowler, W., "Cognitive Learning in Infancy and Early Childhood," *Psychological Bulletin,* 59 (1962), pp. 116–152.

Fromm, Erich, "The Creative Attitude," in Harold H. Anderson (Ed.), *Creativity and Its Cultivation,* New York: Harper & Row, 1959.

Gagné, John, "The Learning of Concepts," *School Review,* 73:3 (Autumn 1965), pp. 187–196.

Getzels, J. S. and P. W. Jackson, "Family Environment and Cognitive Style: A Study of the Sources of Highly Intelligent and of Highly Creative Adolescents," *American Sociological Review,* 26 (1961), pp. 351–359.

Gordon, Ira J., "New Conceptions of Children's Learning and Development," in Walter B. Waetjen (Ed.), *Learning and Mental Health in Schools.* Washington D. C.: Association for Supervision and Curriculum Development, NEA, 1966.

Grotberg, Edith L., "Role of that Parent in Fostering Early Learning," *Education* (September–October 1968), 89:1, pp. 35–39.

Hunt, J. McV., "Experience and the Development of Motivation: Some Reinterpretations," *Child Development,* 31 (1960), pp. 489–504.

Hunt, J. McV., *Intelligence and Experience.* New York: Ronald Press, 1961.

Hunt, J. McV., "How Children Develop Intellectually," *Children,* 11 (1964), pp. 83–91.

Jensen, Arthur, "Learning in the Preschool Years," *Journal of Negro Education,* (January 1963), pp. 133–138.

Jensen, Arthur and H. M. Lambert, "Perspectives from Research: Review of Social Class and Perceptual Learning," *Young Children,* 24 (1969), pp. 242+.

Klopf, Gordon J. and William A. Hohman (Eds.), *Perspectives on Learning.* New York: Mental Health Materials Center, 1967.

Mukerji, Rose, "Roots of Early Childhood for Continuous Learning," *Young Children,* (September, 1965), pp. 343–350.

Murphy, Lois B., "Child Development Then and Now," *Childhood Education* (January 1968), pp. 320–306.

Murphy, Lois B., and others, *The Widening World of Childhood. Paths Toward Mastery.* New York: Basic Books, 1962.

Murphy, Lois B., and others, "Children under Three: Finding Ways to Stimulate Development," *Children,* 16 (March 1969), pp. 46–42.

Leovinger, Jane, "Patterns of Parenthood as Theories of Learning," *Journal of Abnormal and Social Psychology,* 59 (1959), pp. 148–150.

Pines, Maya, *Revolution in Learning: The Years from Birth to Six.* New York: Harper & Row, 1967.

Roeper, Annemarie, and Irving Sigal, "Finding the Clues to Children's Thought Processes," *Young Children,* 26, 6 (September 1966), pp. 335–349.

Sigal, Irving, "Developmental Considerations of the Nursery School Experience," in Peter Neubauer (Ed.), *Concepts of Development in Early Childhood.* Springfield, Ill.: Charles C Thomas, 1965.

Waetjen, Walter B. (Ed.), *Learning and Mental Health in the Schools.* Washington, D.C.: Association for Supervision and Curriculum Development, 1966.

Wann, Kenneth D., Miriam Down, and Elizabeth Little, *Fostering Intellectual Development in Young Children.* New York: Teachers College Press, 1962.

White, Burton, "Informal Education During the First Months of Life," in Robert D. Hess and Roberta Meyer Bear (Eds.), *Early Education.* Chicago: Aldine, 1968, pp. 143–170.

White, Robert, "Motivation Reconsidered: The Concept of Competence," *Psychological Review,* 66, 5 (September 1959), pp. 297–333.

White, Sheldon H., "Some Educated Guesses About Cognitive Development in the Preschool Years," in Robert D. Hess and Roberta Meyer Bear (Eds.), *Early Education.* Chicago: Aldine, 1968, pp. 203–214.

Woodring, Paul, "Freedom-Not Licence," *Saturday Review of Literature,* (February 18, 1967), p. 97.

Wright, J. C., and J. Kagan (Eds.), "Basic Cognitive Processes in Children," *Social Research and Child Development Monographs,* 28, 2 (1963), (Entire issue).

VALUING PROCESS

Consideration of contemporary value systems, conflicts, and contradictions; effect on family life; the process of valuing and value change:

Albert, Ethel M., "Conflict and Change in American Values," *Ethics,* 74:1 (October 1963), pp. 19–33.

Baier, Kurt, and Nicholas Reacher, *The Impact of Technological Change on American Values.* New York: Free Press, 1969.

Chaffee, S. H., and J. S. Lindner, "Three Process of Value Change Without Behavioral Change," *Journal of Communication,* 19 (March 1969), pp. 30–40.

Cox, Christine, "A Study of the Religious Practices, Values and Attitudes of a Selected Group of Families," *Dissertation Abstracts,* 17 (1957), pp. 2703–2704.

Fults, Anne Carol, "Examining Socio-Economic Values in Terms of Family Welfare," *Journal of Home Economics,* 51, 4 (April 1959).

Hamilton, J. T., "Values Held by Teachers," *Peabody Journal of Education,* 46 (March 1969), pp. 278–81.

Hill, W. F., "Learning Theory and the Acquisition of Values," *Psychological Review,* 67 (1960), pp. 317–331.

Hobart, Charles, "Commitment, Value Conflict and the Future of the American Family," *Marriage and Family Living,* 25 (November 1963), pp. 405–412.

Liberman, Sally, *A Child's Guide to a Parent's Mind.* New York: Henry Schuman, 1951.

Luckey, Eleanor Braun, "Family Goals in a Democratic Society," *Journal of Marriage and the Family,* 26, 3 (August 1964).

Luckey, Eleanor Braun, "Changing Values: Effects on Parents and Children," *Child Welfare,* 47, 4 (April 1968).

McCormick, Mary, "The Role of Values in the Helping Process," *Social Casework,* 42, 1 (January 1961), pp. 3–10.

McKee, William W. "Values, Ethics and Behavior," *Values: Proceedings of the National Training Conference on Extension Education in Family Life.* Detroit: Merrill-Palmer Institute, September 8–13, 1963, pp. 1–8.

Nye, F. Ivan, "Values, Family and a Changing Society," *Journal of Marriage and the Family,* 29 (May 1967), pp. 241–248.

Opler, Marvin, "Cultural Values and Attitudes on Child Care," *Children,* 2, (1955), pp. 45–50.

Raths, Louis, Merrill Harmin, and Sidney Simon, *Values and Teaching.* Englewood Cliffs, N.J.: Merrill, 1966.

Riley, M. H., J. W. Riley, Jr., and M. E. Moore, "Adolescent Values and the Riesman Topology: An Empirical Analysis," in S. M. Lipset and L. Lowenthal (Eds.), *Culture and Social Character.* New York: Free Press, 1961.

Rogers, Carl R., "Toward a Modern Approach to Values," *Journal of Abnormal and Social Psychology,* 68, 2 (1964), pp. 160–167.

Rokeach, Milton, "A Theory of Organization and Change Within Value-Attitude Systems," *Journal of Social Issues,* 24, 1 (1968), pp. 13–33.

Shaftel, Fannie R., and George Shaftel, *Role-Playing for Social Values.* Englewood Cliffs, N.J.: Prentice-Hall, 1967.

Shalock, Del, "Implications of Changing Values in Family Life," *Proceedings of the National Training Conference on Extension Education in Family Life.* Detroit: Merrill-Palmer Institute, 1963, pp. 20–33.

Strodbeck, F. L., "Family Interaction, Values and Achievement," in D. C. McClellands, and others (Eds.), *Talent and Society.* Princeton: Van Nostrand, 1958, pp. 135–194.

Wrightsman, Lawrence S., "Measurement of Philosophies of Human Nature," *Psychological Reports,* 14 (1964), pp. 743–751.

ISSUES IN ADULT EDUCATION

Readings focused on philosophical issues in the field of adult education as they pertain to the education of parents; the adult learning process, socialization, and role learning in the adult years:

Benne, Kenneth B., "The Uses of Fraternity," *Daedalus,* 90, 2 (Spring 1961), pp. 239–40.

Benne, Kenneth D., "Some Philosophic Issues in Adult Education," *Adult Education,* 7, 2 (Winter 1957), pp. 67–82.

Birnbaum, Max, "Mind and Emotion in Adult Education," *Adult Education,* 7, 3 (Spring 1957), pp. 144–151.

Birron, James E., "Adult Capacities to Learn," in Raymond G. Kuhlen (Ed.), *Psychological Backgrounds of Adult Education.* Chicago: Adult Education Association of the U. S. A., 1963.

Blakely, R. J., "The Path and the Goal," *Adult Education* 7, 2 (Winter 1957), p. 95.

Brim, Orville, and Stanton Wheeler, *Socialization After Childhood: Two Essays.* New York: Wiley, 1966.

Broudy, Harry S., "A Philosopher Looks at Adult Education," *Seeking Common Ground in Adult Education.* Chicago: Adult Education Association of the U. S. A., 1958.

Brunner, Edmund, et al. *An Overview of Adult Education Research.* Chicago: Adult Education Association of the U. S. A., 1959.

Clark, Burton R., *Adult Education in Transition.* Berkeley and Los Angeles: University of California Press, 1958.

Commission of the Professors of Adult Education, "Adult Education: A New Imperative for Our Times," Chicago: Adult Education Association of the U. S. A., 1961.

Cotton, Webster, "The Need for Adult Education—Some Major Themes," *Adult Education* 13, 1 (Autumn 1962), pp. 3–12.

Fay, Jean B., "Psychological Characteristics Affecting Adult Learning," in Frank W. Lanning and Wesley A. Many, *Basic Education for Disadvantaged Adults.* Boston: Houghton Mifflin Co., 1966, pp. 87–90.

Guerin, Quentin, and Robert McKeand, "Attitudes that Hinder Self-Improvement," *Adult Leadership,* 16, 4 (October 1967), pp. 144–162.

Knowles, Malcolm S., "Tensions and Gaps from Philosophical Differences," *Seeking Common Grounds in Adult Education.* Chicago: Adult Education Association of the U.S.A., 1958.

Knox, Alan B., and Douglas Sjogren, "Research on Adult Learning," *Adult Education* (Spring 1965), pp. 133–137.

Kuhlen, Raymond G., "Motivational Changes During the Adult Years," *Psychological Backgrounds of Adult Education.* Chicago: Center for the Study of Liberal Education of Adults, 1963.

Liverright, A. A., "Some Observations on the Status of Adult Education," *Adult Education,* 16, 4 (Summer 1966), pp. 239–244.

Lorge, Irving, "Thorndike's Contribution to the Psychology of Learning of Adults," in Frank W. Lanning and Wesley A. Many, *Basic Education for the Disadvantaged Adult.* Boston: Houghton Mifflin, 1966, pp. 69 ff.

Lypoldt, Martha M., "The Teaching-Learning Process with Adults," *Adult Leadership,* 16, 6 (December 1967), pp. 212–233.

Mann J., *Changing Human Behavior.* New York: Scribner's, 1965.

McKeachie, W. J., "Psychological Characteristics of Adults and Instructional Methods in Adult Education," in Raymond G. Kuhlen (Ed.), *Psychological Backgrounds in Adult Education.* Chicago: Adult Education Association of the U.S.A., 1963.

Neugarten, Bernice L., "Personality Changes During the Adult Years," in Raymond G. Kuhlen (Ed.), *Psychological Backgrounds of Adult Education.* Chicago: Center for Study of Liberal Education for Adults, 1963, pp. 43–76.

Scriven, E. G., "How Inconsistent are Professional Educators on Aims for Education," *Journal of Teacher Education,* 20 (Spring 1969), pp. 45–48.

Scriven, E. G., "To Redefine Adult Education," *Times Education Supplement,* 2803 (February 7, 1969), p. 406.

ISSUES IN PARENT EDUCATION

The history of parent education as an educative effort; review of theory, critique of practice, range of research:

Albert, Gerald, "Learning Theory and Parent Education: A Summing Up," *Marriage and Family Living,* 24, 3 (August 1962), pp. 249–253.

Becker, Wesley C., and Ronald S. Krug, "The Parent Attitude Research Instrument: A Research Review," *Child Development,* 36 (1965), pp. 329–365.

Brieland, Donald, "Uses of Research in Recent Popular Parent Education Literature," *Marriage and Family Living,* 19, 2, pp. 60–65.

Brim, Orville G., Jr., "Evaluating the Effects of Parent Education," *Marriage and Family Living,* 19, 1 (February 1957), pp. 54–60.

Brim, Orville G., Jr., *Education for Child Rearing.* New York: Free Press, 1965.

Bruch, Hilda, "Parent Education or the Illusion of Omnipotence," *American Journal of Orthopsychiatry* (1954), pp. 723–732.

Buchmueller, A. D., "The Place of Values in Parent Education," *Child Study,* (Spring 1960), pp. 16–20.

Chandler, B. A., "An Exploratory Study of the Professed Parent-Role Concepts and Standards of Child Behavior of Mothers in a Parent

Education Project," *Dissertation Abstracts,* 15 (1955), pp. 219–220.

Endres, Mary P., and Merry J. Evans, "Some Effects of Parent Education on Parents and Their Children," *Adult Education Journal,* 18, 2 (1967), pp. 101–111.

Grams, Armin, *Parent Education and the Behavioral Sciences.* Washington, D .C.: Children's Bureau No. 379, Dept. of Health, Education and Welfare, Social Security Administration, 1960.

Hendrickson, Norejane Johnston, *A Brief History of Parent Education in the United States.* Columbus, Ohio: Ohio State University College of Education, 1963. Reproduced by the Center for Adult Education.

Jefferson, R. B., "Interracial Understanding: A Challenge to Home and Family Life Education," *Journal of Home Economics,* 51 (1959), pp. 87–93.

Kawin, Ethel, *Parenthood in a Free Nation.* Vol. I: *Basic Concepts for Parents,* Vol. II: *Early and Middle Childhood,* Vol. III: *Later Childhood and Adolescence.* New York: MacMillan, 1963.

Luckey, Eleanor Braun, "Value as the Content of Parent Education Programs," *Marriage and Family Living,* 23, 2 (August 1961), pp. 263–266.

LeShan, Lawrence, and Eda LeShan, "Some Recent Trends in Social Science Research Relevant to Parent Education," *Marriage and Family Living,* 23 (February 1961), pp. 31–37.

Mannino, Fortune V., Julia Kisielewski, Exall L. Kimbro, and Barbara Morgenstern, "Relationships Between Parental Attitudes and Behavior," *The Family Coordinator* (October 1968), pp. 237–240.

Mawby, Russell G., Joe A. Miller and Andrew L. Olson, "Parental Aspirations: A Key to the Educational and Occupational Achievements of Youth," *Adult Leadership* (May 1965), pp. 8–10.

McCandless, Boyd, "The Devil's Advocate Examines Parent Education," *The Family Coordinator* (July 1968), pp. 149–154.

Schaefer, E. S., and R. Q. Bell, "Development of a Parent Attitude Research Instrument," *Child Development,* 29 (1958), pp. 339–361.

Stern, H. H., *Parent Education: An International Survey.* Hamburg: Studies in Education, the University of Hull with the UNESCO Institute for Education, 1960.

Taylor, Katherine Whiteside, *Parents and Children Learn Together.* New York: Teachers College Press, 1967.

Zuckerman, M. B. B. Ribback, E. Monashkin, and J. A. Norton, "Normative Data and Factor Analysis on Parental Attitude Research Instrument," *Journal of Consulting Psychology,* 22 (1958), pp. 165–171.

METHODOLOGY IN PARENT EDUCATION

Consideration of programs, curriculum, methods, and materials in parent education; group process, the discussion method, decision-making, the role of the parent educator, guidance techniques:

Argyris, Chris, *Roleplaying in Action.* New York: New York State School of Industrial and Labor Relations, Bulletin No. 14, May 1951.

Auerbach, Aline B., *Parents Learn Through Discussion: Principles and Practices of Parent Group Education.* New York: Wiley, 1968.

Babitz, Milton, *Parent Education Curriculums, Methods and Materials.* Sacramento, Calif.: Bulletin of the California State Department of Education, Vol. 30, May 1961.

Barnlund, Dean C., and F. S. Haiman, *Dynamics of Discussion.* Boston: Houghton Mifflin, 1960.

Barrett-Lennard, G. R., "Significant Aspects of a Helping Relationship," *Canada's Mental Health,* Supplement No. 47 (July–August 1965).

Bennett, Margaret E., *Guidance in Groups: A Resource Book for Teachers, Counselors and Administrators.* New York: McGraw-Hill, 1955.

Cantor, Nathaniel, *Learning Through Discussion.* Buffalo: Human Relations for Industry, 1951.

Cartwright, Dorwin, and A. Zander (Eds.), *Group Dynamics: Research and Theory.* New York: Row, 1960, (2nd Ed.).

Cartwright, R. L., and G. L. Hinks, *Creative Discussion.* New York: Mac-Millan, 1959.

Crow, Maxine S., "Preventive Intervention Through Parent Group Education," *Social Casework,* 18, 3 (March 1967), pp. 161–166.

Driver, Helen, *Multiple Counseling: A Small Group Method for Personal Growth.* Madison, Wisconsin: Monona Publications, 1954.

Gordon, Thomas, *Group-Centered Leadership.* New York: Houghton Mifflin, 1955.

Hall, D. M., *Dynamics of Group Action.* Danville, Ill.: Interstate Printers and Publishers, 1957.

Harnack, R. Rictor, and Thorrell B. Fest, *Group Discussion: Theory and Technique.* New York: Appleton-Century-Crofts, 1964.

Hare, A. Paul, *Small Group Process.* New York: Free Press, 1969.

Hareford, Carl S., *Changing Parental Attitudes Through Group Discussion.* Austin: University of Texas Press, 1964.

Hoffman, Randall W., and Robert Plutchik, *Small Group Discussion in Orientation and Teaching.* New York: Putnam, 1959.

Jersild, Arthur T., *When Teachers Face Themselves*. New York: Teachers College Press, 1955.

Keltner, John W., *Group Discussion Process*. New York: Longmans, Green, 1957.

Knowles, Malcolm, *Introduction to Group Dynamics*. New York: Association Press, 1959.

Levine, Jacob, and John Butler, "Lecture Vs. Group Decision in Changing Behavior," in D. Cartwright, and A. Zander (Eds.), *Group Dynamics: Research and Theory*, Evanston, Ill.: Row, Peterson, 1953, pp. 280–286.

Lorge, Irving, "Effective Methods in Adult Education," *Report of the Southern Regional Workshop for Agricultural Extensions Specialists*. Raleigh, N.C.: North Carolina State College, June 1947.

Maier, Norman R. F., and Allen R. Solem, "The Contributions of a Discussion Leader to the Quality of Group Thinking: The Effective Use of Minority Opinions," in D. Cartwright and A. Zander (Eds.), *Group Dynamics: Research and Theory*. Evanston, Ill.: Row, Peterson, 1953.

Malinowski, Bronislaw, *The Group and the Individual in Functional Analysis*. New York: Bobbs-Merrill Reprint Series in the Social Sciences No. 183.

Mayer, G. Roy and John J. Cody, "Festinger's Theory of Cognitive Dissonance Applied to School Counseling," *Personnel and Guidance Journal*, 47, 3 (November 1968), pp. 233–239.

McBurney, James H., and Kenneth G. Hance, *Discussion in Human Affairs*. New York: Harper, 1950.

Middlewood, Esther, "Lay Leadership Through Parent Education Associates," *The Family Coordinator*, 17, 4 (October 1968), pp. 264–270.

Olmstead, Michael, *The Small Group*. New York: Random House, 1959.

Phillip, Gerald M., *Communication and the Small Group*. New York: Bobbs-Merrill, 1966.

Rogers, Carl, "Techniques of a Helping Relationship," in Morris Stein (Ed.), *Contemporary Psychotherapies*. New York: Free Press, 1961.

Rokeach, Milton, *The Open and Closed Mind*. New York: Basic Books, 1960.

Ryan, T. Antoinette, and John D. Krumholtz, "Effect of Planned Reinforcement Counseling on Client Decision-Making Behavior," *Journal of Counseling Psychology*, 11, 4 (Winter 1964), pp. 315–323.

Santestefano, Sebastiano, and Samuel Stayton, "Training the Preschool Retarded Child in Focusing Attention: A Program for Parents," *American Journal of Orthopsychiatry*, 37, 4 (July 1967), pp. 723–743.

Schwartz, Anne C., and Carole M. Olson, "Parent Guidance: A Community Mental Health Service," *Social Casework,* 48, 3 (March 1967), pp. 141–147.

Thelen, Herbert, *Dynamics of Groups at Work.* Chicago: Chicago University Press, 1954.

Westerville, Evelyn, "Role Playing: An Educational Technique," *Journal of Marriage and the Family,* 21, 1 (February 1958), pp. 78–79.

Willsey, Frank Richard, Jr., "An Experimental Study of an Adult Learning Situation Involving three Levels of Training in the Group Discussion Process," *Dissertation Abstracts,* 23 (1963), pp. 2407–2408.

Zaccaria, Joseph S., "Some Aspects of Developmental Guidance Within an Existential Context," *Personnel and Guidance Journal,* 47, 5 (January 1969), pp. 440–455.

IMPACT OF POVERTY ON FAMILY LIFE

Readings on lower class status, poverty and race: the impact on families and their capacity to function in relation to the demands of the middle-class norm:

Billingsley, Andrew, *Black Families in White America.* Englewood Cliffs, N.J.: Prentice-Hall, 1968.

Cavan, Ruth, "Lower Class Families," in *The American Family.* New York: Crowell, 1963, pp. 141–153.

Cohen, Albert K. and Harold M. Hodges, "Characteristics of the Blue-Collar Class," *Social Problems,* 10, 4 (Spring 1963), pp. 303–333.

Dick, Kenneth, and Lydia J. Strand, "The Multi-Problem Family and Problems of Service," *Social Casework,* 39, 6 (1958), pp. 349–355.

Elam, S. L., "Poverty and Acculturation in a Migrant Puerto Rican Family," *Record,* 70 (April 1969), pp. 617–626.

Fernandez, J. S., and others, "Three Basic Themes in Mexican and Puerto Rican Family Values," *Journal of Social Psychology,* 48 (1958), pp. 167–181.

Ford, Thomas R., "Value Orientations of a Culture of Poverty: The Southern Appalachian Case," in *Working with Low-Income Families.* Washington, D. C.: American Home Economics Association, 1965.

Freedman, P. I., "Middle Class Values, Lower Class Rights," *Clearing House,* 43 (April 1969), pp. 469–470.

Gans, Herbert J., *The Urban Villagers*. New York: Free Press of Glencoe, 1962.

Gavron, Hannah, *The Captive Wife*. London: Pelican, 1968.

Geismar, Ludwig, "The Social Functioning of the ADC Family," *The Welfare Reporter*, 41, 3 (July 1963), pp. 43–54.

Geismar, Ludwig and Michael A. La Sorte, *Understanding the Multi-Problem Family*. New York: Association Press, 1964.

Glasser, Paul H., and Elizabeth L. Navarre, "The Problems of Families in the ADC Program," *Children*, 12, 4 (July–August 1965), pp. 151–156.

Harrington, Michael, *The Other America: Poverty in the United States*. New York: Macmillan, 1962.

Hawkes, Glenn R., "Human Needs and the Community," in Loe L. Froste and Glenn R. Hawkes (Eds.), *The Disadvantaged Child: Issues and Innovations*. Boston: Houghton Mifflin, 1966, pp. 419–426.

Herzog, Elizabeth, "Is There a 'Breakdown' of the Negro Family?" *Social Work*, 11, 1 (January 1966).

Herzog, Elizabeth, *About the Poor: Some Facts and Some Fictions*. Washington, D. C.: Department of Health, Education and Welfare, Social and Rehabilitation Service, Children's Bureau No. 451, 1967.

Hines, Ralph H., "Social Expectations and Cultural Deprivation," *Journal of Negro Education*. (special edition, Summer 1964), pp. 136–142.

Irelan, Lola M. (Ed.), *Low-Income Life Styles*. Washington D. C.: Department of Health, Education and Welfare, 1966.

Keller, Suzanne, *The American Lower Class Family*. Albany, N. Y.: New York State Division for Youth, 1966.

Jeffers, Camille, *Living Poor*. Ann Arbor, Mich.: Ann Arbor Publications, 1967.

Kushnick, Louis, "The Negro Family in the United States: A Review," *Race*, 8, 4 (April 1967), pp. 409–414.

Lewis, Hylan, "The Changing Negro Family," in Eli Ginzberg (Ed.), *The Nation's Children*, Vol. 1. New York: Columbia University Press, 1960, pp. 108–135.

Lewis, Hylan, "Culture, Class and the Behavior of Low Income Families," Paper presented at the Conference on Lower Class Culture, New York City, June 1963. Mimeo.

Lewis Oscar, *Five Families*. New York: Basic Books, 1959.

Lipset, S. M., "Working Class Authoritarianism," in *Political Man*. New York: Anchor Books, 1963, pp. 87–126.

Miller, S. M., and Frank Riessman, "Working-Class Authoritarianism: A

Critique of Lipset," *The British Journal of Sociology*, 12 (September 1961), pp. 263–273.

Miller, S. M., "The American Lower Classes: A Topological Approach," in Frank Riessman, Jerome Cohen, and Arthur Pearl (Eds.), *Mental Health of the Poor*. New York: Free Press, 1965, pp. 139–154.

Miller, S. M., Martin Rein, Pamela Roby, and Bertram M. Gross, "Poverty, Inequality and Conflict," *Annals of American Academy of Political and Social Science*, 373 (September 1967), pp. 16–52.

Mizruchi, Ephraim Harold, *Success and Opportunity*. Glencoe, Ill.: Free Press, 1964.

Moynihan, Daniel Patrick, "Employment, Income and the Ordeal of the Negro Family," *Daedulus* (Fall 1965), pp. 760–761.

Pettigrew, Thomas F., *A Profile of the Negro American*, Princeton, N. J.: D. Van Nostrand, 1964.

Rainwater, Lee, Richard P. Coleman, and Gerald Handel, *Workingman's Wife*. New York: Oceano Publications, 1959.

Rainwater, Lee, "Fear and the House-as-Haven in the Lower Class," *Journal of the American Institute of Planners* (February 1966).

Rainwater, Lee, "Crucible of Identity: The Negro Lower-Class Family," *Daedulus*, 95 (1966), pp. 172–216.

Riessman, Frank, Jerome Cohen, and Arthur Pearl (Eds.), *Mental Health of the Poor*. New York: Free Press, 1964.

Riessman, Leonard, "Levels of Aspiration and Social Class," *American Sociological Review*, 18 (1953), pp. 233–243.

Rodman, Hyman, "On Understanding Lower-Class Behavior," *Social and Economic Studies* (December 1959), pp. 441–450.

Rodman, Hyman, "The Lower Class Value Stretch," *Social Forces*, 42, 2 (December 1963), pp. 205 ff.

Rodman, Hyman, "Middle-Class Misconceptions About Lower-Class Families," in H. Shostak, and W. Gomberg (Eds.), *Blue Collar World*. Englewood Cliffs, N. J.: Prentice-Hall, 1964, pp. 59–69.

Schneiderman, Leonard, "Value Orientation Preferences of Chronic Relief Recipients," *Journal of Social Casework* (July 1964).

Schneiderman, Leonard, "Social Class, Diagnosis and Treatment," *American Journal of Orthopsychiatry* (January 1965), pp. 99–105.

Stucky, William G., "Poverty is the Consequence of Obsolescence in Social Institutions," in *Working with Low-Income Families*. (Proceedings of the American Home Economist Association Workshop, (March 1965), pp. 81 ff.

Willie, Charles V., and Janet Weinandy, "The Structure and Composition of 'Problem' and 'Stable' Families in a Low-Income Population," *Marriage and Family Living*, 25, 4 (November 1963), pp. 439–447.

CHILD-REARING AND THE POOR

Readings on lower class status, poverty and race: the impact on child-rearing practices and development of children:

Alman, Emily, "The Child of the American Poor," in Milly Cowles (Ed.), *Perspectives in the Education of Disadvantaged Children.* Cleveland, Ohio: World Publishing, 1967, pp. 5–32.

Ausubel, David P., "The Effects of Cultural Deprivation on Learning Patterns," *Audiovisual Instruction* (January 1965), pp. 10–12.

Bell, Robert R., "Lower Class Negro Mothers and Their Children," *Integrated Education,* 2 (December–January 1964–1965), pp. 23–27.

Bloom, B. S., Allison Davis, and Robert Hess, *Compensatory Education for Cultural Deprivation.* New York: Holt, Rinehart and Winston, 1965.

Blum, Alan F., "Social Structure, Social Class and Participation in Primary Relationships," in Arthur B. Shostak and W. Gomberg (eds.) *Blue Collar World.* Englewood Cliffs, .J.: Prentice Hall, 1964, pp. 195–207.

Caldwell, Bettye M., and Julius B. Richmond, "Social Class Level and Stimulation Potential of the Home," in *Exceptional Infant: Volume I, The Normal Infant.* Seattle, Washington: Special Child Publications, 1967, pp. 455–465.

Chilman, Catherine S., "Child-Rearing and Family Relationship Patterns of the Very Poor," *Welfare in Review,* 3 (January 1965), pp. 9–19.

Chilman, Catherine S., *Growing Up Poor.* Washington, D. C.: Department of Health, Education and Welfare, Welfare Administration, Division of Research, (May 1966), Publication No. 13.

Deutsch, Martin, "Disadvantaged Children and the Learning Process," in Martin Deutsch and associates, *The Disadvantaged Child.* New York: Basic Books, 1967.

Edwards, T. B., "Deliberate Attitudes, IQ and Social Class," *Journal of Experimental Education,* 37 (Winter 1968), pp. 7–18.

Epstein, Leonore A., "Some Effects of Low-Income on Children and Their Families," *Social Security Bulletin,* Washington, D. C.: U. S. Government Printing Office, February, 1964.

Fantini, Mario D., and Gerald Weinstein, *The Disadvantaged.* New York: Harper, 1968.

Frazier, Franklin, "Problems and Needs of Negro Children and Youth Resulting from Family Disorganization," *Journal of Negro Education* (Spring 1950), pp. 269–277.

Goldstein, Bernard, *Low Income Youth in Urban Areas: A Critical Review of the Literature.* New York: Holt, Rinehart and Winston, 1967.

Hertzig, Margaret E., Herbert G. Birch, Alexander Thomas, and Olga Aran Mendez, *Class and Ethnic Differences in the Responsiveness of Preschool Children to Cognitive Demands.* Chicago: University of Chicago Press for Society for Research in Child Development, Monography, 117, 1968.

Herzog, Elizabeth and Cecelia E. Sudia, "Fatherless Homes: A Review of Research," *Children,* 15, 5 (September–October 1968).

Hess, Robert, "Educability and Rehabilitation: The Future of the Welfare Class," *Journal of Marriage and the Family* (November 1964), pp. 422–429.

Hess, Robert, "Material Teaching Styles and Educational Retardation," in E. Paul Torrance and Robert D. Strom (Eds.), *Mental Health and Achievement.* New York: Wiley, 1965.

Jensen, Arthur, "Social Class and Verbal Learning," in Martin Deutsch, Irwin Katz, and Arthur Jensen (Eds.), *Social Class, Race and Psychological Development.* New York: Holt, Rinehart and Winston, 1968, pp. 115–174.

John, Vera P., "Intellectual Development of Slum Children," *American Journal of Orthopsychiatry,* 33 (1963), pp. 813–822.

Keller, Suzanne, "The Social World of the Urban Slum Child: Some Early Findings," *American Journal of Orthopsychiatry,* 33 (October 1963), pp. 813–822.

Lewis, Hylan, *Child Rearing Practices Among Low Income Families in the District of Columbia.* Health and Welfare Council of the National Capital Area. Presented at National Conference of Social Welfare, May 1961, Minneapolis, Minn. Mimeo.

Maccoby, Eleanor E., and P. K. Gibbs, "Methods of Child-Rearing in Two Social Classes," in W. E. Martin, and C. B. Stendler (Eds.), *Readings in Child Development.* New York: Harcourt, Brace, 1954, pp. 380–396.

Meier, Elizabeth G., "Culturally Deprived Children: Implications for Child Welfare," *Child Welfare,* 45, 2 (February 1966).

Moles, Oliver C., Jr., "Training Children in Low-Income Families for School," *Welfare in Review,* 3 (June 1965), pp. 1–11.

Moles, Oliver C., Jr., "Child Training Practices Among Low Income Families," *Welfare in Review,* 3 (December 1965), pp. 1–19.

North, George E., and O. Lee Buchanan, "Maternal Attitudes in a Poverty Area," *Journal of Negro Education,* 107, 4 (Fall 1968), pp. 418–425.

Olin, E. G., Robert Hess, and V. Shipman, "Maternal Language Styles and Their Implications for Children's Cognitive Development," Presented at a symposium on The Effect of Maternal Behavior on Cognitive Development and Impulsivity. American Psychological Association, Chicago, Ill., 1965. Mimeo.

Pavenstadt, Eleanor, "A Comparison of the Child-Rearing Environment of Upper-Lower and Very Low-Lower Class Families," *American Orthpsychiatric Journal* (January 1965), pp. 89–98.

Radin, Norman, and Constance Kamii, "The Child-Rearing Attitudes of Disadvantaged Negro Mothers and Some Educational Implications," *Journal of Negro Education*, 34, 2 (Spring 1965), pp. 138–146.

Stendler-Lavatelli, Celia, B., "Environmental Intervention in Infancy and Childhood," in Martin Deutsch, Irwin Katz, and Arthur Jensen (Eds.), *Social Class, Race and Psychological Development*. New York: Holt, Rinehart and Winston, 1968, pp. 347–380.

Walters, James and Ruth Connor, "Interaction of Mothers and Children from Lower-Class Families," *Child Development*, 35 (1964), pp. 433–440.

Wortis, H., J. G. Bardash, R. Rue Culter, and A. Freedman, "Child-Rearing Practices in Low Socio-Economic Group," *Pediatrics*, 32 (August 1963), pp. 298–307.

METHODS OF PARENT EDUCATION
WITH LOW-INCOME FAMILIES

Readings on innovations in philosophy, content and methodology in the development of relevant programs for low-income parents.

Calia, Vincent, "The Culturally Deprived Client: A Re-Formulation of the Counselor's Role," *Journal of Counseling Psychology*, 13, 1 (1966), pp. 100–105.

Chilman, Catherine S., and Ivor Kraft, "Helping Low-Income Parents Through Parent Education Groups," *Children*, 10, 1 (July–August 1963), pp. 127–132.

Clarizio, Harvey F., "Maternal Attitude Change Associated with Involvement in Head Start," *Journal of Negro Education*, 37, 2 (Spring 1968), p. 106–113.

Cloward, Richard A., and James A. Jones, "Social Class: Educational Attitudes and Participation," in A. Harry Passow (Ed.), *Education in Depressed Areas*. New York: Columbia University Teachers College Bureau of Publications, 1963, pp. 190–216.

Daniel, Walter G., "Some Essential Ingredients in Educational Programs for Socially Disadvantaged," in Jerone Hellmuth (Ed.), *Disadvantaged Child*. Vol. I, Seattle: Special Child Publications, 1967.

Delano, June S., "Ten O'Clock Scholars," *Young Children* (October 1967), pp. 44–50.

Dodson, D. W., "Power as a Dimension of Education," *Journal of Educational Sociology,* 35 (1962), pp. 203–215.

Faust, Margaret, "What is a Good Program for Economically Deprived Children," *California Journal for Instructional Improvement,* 8, 4 (December 1965).

Fraser, Roberta, *Helping Parents Teach Young Children.* Washington, D. C.: Federal Extension Service, Department of Agriculture, March 1966, FES Packet A.

Fusco, Gene, *School-Home Partnership in Depressed Urban Neighborhoods.* Washington, D.C.: Department of Health, Education and Welfare, Bulletin No. 20, 1964.

Fusco, Gene, "Reaching the Parents," in Robert D. Strom (Ed.), *The Inner City Classroom: Teacher Behaviors.* Columbus, Ohio: Charles E. Merrill Books, 1966.

Goldberg, Sidney J., Barbara Rice, and Geneva Erickson. "Working with Head Start Parents in Public Schools: A Community-Agency-School Approach," *Adult Leadership* (February 1969), pp. 345–375.

Gordon, Ira J., and associates, *Reaching the Child Through Parent Education: The Florida Approach,* Gainesville, Fla.: Institute for Development of Human Resources, University of Florida Research Reports, 1969.

Gould, Robert E., "Dr. Strangeclass: or How I Stopped Worrying About the Theory and Began Treating the Blue Collar Worker," *American Journal of Orthopsychiatry* (January 1967), pp. 78–86.

Grams, Armin, and John G. Chantiny, "Parent Education," *Journal of Cooperative Extension,* 4, 2 (Summer 1966), pp. 75–79.

Guerney, Bernard, and Lillian Stover, "On Educating Disadvantaged Parents to Motivate Children for Learning: A Filial Approach," *Community Mental Health Journal,* 3, 1 (Spring 1967), pp. 66–76.

Haggstrom, Warren C., "Poverty and Adult Education," *Adult Education,* 15 (Spring 1965), pp. 145–160.

Harding, Gene, "Operation Family—An Experiment in Family Life Education," *Adult Leadership* (October 1968), pp. 169–194.

Hoffman, W. K., "Parents Help Preschoolers Get Their Start In Chicago," *Nations Schools,* 83 (April 1969), pp. 81–82.

Horton, Della M., "A Training Program for Mothers," *Report from Demonstration and Research Center for Early Education.* Nashville: George Peabody College for Teachers Publication, 1968.

Karnes, Merle B., William M. Studley, and Willis R. Wright, *An Approach for Working with Parents of Disadvantaged Children: A Pilot*

Project. Urbana, Ill.: Manual, Institute for Research on Exceptional Children, Research Program on Preschool Disadvantaged Children, University of Illinois, August 1966.

Keliher, A. V., "Parent and Child Centers: What They Are, Where They Are Going," *Children,* 16 (March 1969), pp. 63–66.

Kerckoff, Richard K., "Strategy II Teaches Parents to Teach Children," *Journal of Home Economics,* 60, 5 (May 1968), pp. 346–349.

Kevin, David, "Group Counseling of Mothers in an AFDC Program, *Children,* 14, 2 (March-April 1967).

King, Charles H., "Family Therapy with the Deprived Family," *Social Casework,* 48, 4 (April 1967), pp. 203–208.

Klaus, Rupert and Susan W. Gray. *The Early Training Project.* Murfreesburo, Tenn.: Proceedings of Section II, American Psychological Association Conference, St. Louis, August 1962.

Levenstein, Phyllis, and Robert Sunley, "Stimulation of Verbal Interaction Between Disadvantaged Mothers and Children," *American Journal of Orthopsychiatry,* 38, 1 (January 1968), pp. 116–121.

Lipchik, M. A., "Saturday School for Mothers and Preschoolers," in Fred M. Hechinger (Ed.), *Preschool Education Today.* New York: Doubleday, 1966, pp. 137–143.

McBroom, Elizabeth, "The Socialization of Parents," *Child Welfare,* 46, 3 (1967).

McCarthy, Janet Lee Gorrell, "Changing Parent Attitudes and Improving Language and Intellectual Abilities of Culturally Disadvantaged Four-Year-Old Children Through Parent Involvement," *Contemporary Education,* 40, 3 (January 1969), pp. 166–168.

Moses, Lois, "Homework for Preschoolers," 1, *Young Children* (October 1967), pp. 19–22.

Pickarts, Evelyn W., *Recruiting Low-Income Families for Family Life Education Programs.* New York: Child Study Association of America, 1965. Article II.

Pickarts, Evelyn W., "Parent Education Is More Than a Head Start," *California Parent-Teacher* (January 1966), pp. 26–27.

"Project Enable," *Social Casework,* 48, 10 (December 1967). Entire issue on Child Study Association of America, Family Service Association and National Urban League Project: Education and Neighborhood Action for Better Living Environment.

Radin, Norma, and David Weikart, "A Home Teaching Program for Disadvantaged Preschool Children," *Journal of Special Education* (Spring 1966).

Regal, J. M. and Dorothy Rizer, *Parent Education Experimental Program.* Presented at the American Educational Research Association Conference, 1962. Mimeo.

Reissman, Frank and Jean Goldfarb, "Role Playing and the Poor," New York Mobilization for Youth, Inc., (December 1964). Mimeo.

Robinson, H. L., "From Infancy Through School: Frank Porter Graham Child Develpoment Center," *Children,* 24 (March 1969), pp. 61–62.

Samenfink, J. Anthony, Julie W. Lepeschkin, and Nancy Hall, "Parent-Child Education for Low-Income Families," *Journal of Home Economics,* 59, 1 (January 1967).

Scott, Carl A., "Some Concerns of Parents in Low-Income Groups as Seen in Parent Group Education Program," Presented at National Conference on Social Welfare, Child Study Association of America, New York, May 1963.

Sharock, A., "Relations between Home and School," *Educational Research* (January 1968), pp. 185–196.

Shea, Margaret C., "The Uniqueness of Family Life Education with Low-Income People," Presented at Annual Leadership Institute in Family Life Education, Nassau County Mental Health Association, January 22, 1965.

Shepard, Samuel, "Working with Parents of Disadvantaged Children," in C. W. Hunnicutt (Ed.), *Urban Education and Cultural Deprivation.* Syracuse, N.Y.: Syracuse University Press, 1964.

Stein, Lisa, "Techniques for Parent Discussions in Disadvantaged Areas," *Young Children,* 19, 4 (March 1967), pp. 210–217.

Smilansky, Moshe, "Fighting Deprivation in the Promised Land," *Saturday Review of Literature* (October 5, 1966), pp. 82–91.

White, Gladys O., Alberta D. Hill, and Edna P. Amidon, *Improving Home and Family Living Among Low Income Families.* Washington, D.C.: Department of Health, Education and Welfare, Social Security Administration, Bureau of Family Services and Office of Education, May 1962, p. 24.

Wolf, Anna W. M., and Adel B. Tunick, *Reaching the Neighborhood Parent.* New York: Public Education Association, 1966, p. 12.

Index